Precarious childhood in post-independence Ireland

MANCHESTER
1824

Manchester University Press

Precarious childhood in post-independence Ireland

Moira Maguire

Manchester University Press
Manchester and New York
distributed in the United States exclusively
by Palgrave Macmillan

The right of Moira J. Maguire to be identified as the author of this work has been asserted by her in accordance with the Copyright, Designs and Patents Act 1988.

Published by Manchester University Press
Oxford Road, Manchester M13 9NR, UK
and Room 400, 175 Fifth Avenue, New York, NY 10010, USA
www.manchesteruniversitypress.co.uk

Distributed in the United States exclusively by
Palgrave Macmillan, 175 Fifth Avenue,
New York, NY 10010, USA

Distributed in Canada exclusively by
UBC Press, University of British Columbia, 2029 West Mall,
Vancouver, BC, Canada V6T 1Z2

British Library Cataloguing-in-Publication Data is available

Library of Congress Cataloging-in-Publication Data is available

ISBN 978 0 7190 8774 5 paperback

First published by Manchester University Press in hardback 2009

This paperback edition first published 2012

The publisher has no responsibility for the persistence or accuracy of URLs for any external or third-party internet websites referred to in this book, and does not guarantee that any content on such websites is, or will remain, accurate or appropriate.

Printed by Lightning Source

Contents

Acknowledgements

This book has its roots in a doctoral dissertation completed at American University, Washington DC in 2000, although it has undergone a drastic transformation since then. Thanks, therefore, must go to the people who were part of the original project. Vanessa Schwartz and Eileen Findlay provided feedback and support and helped me to see the dissertation to fruition. Gail Savage and Liz Sheehan shared their time and insights with me at critical stages of the process. And Liz Stewart provided friendship and encouragement when it was most desperately needed.

I had the good fortune to spend six years living, researching, and teaching in Ireland, and the intellectual community I found there was instrumental to this work. Professor Vincent Comerford welcomed me into the Department of Modern History at National University of Ireland, Maynooth and was unbelievably generous in sharing his time, insights, and feedback. He has been a constant and unflagging supporter of my work, and a steady source of encouragement and absolute conviction in the value of this work. Without his support, kindness, and generosity this book may never have been completed. Ann Matthews has been a stalwart supporter and fellow traveler on the intellectual journey that led to this book. Her friendship, warmth, generosity, and encyclopedic knowledge never cease to amaze me.

The transformation that occurred between the dissertation and this finished product would not have been possible without access to archival and other material made possible by my participation in a research project commissioned by the Irish Sisters of Mercy. I am most grateful to Seamus O'Cinneide for taking me on as his assistant and colleague. He was a generous and insightful colleague who has contributed enormously to the finished product that is this book. I also owe a debt of gratitude to the law firm of Arthur O'Hagan who provided material support and helped pave access to archival material that might otherwise have been inaccessible to me.

My UALR colleagues Laura Smoller, Kristin Mann, and Charlie Bolton have provided conversations and encouragement that kept me going through the arduous process of whipping the manuscript into shape. My parents, Patricia and Dexter Merry, have been a constant source of support and encouragement (and lots of bragging). Their love and support mean more to me than they know. Many others have contributed to this book in ways both big and small. I cannot possibly name everyone here, but I am grateful to everyone who has shown an interest in my work over the years, who has encouraged me, and who promised to buy the book when it was finished.

Some of the research for this book was supported by a post-doctoral fellowship from the Irish Research Council for the Humanities and Social Sciences. I am grateful for that support, which allowed me a full year to immerse myself in some critical sources.

Finally I would like to thank Emma Brennan and the anonymous Manchester University Press readers whose comments and feedback were invaluable in shaping the finished product. Any errors, omissions, or oversights are, of course, entirely my own.

Introduction

The Democratic Programme of the First Dáil, which could be read as a "blueprint" for the independent Irish state's social agenda, acknowledged the concept of public responsibility for the care and well-being of children, not only as the human resources upon which the future social, political, and economic viability of the state rested, but as valued members, in their own right, of post-independence Irish society.[1] Specifically, it asserted the state's fundamental responsibility to feed, clothe, shelter, and educate children as the future citizens of the independent Irish state: "It shall be the first duty of the Government of the Republic to make provision for the physical, mental, and spiritual well-being of the children to secure that no child shall suffer hunger or cold from lack of food, clothing, or shelter, but that all shall be provided with the means and facilities requisite for their education and training as citizens of a Free and Gaelic Ireland."[2] Although the role and responsibility of parents was not explicitly mentioned in the Democratic Programme, there is no reason to assume its architects envisioned supplanting parents as the natural carers, protectors, and educators of children. The Democratic Programme could, therefore, be read as a commitment on the part of the state to aid parents in providing for their children, rather than an intention to assume the parental role entirely. It signaled that the independent Irish state would (or intended to) be child- and family-centered.

But the commitments outlined in the Democratic Programme were not enshrined in the 1937 Constitution or in legislative initiatives, so the republican ideal was not translated into specific rights for children or specific responsibilities on the part of the state to aid families. What was enshrined in the Constitution was the state's right to strip "unfit" parents of their parental rights: "In exceptional cases, where the parents for physical or moral reasons fail in their duty towards their children, the State as guardian of the common good, by appropriate means shall endeavour to supply the place of the parents, but always with due regard for the natural and imprescriptible rights of the child."[3] This might appear to be a strong endorsement of children's rights, but the children's "natural" and "imprescriptible" rights were never clearly defined or supported by legislative initiative. And it would be easy to assume that this prerogative was applied only sparingly, and only against a small number of parents who flagrantly and blatantly abdicated their parental responsibilities. In fact, however, parents were stripped of their parental rights with relative ease, often for no other reason than abject poverty. Others were shamed and humiliated (and rejected) when they sought public assistance to provide for their children's most basic needs. The way the state put republican ideals and constitutional imperatives into practice reveals the extent to which definitions of childhood, family, and parental roles were politicized to suit a post-independence agenda. Throughout the first two-thirds of the twentieth century lawmakers presented a façade of caring and compassion while their social policies repeatedly ignored the needs and best interests of the neediest of Irish children – those who were illegitimate, poor, neglected, and abused.

Life could be precarious for illegitimate children in twentieth-century Ireland, because of poverty and prejudice. But life also could be precarious for legitimate children whose parents were too poor to provide for them adequately, who lost one or both parents to death or desertion, or who were neglected or abused by their parents. Legitimate children were as likely as their illegitimate counterparts to be sent to industrial schools, primarily on the grounds of parental poverty, neglect, death or desertion. Even children who lived at home in a "normal" family environment experienced endemic poverty and the malnutrition and substandard housing that went along with it, excessive corporal punishment at home and in school that at times bordered on abusive, and sexual abuse that was often covered up. All of this served to mask the gap between the idealized Ireland of republican fantasy, and the reality of everyday life for Ireland's poor and marginalized children.

One of the most obvious but unspoken idiosyncrasies of twentieth-century Irish society was the gap between Catholic rhetoric that insisted on abundant fertility, and economic and social conditions that made abundant fertility a foolish aspiration. At least into the 1950s successive Irish governments shied away from industrial and economic planning, which translated into extended periods of economic stagnation and high rates of unemployment and under-employment. Economic conditions were such that a significant proportion of the population lived in poverty characterized by seasonal unemployment and migration, malnutrition, and sub-standard housing and housing shortages that contributed not just to overcrowding but to dangerous and sometimes potentially deadly home environments. Meanwhile the Catholic Church, through its teachings and its influence in the legislative arena, insisted on abundant fertility: women were expected to bear as many children as they could during the course of their reproductive lives. This created a situation where families, poor families more so than middle- and upper-class, had more children than they could house, clothe, feed, and educate according to middle-class standards. The state inevitably asserted its constitutional right to care for these "excess" children in whatever way it saw fit. Sometimes this meant that local authorities granted home assistance to enable parents to provide for their children's basic needs in their own homes.[4] More often, however, it meant that children were removed from their parents' care and custody and placed in industrial schools or other state-funded institutions. Countless tens of thousands of children suffered, over the course of the twentieth century, for the Catholic Church's teachings on sex and reproduction, and for the narrow and often mean-spirited ways that the Irish state interpreted the rights and responsibilities enshrined in the 1937 Constitution.[5]

There was also a gap between the Catholic "sanctity of life" doctrine, and the way church and state dealt with poor, illegitimate, and abused children. Catholic writers and the Catholic hierarchy (consisting of bishops and archbishops) waged a sustained battle against abortion on the grounds that child life was sacred. They were supported in this by lawmakers and by Irish society as a whole, which voted in 1983 to embed a ban on abortion in the Irish Constitution. But this sanctity of life doctrine was applied inconsistently throughout the twentieth century, and it becomes clear that child life was only sacred when upholding its sanctity did not conflict with more pressing political and social imperatives. These inconsistencies were illustrated in official responses to adoption and infanticide legislation. By the late 1930s lawmakers were aware of the need for a law legalizing adoption. But the Catholic hierarchy refused to support a legislative initiative that might have allowed Catholic children to fall into the hands of Protestant proselytizers; and politicians were reluctant to move forward on a measure that the hierarchy did not endorse. When adoption legislation finally was passed in 1952, it was thanks to a series of high-profile scandals that had shamed the government into it, and not to official recognition of what was best for children. When the government passed the Infanticide Act in 1949 the hierarchy had little to say about it, which was remarkable given how vociferous its anti-abortion rhetoric could be. Many members of the political and religious establishment seem to have believed that the murder of innocent newborn infants was a small price to pay to uphold the nationalist façade of moral purity and superiority.

In foregrounding policy and practice as it related to poor, illegitimate, and abused children this book gives voice to historical actors who formed a significant proportion of the Irish population but who have been ignored or marginalized in the historical record. More importantly, this book uses poor, illegitimate, and abused children as lenses through which to re-evaluate Catholic influence in post-independence Irish society. The historiography on church and state in modern Ireland tends to emphasize the formal means through which the church sought to ensure that Irish social policy was infused with Catholic principles. It is almost cliché to suggest that the Catholic Church exerted influence over many aspects of Irish life, but there has as yet been no attempt to examine what that meant in practical terms. How, for example, was the Catholic sanctity of life doctrine implemented in policy and practice, and how did that shape and affect the lives and experiences of poor children? What effect did bans on contraception have on working-class mothers who were more likely than their middle-class counterparts to have large families, but who were least able to support and care for them? In short, this book offers a different interpretation of the relationship between and among the Catholic hierarchy, the political establishment, and Irish people.

One final anomaly this book examines relates to the place of the family in Irish society. Articles 41.1.1 and 41.1.2 of the Irish Constitution recognize the family as "the natural primary and fundamental unit group of Society" and, as such, as worthy of protection in its "constitution and authority."[6] The central argument of this book, however, is that far from protecting and upholding the family, Irish social policy had the effect of destroying family life when it did not conform to middle-class norms and expectations, or when it threatened the nationalist ideal of simple, content if poor, morally pure Irish society. The constitutional rights of poor parents were regularly trampled with impunity throughout the twentieth century as thousands of children were removed from their homes on the grounds of poverty, neglect, and illegitimacy, and their parents stripped of their custodial rights.

The extent to which parental rights were trampled is illustrated by the Doyle case from 1955.[7] In 1953 Evelyn Doyle and her younger brothers were committed to industrial schools in the Dublin area after their mother deserted the family.[8] It was not unusual for children to be committed to industrial schools under these circumstances, because it was widely assumed that fathers could not care for their children properly and that they should not have sole responsibility for the care of their daughters. Evelyn's father Desmond did not want his children to be sent to industrial schools, but great pressure was brought to bear on him by both the Irish Society for the Prevention of Cruelty to Children (ISPCC) inspector and by family and friends.

In 1955 Doyle applied to the Minister for Education to have Evelyn and her brothers returned to him. His request was denied on the grounds that the law required the consent of both parents on an application for a child's release from an industrial school. Doyle pointed out that the consent of Evelyn's mother had not been necessary when Evelyn and her brothers were committed to the industrial school in the first place, and that as the mother could not be traced her consent could not be secured. After additional un-successful petitions to the Minister for Education, Doyle appealed to the High Court on the grounds that there was a fundamental flaw in a law that allowed a child to be removed from his or her home with the consent of only one parent, but that the consent of *both* parents was necessary in order for the child to be returned to their home. The High Court upheld the Department of Education's position on the matter.[9] In desperation Doyle petitioned the Supreme Court on the grounds that his constitutional rights had been violated.

The Supreme Court ruled in Doyle's favor but the question of parental consent was never addressed. Instead, the case was decided on the consti-tutionality of the Children Act of 1941. The Supreme Court ruled that the relevant sections of the Act were unconstitutional in that they infringed the rights guaranteed in Article 40.0. of the Constitution. The ruling centered on the constitutional right of parents to determine the course of their children's education; it did not explicitly comment on the state's right to deny parents the custody of their children solely on the grounds of poverty.[10] However, in the months following the Supreme Court decision in the Doyle case the district justice in Dublin refused to commit children to industrial schools solely on the grounds of parental destitution, and it is likely that the Doyle case was one factor in the decrease in committals to industrial schools from the late 1950s.[11] At the time the Doyle case was extraordinary, and received a great deal of press attention, mainly because it was seen by many as a case of a poor, unemployed man taking on "the system" and winning.

The Doyle case revealed the injustice, and mean-spirited attitudes, in-herent in the system of state care for children whose family life did not conform to a middle-class ideal. Ostensibly the Minister for Education re-jected Doyle's application for Evelyn's release because of a legal technicality.

However, it is likely that the staff responsible for reviewing Doyle's application believed him to be an unfit parent: his wife had deserted him, for which he likely would have been held responsible; he was poor and unemployed; he probably enjoyed the odd pint with his friends; but most importantly, he was a single man fighting for the custody of his daughter. For all of these reasons Doyle did not conform to the "official" image of respectable and acceptable parenthood, and Department of Education staff assumed that the industrial school was a better environment for his children than their own home. Surely they never anticipated that someone like Doyle would challenge the system in such a profound and significant way, or that he would ultimately prevail.

The Doyle case, which has been the subject of autobiography and a major motion picture but not historical examination, is but one example of what is missing in twentieth-century Irish historiography. Modern Irish history tends to be written from a nationalist and Catholic perspective that highlights Ireland's "heroic struggle" for independence from a "tyrannical" British oppressor or that stresses the role of the Catholic Church in building the modern Irish state. J.H. Whyte's pathbreaking *Church and state in modern Ireland* was one of the first to examine, in a comprehensive way, the influence of the Irish Catholic Church on the development of the independent Irish state.[12] Whyte examined the evolution of some social policy issues, such as the mother and child scheme and adoption legislation, to illustrate the Catholic Church's enormous influence over political and social policy through the 1960s.[13] Whyte's work was valuable in its time, and still holds an esteemed place in the historiography of twentieth-century Ireland. But the availability of new sources, and fresh analyses of existing sources have rendered his work somewhat obsolete. (For example, Whyte argues that the Adoption Society, an organization formed specifically to lobby the Irish government for legal adoption, was the single most important factor in the government's decision to pass adoption legislation in 1952. It is clear, however, from a reading of sources that have become available since Whyte's work was published, that the Adoption Society was not as influential as Whyte believed. Rather, a number of high-profile scandals were behind the government's about-face in 1952.) Furthermore, Whyte emphasizes the institutional and structural relationships between church and state, but there is little consideration of the practical impact on the lives of Ireland's poor and marginalized, of the church's influence in the political and social arenas.

Tom Inglis, in several published works, examines the Catholic Church's role in broader perspective – not just in social policy but also in the shaping of attitudes and behaviors.[14] Inglis's *Moral monopoly: The rise and fall of the Catholic Church in modern Ireland* examines how the Catholic Church became powerful in independent Irish society, and the forces that contributed to its decline beginning in the 1980s. Inglis argues that women gained power and influence in the home through their relationship with the Catholic Church: "Emphasis is given to the Church's influence in Irish family life and, in particular, the dependence of mothers on the Church for moral power within the home. It was primarily through this dependence that the Church maintained control of women and sex and was able to develop a rigid adherence to its rules and regulations."[15] While it is true that Catholic doctrine and teaching influenced individual behavior, to some extent, the copious materials examined here would in no way support the view that working-class women exercised any sort of "moral power" within the home. Many working-class mothers appear to have lived in mortal fear that their children would be taken from them because endemic poverty made it impossible for them to raise their children according to middle-class standards and expectations. In their efforts to fulfill their religious obligations (for example, in not using contraception) poor and working-class women were saddled with more children than they could adequately care or provide for. In short, some aspects of Catholic social teaching made women's lives extremely difficult and contributed to the misery of countless thousands of poor and working-class children, who lived a precarious existence on the margins of survival.

Inglis revised *Moral monopoly* in 1998 to re-evaluate the church's role in Irish society in light of the growing scandals that had, since the early 1990s, rocked the Catholic Church at its core. Inglis suggests that Catholic influence has begun to decline in part because Irish Catholics are becoming more "Protestant" in the way they practice their faith, but also because they are becoming more secular. This is evidenced by declining attendance at Mass and other sacraments, and a declining belief in basic Catholic principles.[16] But this decline cannot be attributed only to the behavior of Irish Catholics. The church's influence has also been undermined in the many social service areas where they once predominated: health care, education, and philanthropy. And mounting scandals since the early 1990s have chipped away at the church's moral authority. Inglis is probably correct that the Catholic Church's power and influence in Irish society has declined significantly since the mid-1980s. But a central, if often unspoken, tenet of this book is that the Catholic Church's power and influence were never as complete as historians have previously assumed or suggested.

It has become fashionable in recent years to criticize the Irish Catholic Church for all of its sins, real and imagined. Just as it was customary at the beginning of the twentieth century to place all of the blame for Ireland's social ills at the feet of British mis-rule in Ireland, at the beginning of the twenty-first century those same problems are attributed to the Catholic Church's singular and allegedly repressive influence over all facets of Irish social, cultural, and political life. This is not to deny that the Catholic Church attempted to enforce conformity to narrowly defined codes of behavior. But placing the entire blame for the attitudes and events that have come to light in recent years assumes that Irish lawmakers and politicians, and the Irish population as a whole, lacked any sort of social, political, or religious agency. As this book suggests, people at all levels of Irish society often acted out of little more than self-interest and self-preservation, especially when it came to the treatment of poor, illegitimate, and abused children; Catholic moral teachings were not always at the top of their list of priorities.

The tendency to bash the Catholic Church has become more pronounced in the last ten or so years as allegations have surfaced about the treatment of children in industrial schools in the 1940s, 1950s, and 1960s. The first public rumblings about the industrial school system arose in 1996 when the documentary *Dear daughter* aired on Irish television.[17] The documentary chronicled the life of Christina Buckley, a woman who spent her childhood in Goldenbridge industrial school. In recent years the media has found the stories of former industrial school residents worthy of media attention. However, Christina Buckley's story was particularly noteworthy because she was a woman of mixed race. Because of its poor economic position until the early 1990s, combined with a conservative Catholic ethos that outsiders may have found stifling, Ireland did not attract the same scale of immigration, legal or otherwise, that occurred elsewhere in Europe. This meant that Ireland was, until the late 1990s, one of the most ethnically and religiously homogenous countries in the West. But it has been a well-kept secret in Irish history that a significant number of men came to Ireland from Africa in the 1950s to study medicine at Trinity and the Royal College of Surgeons. This influx resulted in a small but not insignificant population of mixed-race children, most of whom were born outside of marriage and ultimately ended up in one form of state care or another.

Christina Buckley was one of these children, and *Dear daughter* documented her efforts to trace her father in Nigeria. The main theme of the documentary was Buckley's search not only for her father, but also for the Irish mother who abandoned her shortly after her committal to Goldenbridge in 1952. In fact, the documentary opens with Buckley admitting "I wanted to find my parents and kill them."[18] Buckley also acknowledged that her search for her mother had a disappointing outcome: "There was nothing about her I recognised. I had looked forward to this day and I thought that we would be able to become friends and I thought we would be able to have many an hour sipping coffee in Bewley's ... as I looked at this woman I knew it could never be like this."[19] But the documentary also gave voice to an undercurrent of anger at the Sisters of Mercy, who ran Goldenbridge and a number of other industrial schools for girls. Buckley made a litany of allegations, ranging from starvation and neglect, to denial of educational opportunities, overwork, and severe physical abuse. In the days and weeks after *Dear daughter* aired, public outrage was palpable. This outrage was short-lived, however, and it failed to spark the Irish imagination the way subsequent events would.

A more sustained public debate arose in April 1999 when RTÉ, the Irish state television network, aired a 3-part series, *States of fear* that documented the experiences of former residents of Irish industrial schools in the 1940s, 1950s, and 1960s.[20] In the weeks after this documentary aired former industrial school residents began to make their voices heard in record numbers, forming support groups, appearing on television, writing letters to newspaper editors, and phoning in to radio chat shows across the country. Irish society quickly became convulsed with misery, grief, and anger, and all of that emotion was directed almost entirely at the Catholic Church.

In the years between *Dear daughter* and *States of fear*, small numbers of former industrial school residents had taken civil cases against the religious orders who ran the industrial schools; in most cases the Department of Education and/or the Department of Health, both of whom had oversight and financial responsibilities, were named as co-defendants. After *States of fear* aired the number of civil cases increased exponentially. The Irish government, faced with an extraordinary level of public anger and scrutiny, not to mention millions of Punts in possible compensation to former industrial school residents, issued an unprecedented public apology on 11 May 1999: "On behalf of the State and of all citizens of the State, the Government wishes to make a sincere and long overdue apology to the victims of childhood abuse for our collective failure to intervene, to detect their pain, to come to their rescue."[21] They also announced the establishment of a commission to investigate allegations made by former residents.[22]

The historiography on the Irish industrial school system is nearly non-existent and is, for the most part, limited to non-scholarly media sources whose credibility and objectivity are questionable. Jane Barnes's *Irish industrial schools* is the only scholarly monograph on the subject; it is useful in explaining how the Irish industrial school system came into existence, and how it developed and evolved during its first fifty years.[23] However, the study stops at 1908, with the introduction of the Children Act of 1908, and therefore is of limited use in understanding how the system changed and evolved throughout the first half of the twentieth century, and how the system contributed to contemporary scandals. More recently Mary Raftery and Eoin O'Sullivan published *Suffer the little children*, based on O'Sullivan's doctoral thesis and the *States of fear* documentary.[24] Although based in part on research conducted for a doctoral thesis, *Suffer the little children* could not be categorized as a scholarly work but is, rather, a polemic and sensationalist piece of journalism that aimed more to incite popular feeling than to educate or elucidate. *Suffer the little children*, like O'Sullivan's doctoral thesis "Child welfare in Ireland," makes selective use of Department of Education files to present grand and sensational claims about the state of Ireland's industrial schools. The limited and selective use of primary source material in these two works is disappointing, given that O'Sullivan was the only scholar to have had access to Department of Education files before public access was withdrawn in May 1999.[25]

In recent years the industrial school system, and especially the male and female religious orders that administered them, have come under enormous fire in Ireland; the religious orders have essentially been forced to bear the full brunt of public outrage. And while no one would deny that children who may have been abused in these institutions deserve to have their stories told and validated, the public discussion has become polarized to such an extent that no one questions the accuracy or validity of any "survivor accounts," nor have they considered the role that other parties played in the system. The industrial school system would not have existed in the first place if it did not serve some purpose to the state, and if it was not upheld and supported, every day, by an army of ISPCC inspectors and district court justices who sat in judgment on poor Irish families, and consigned to industrial schools children whose parents did not fit the mould of appropriate and respectable Irish parenthood.

Contemporary media discussions of industrial schools have begun to link the industrial school system with a broader network of institutions, including magdalen asylums that served to rid Irish society of potentially harmful or dangerous elements. Indeed, James Smith argues, in *Ireland's magdalen laundries and the nation's architecture of containment*, that the institutional network underpinned a "culture of containment" whereby those guilty of sexual indiscretions of any kind, especially unmarried mothers, were banished from Irish society and forced to spend an eternity behind the walls of institutions like magdalen asylums.[26] Smith acknowledges that his work is primarily a piece of literary criticism, and a significant portion of the book analyzes various genres of text that deal with magdalen asylums. But he does purport to provide a historical context for his textual analysis and herein lies the danger. Smith's work is seriously under-sourced as a work of history, and he draws broad conclusions and makes sweeping generalizations with scant evidence. He tends to take at face value the autobiographical accounts of former industrial school and magdalen asylum residents, and he is uncritical in his acceptance of the conviction that the male and female religious who ran Ireland's institutions were abusive, corrupt, and selfish. He alludes to the "responsibility" or complicity of Irish society as a whole, but most of his ire is directed at the Catholic Church.

Frances Finnegan's *Do penance or perish: A study of magdalen asylums in Ireland* suffers from the same problem.[27] The potential of Finnegan's subtitle, *A study of magdalen asylums in Ireland* is never fully realized, for two main reasons. First, Finnegan is unapologetic in asserting the bias that underpins her work. She insists that women who were admitted to magdalen asylums in the nineteenth and twentieth centuries were victims of "indifference" and "injustice." Women probably were victims of injustice and indifference (although it is likely that they were victimized by their families and communities as much as they were victimized by the Good Shepherds). However, because Finnegan insists on portraying women only as victims, she rejects other possible interpretations of her source material. Furthermore, Finnegan reaches conclusions about women's experiences and motivations that are not entirely supported by the available evidence. For example, she concludes, solely on the basis of the scant information included in admission registers, that the majority of women admitted to the asylums were admitted against their will. This may, in fact, be true, but lacking personal accounts from the women themselves, we can never know definitively. But, in reaching these conclusions, Finnegan effectively strips women of their agency and reduces them to infants incapable of or unwilling to assert their power and individuality.

The institutional network is just one area of Irish social history that has been shortchanged in the historiography of twentieth-century Ireland. In recent years there have been scholarly works that touch on the history of childhood and families in Ireland, although they touch only tangentially on the issues that are central to this book. Maria Luddy briefly examines the treatment of unmarried mothers, and links it to prostitution in her 2007 book *Prostitution in Irish Society*.[28] In addressing unmarried motherhood, this work focused on the punitive treatment meted out to unmarried mothers, and projects the view that they were, across the board, condemned and vilified and banished from "respectable" society through institutionalization or desperate journeys to Britain. A recent volume on single motherhood in Ireland, *Single motherhood in twentieth-century Ireland*, follows Luddy's lead in focusing on one aspect of single motherhood: the use of magdalen asylums to "punish" unmarried mothers for their sins.[29] Most of the essays in this volume deal with single motherhood from a contemporary perspective; three of the four that deal with the historical perspective are narrowly focused on magdalen asylums (two essays) and women who committed infanticide.[30]

A more general study of motherhood in twentieth-century Dublin is Lindsey Earner-Byrne's *Mother and child: Maternity and child welfare in Dublin*.[31] This work is concerned with public and private social welfare and health services available to Dublin women to help them provide for their families. In drawing heavily on the papers of Edward Byrne and John Charles McQuaid, Archbishops of Dublin, Earner-Byrne foregrounds the role of the Catholic Church in shaping public and private services. The central role of the Catholic Church in the development of social services for mothers apparently guaranteed that there were few public services available to unmarried mothers before the 1970s. Earner-Byrne is correct, technically, that no public services were explicitly available to unmarried mothers to care for their children in their own homes. However, an examination of public assistance records and ISPCC case files reveals that unmarried mothers did, on occasion, successfully petition local authorities for home assistance. And while Earner-Byrne correctly identifies the "moral angst" that shaped official attitudes to unmarried motherhood in post-independence Ireland, it is also true that many unmarried mothers and their children lived within families and communities just as "legitimate" children did. A valuable examination of changes in attitude towards the family, as well as the role and function of families in Irish society, is Finola Kennedy's *Cottage to creche*.[32] Kennedy's book deals primarily with changes that have occurred in the family since the 1970s, but it does offer some tantalizing glimpses into the more distant past.

Overall, the field of Irish social history generally is significantly underdeveloped when compared with other European societies. Diarmaid Ferriter's recent *The transformation of Ireland* seeks to fill some of the gaps in twentieth-century Irish social history.[33] Ferriter's ambitious project raises some interesting questions about how twentieth-century Irish history has traditionally been written, and sheds some light on people and issues that have long been ignored in historical scholarship. Ferriter wonders why, if the family was in fact the integral building block of Irish society, as stated in the Constitution, it has been all but ignored by historians: "Scholars seem to concur that twentieth-century Ireland nurtured a caring community bound together by a high degree of social consensus, underpinned by an underdeveloped but viable economy, a stable multi-party political system, and a distinctive foreign policy. But if the family is placed at the top of this achievement, why hasn't it been subjected to more sustained examination?"[34] *Precarious childhood in post-independence Ireland* takes issue with the view that "Ireland nurtured a caring community bound together by a high degree of social consensus" and in fact argues just the opposite. On the other hand, it seeks to remedy what Ferriter rightly points out as a flaw in twentieth-century Irish historiography: the absence of any discussion of family (and childhood). This book argues that definitions of family and childhood and, indeed, real families and children, were manipulated, used, and sometimes abused to reinforce an image of independent Irish society that was little more than a myth.

Ferriter also correctly points out that issues of class are markedly absent from twentieth-century Irish historiography. Much of twentieth-century Irish history seems to assume that social class distinctions did not exist; this perspective is evident, for example, in Inglis's argument that mothers gained moral authority from their relationship with the Catholic Church. *Middle-class* mothers might have earned such moral authority but working-class mothers did not. In fact, working-class mothers often had their constitutional rights trampled when their children were taken from them, for no reason other than abject poverty, and placed in industrial schools or foster homes. The constitutional rights of unmarried mothers were equally ignored as their children were boarded-out, sent to industrial schools and, occasionally, adopted by American couples under a legally and constitutionally questionable informal adoption scheme. No one suffered more, as a result of these circumstances, than working-class children. The precariousness of working-class childhood in the twentieth century shows the lie to many of the assumptions that have been made about twentieth-century Irish society, about the value of the family as the "fundamental unit group of society," about the "caring community" that allegedly characterized post-independence Irish society, about the Catholic Church's sanctity of life doctrine, and about the independent state's professed commitment to "cherish all the children equally." An examination of social policy as it related to children and families, and of the experiences of children themselves, begs a re-examination of the nature and character of post-independence Irish society.

This book draws on a wide array of sources, many of which have not been utilized fully or even used by historians. Legislation and parliamentary debates, government commission reports, annual reports of the Departments of Health, Education, and Social Welfare, and the archival material of various government departments offer insight into official attitudes towards the state's responsibility in caring for poor, neglected, and abused children. The Catholic hierarchy's attitude is evident in writings (including pastorals, penny pamphlets, articles in scholarly and popular journals, and the Catholic press) and archival material from various arch-bishops. The experiences of families and children are evident, to some extent, in the ISPCC case files, newspaper articles, and the minutes of local boards of health and public assistance.

A source that has been overlooked by historians is the case files of the Irish Society for the Prevention of Cruelty to Children (ISPCC).[35] These files are enormously valuable for the glimpses they give into the lives of poor families, and the way these families utilized the ISPCC and other resources to care for and protect themselves and their families. But ISPCC case files are not unproblematic, for all of their value. The staff of the current ISPCC had no connection with or knowledge of how the Society operated prior to the 1970s and, indeed, they appear to have been two entirely different organizations in approach, outlook, and attitude. Until about ten years ago it seemed, indeed, that no case files from the years before the 1970s had survived. Hundreds of case files were eventually discovered in unused closets and cabinets. For some reason that is impossible to explain, these case files all relate to three counties: Wexford, Wicklow, and Mayo, and they are all confined to the period from the late 1930s to the mid-1950s. Although limited in geography and time-frame, however, one can assume that they are representative of the kinds of cases that came to the attention of the ISPCC, and how the ISPCC inspectors responded.

Because this book is concerned, to some extent, with contemporary al-legations of abuse in industrial schools, it also utilizes autobiographies and documentaries that are, essentially, oral histories. Other authors who look at the Irish industrial school system have been uncritical in their use of per-sonal testimonies – a flaw this book will avoid without dismissing outright the painful experiences of hundreds, if not thousands, of poor, neglected, and abused children, An example of the problematic nature of oral histories is evident in the case of Christina Noble and her sister Philomena Byrne. In her autobiography, published several years before the current scandals broke, Noble recounts the story of her mother's funeral, and specifically, her sister Philomena being pushed into the coffin by a thoughtless relative so she could kiss her mother goodbye. Noble recalled that the same was done to her: "When I was at last released I fell to the floor and vomited. What happened afterwards is dim and vague. I only remember that very faintly I heard Philomena's screams as she in turn was pushed into the coffin and held against mother's cold face."[36] Noble also detailed a horrific pattern of physical and sexual abuse inflicted by relatives on her and her sisters. In a 2000 documentary aired on TV3, *20/20: Stolen lives*, Philomena alleged that the nuns who ran the industrial school to which she had been com-mitted used to lock the children in coffins as punishment, and that she was taken from her bed at night to have sex with priests and other men.[37] It is not unreasonable to question the extent to which Byrne's memories of her life before being committed to the industrial school were blurred and distorted. This is true of many children who were sent to industrial schools at very young ages after having experienced severe trauma at home. It is not the intent of this book to deny or dismiss the experiences of former industrial school residents, but rather to attempt to place those memories in a broader historical context.

Notes

1   Dáil Éireann, *Minutes of proceedings of the first parliament of the Republic of Ireland 1919–1921* (Dublin: Government Stationery Office, 1921).
2   Dáil Éireann, *Minutes of proceedings of the first parliament*, p. 23.
3   *Bunreacht na Éireann Constitution of Ireland* (Dublin: Government Stationery Office, n.d.), p. 142.
4   A scheme of children's allowances was introduced in 1944 that paid parents 2s 6d per week for the third and each subsequent child. The scheme was intended to ensure that poor parents were not discouraged from having large families. The measure was influenced in part by first-hand observations by some TDs of the abject poverty that existed in their constituencies, and by the anticipation of the publication of the Beveridge Report in Britain. (TD = teacha dala, or member of the Dáil.)
5   Not all Irish women and men adhered to Catholic teaching with regard to extramarital sexuality and contraception. However, legislation upheld those teachings, making it virtually impossible for couples to legally and safely limit their fertility.
6   *Bunreacht na Éireann Constitution of Ireland*, p. 136.
7   The Doyle case inspired Evelyn Doyle's autobiography as well as the 2002 film *Evelyn*. See Evelyn Doyle, *Tea and green ribbons* (New York: Free Press, 2003) and *Evelyn*, directed by Bruce Beresford, MGM, 2003.
8   *Evening Mail* (17 December 1954), p. 9.
9   *Evening Mail* (24 January 1955), p. 5.
10   *Evening Mail* (21 December 1955), p. 5.
11   *Evening Mail* (8 February 1956), p. 5.
12   J.H. Whyte, *Church and state in modern Ireland 1923–1979* (Dublin: Gill and Macmillan, 1980).
13   The "mother and child" controversy erupted in 1950 when the Minister for Health, Dr Noel Browne, introduced a new health bill, the centerpiece of which was a comprehensive scheme of health care for pregnant women, new mothers, and children under five years of age. Browne's scheme was a response to growing concerns about high maternal and infant mortality, and it represented a new departure in that it committed the state to providing free health care to mothers and their children. Under Browne's proposed scheme women would have been free to select their own GPs, even if the GP was not already on the government's list of approved doctors; this provision was the scheme's fatal flaw. The Catholic

hierarchy objected in the strongest terms to the idea that women would be free to choose their own GPs, but that the state would foot the bill. (They feared that the state would end up paying the fees of doctors who did not practice according to Catholic teachings.) The debate over the mother and child scheme became so heated that Browne was compelled to resign. The scheme that was finally introduced was a significantly watered-down version of what Browne had originally proposed. See Noel Browne, *Against the tide* (Dublin: Gill and Macmillan, 1986) and John Horgan, *Noel Browne: Passionate outsider* (Dublin: Gill and Macmillan, 2004).

14   Tom Inglis, *Moral monopoly: The Catholic Church in modern Irish Society* (Dublin: Gill and Macmillan, 1987); Tom Inglis, *Moral monopoly: The rise and fall of the Catholic Church in modern Ireland* (Dublin: Gill and Macmillan, 1998); Tom Inglis, *Lessons in Irish sexuality* (Dublin: University College Dublin Press, 1999); Tom Inglis, *Truth, power, and lies: Irish society and the case of the Kerry Babies* (Dublin: University College Dublin Press, 2004).

15   Inglis, *Moral monopoly: The rise and fall of the Catholic Church*, p. 9.

16   Inglis, *Moral Monopoly: The rise and fall of the Catholic Church*, pp. 205–9.

17   *Dear daughter*, Crescendo Concepts, producer/director Louis Lentin, 1996.

18   *Dear daughter*.

19   *Dear daughter*.

20   *States of fear*, narr., Aine Lawlor, writ., prod., dir., Mary Raftery, RTÉ, Ireland, 27 April 1999.

21   *Irish Times* (12 May 1999),p. 1. This apology appeared in all major newspapers on that day.

22   The Laffoy Commission, under the leadership of Justice Mary Laffoy, was appointed in 1999 to investigate allegations of abuse in Ireland's industrial schools. The Commission had two strands that offered former residents a choice on how they wanted their grievances heard. The "listening strand" was intended to offer former industrial school residents a safe and discreet environment to talk about their experiences and have them validated. The "investigative strand" took evidence from former residents and other concerned parties with the intent of bringing to account people accused of abusing former industrial school residents. In September 2003 Mary Laffoy resigned from the Commission because she did not believe the government was giving its full cooperation to its work; Justice Sean Ryan subsequently replaced her.

23   Jane Barnes, *Irish industrial schools, 1868–1908: Origins and development* (Dublin: Irish Academic Press, 1989).

24   Mary Raftery and Eoin O'Sullivan, *Suffer the little children: The inside story of Ireland's industrial schools* (Dublin: New Island Books, 1999). See also Eoin O'Sullivan, "Child welfare in Ireland, 1750–1995: A history of the present," Ph.D. thesis, Trinity College Dublin, 1999; *States of fear*.

25   The Department of Education files examined by O'Sullivan were never released to the National Archives, as they should have been under the National Archives Act (1986). They were held in the department's headquarters in Galway, and researchers had to apply for access to them. Shortly after the airing of the *States of fear* documentaries the department closed these files altogether and, at the time of writing, they have not been re-opened.

26   James Smith, *Ireland's magdalen asylums and the nation's architecture of containment* (Notre Dame, IN: University of Notre Dame Press, 2007).

27 Frances Finnegan, *Do penance or perish: A study of magdalen asylums in Ireland* (Piltown, Co. Kilkenny: Congrave Press, 2001).

28 Maria Luddy, *Prostitution and Irish society, 1800–1940* (Cambridge: Cambridge University Press, 2007). See also Maria Luddy, "Moral rescue and unmarried mothers in Ireland in the 1920s," *Women's Studies*, 30 (2001), pp. 797–817.

29 Maria Cinta Ramblado-Minero and Auxiliadora Perez-Vides (eds), *Single motherhood in twentieth-century Ireland: cultural, historical, and social essays* (Lewiston, NY: Edwin Mellen Press, 2006).

30 See Cliona Rattigan, "'Dark spots' in Irish Society: Unmarried mothers and infanticide in Ireland from 1926 to 1938"; Aida Rosende-Perez, "'Washing away their sins': Unmarried motherhood in Peter Mullan's *The magdalene sisters*"; and Paula Murphy, "'Wayward girls and fallen women': Negotiating fact and fiction in the magdalen laundries," in *Single motherhood in twentieth-century Ireland: Cultural, historical, and social essays*, ed. Maria Cinta Ramblado-Minero and Auxiliadora Perez-Vides (Lewiston, New York: Edwin Mellen Press, 2006).

31 Lindsey Earner-Byrne, *Mother and child: Maternity and child welfare in Dublin, 1922–1960* (Manchester: Manchester University Press, 2007).

32 Finola Kennedy, *Cottage to creche: Family change in Ireland* (Dublin: Institute of Public Administration, 2001).

33 Diarmaid Ferriter, *The transformation of Ireland* (Woodstock, NY: Overlook Press, 2004).

34 Ferriter, *The transformation of Ireland*, p. 5.

35 The Irish Society for the Prevention of Cruelty to Children operated, for the first fifty or so years of its existence, as a branch of the English National Society for the Prevention of Cruelty to Children and was referred to as the National, rather than the Irish, Society. It broke from the English organization in 1956 and changed its official name to the Irish Society for the Prevention of Cruelty to Children. ISPCC is used throughout this book for the sake of consistency.

36 Christina Noble (with Robert Coram), *Bridge across my sorrows: The Christina Noble story* (London: J. Murray, 1994), p. 55.

37 *20/20: Stolen lives*, prod. Louis Lentin, TV3 Ireland, 5 November 2000.

1

Poverty, family dysfunction, and state provision for neglected children

Introduction

The years from the 1920s to the 1950s were characterized by periods of endemic poverty and austerity that had a profound impact on poor families. Children seem to have suffered the most from this poverty: at best they went to bed hungry and lived in home environments that were unhealthy and perhaps even dangerous; at worst, they were removed from homes where parents simply could not care for them out of their meager (and sometimes non-existent) resources. During bouts of particularly high unemployment thousands of men migrated to England in search of work. For some families this strategy literally was their salvation. But many men who went off to England failed to send money home, thereby compounding the misery of their wives and children. This chapter, in an examination of social conditions and social policies, argues that the nationalist vision of frugality and simplicity translated into a lack of initiative on the part of successive Irish governments, and children paid a particularly high price for that lack of initiative.

Standard of living

The kind of Irish society envisioned by Eamon de Valera and other nationalists was frugal and simple, with the majority of people living in the countryside, engaging in agriculture and other rural pursuits. Successive Irish governments, from the 1920s forward, introduced some improvements, such as electrification and water schemes, to build up Ireland's infrastructure and, by extension, improve the quality of life in rural areas. But into the 1950s Ireland remained primarily unindustrialized, and there were few efforts at economic and industrial development. This meant that a significant proportion of the Irish population endured bouts of unemployment and poverty that inevitably had a negative impact on their quality of life and on their ability to provide and care for their children. This, in turn, contributed to substandard and even dangerous living conditions for poor children, and comparatively high levels of institutionalization or neglected children whose parents simply could not provide for them.

Poverty

A significant proportion of the Irish population lived in poverty at least into the 1950s. Successive governments were unwilling or unable to resolve Ireland's endemic economic problems, and it was not until the 1960s that the Irish government began to engage in economic planning in a meaningful way.[1] This shortcoming had a significant impact on the lives of the poor, and particularly poor children, many of whom ended up in industrial schools for no other reason than poverty. An article published in 1922 in the *Journal of the Statistical and Social Inquiry Society* outlined the "poverty problems" that faced the new Irish government. The author, John Dunne, pointed out that much of the widespread poverty that existed in Ireland resulted from seasonal or occasional unemployment, and he called on the new government to strengthen the Irish economy with a view to ensuring full employment for all able-bodied men who wanted to work: "The removal of the plague of poverty, which is the fountain-source of much of our national ills, physical and moral, should be, to my mind, the primal work of an Irish administration ... I do sincerely believe that, given the good will of all classes, an era may yet arrive when absolute destitution, whether affecting adult or child, shall be unknown, and employment for willing workers will be ever abundant."[2] Dunne's optimism proved unfounded, and full employment and economic prosperity continued to be elusive right into the 1960s.

The late 1920s and 1930s were characterized by widespread poverty and poor housing: these were the two factors to which the Irish Society for the Prevention of Cruelty to Children (ISPCC) attributed many of the cases of neglect they encountered during those years. In 1925 the Government established the Commission for the Relief of the Sick and Destitute Poor to "... examine the law and administration affecting the relief of the following destitute classes and to make recommendations: a) widows and their children; b) children without parents; c) unmarried mothers and their children; d) deserted children."[3] The commission's report, published in 1927, commented on the inadequacy of home assistance payments, at that time the only source of relief for poor families outside of the county home (formerly workhouse) system. The report concluded that "boards of health, whilst perhaps acting with more liberality than their predecessors, still fell short of discharging their full obligations in regard to persons eligible for relief who cannot be sent to institutions, and this applies particularly to the cases of widows and children and able-bodied males with dependent families."[4] It recommended a scheme of "mother's pension" to provide relief for widows and their children.

According to an *Evening Herald* article, when the Poor Relief (Dublin) Act of 1929, which provided for the outdoor relief of able-bodied men and women in Dublin city and county, came into force in 1930 people began to line up for applications before six o'clock in the morning, and over 2,000 applications were submitted by the end of the day. The article noted that the majority of the applicants were young, healthy, able-bodied men who could not find work: "Many of the men to the casual passer-by seemed strangely out of place in that great gathering. Some of them were dressed as neatly as bank clerks, with boots well shined, collars immaculately white, and hats worn at a jaunty angle, and it was hard to believe that they were without work and without money. They were, of course, all able-bodied, most of them pictures of health, and their ages ranged from the twenties to the sixties."[5] The observation that these men presented the "picture of health" reinforces the idea that poverty was primarily a function of unemployment (and, by extension, a lack of economic planning on the part of the government) rather than of infirmity or laziness.

Conditions do not appear to have improved in the 1930s. The work of the Society of St Vincent de Paul in the Limerick area reveals the extent of the problem of poverty in Limerick. In 1936 the society provided boots and clothing to nearly 2,000 families, and disbursed nearly £2,000 in assistance. This was in spite of the fact that the society's resources and donations were so diminished that they were forced to reduce by nearly half the number of people they could assist.[6] A 1939 *Standard* article indicated that the unemployment rate throughout the country remained relatively constant at 100,000, with over 83,000 people on home assistance (and further that 34 per cent of those receiving home assistance resided in Dublin city or county). The article suggested that those on home assistance "constitute a vast army of men, women, and children, dragging out a miserable and demoralising existence on pittances and doles."[7] Even those receiving home assistance suffered deprivation, because the amounts were not sufficient to cover rent, much less food, fuel, clothing and other basic necessities.

A number of studies were published in the 1940s that highlighted the extent of poverty and poor housing conditions, especially in Dublin. These studies pointed out both that large families tended to experience more poverty than smaller families, and that poverty and poor housing were more pronounced in urban than in rural areas. A 1945 *Studies* article noted that a recent survey of 10,500 Dublin families found that 55 per cent of them had an income significantly below what experts at the time suggested was a minimum standard, which ranged from £3 5s 0d to £4 18s 0d depending on family size.[8] The article further suggested that "on the whole ... we may take it that there are some 90–100,000 men, women and children in the country who are safeguarded from starvation, but who have not enough – in many cases not nearly enough – money to procure the simple necessities of life."[9] These findings are borne out in the annual reports of the ISPCC. In their 1944–45 annual report the Dublin branch of the ISPCC reported that the number of cases dealt with by the society had risen steadily, and they attributed this increase to the "conditions of squalor and poverty" in which many families lived.[10] These conditions, according to the report, were not entirely the fault of parents but could be attributed to the inadequacy of existing public assistance and housing schemes.

The government enacted a series of emergency measures in the 1920s, 1930s, and 1940s during periods of particularly severe economic depression and unemployment, suggesting that they realized the dire conditions in which many working-class families lived. For example, in the early years of the Irish Free State the government observed with alarm and concern the ever growing rate of unemployment; one of the first measures undertaken by the new government was the introduction of a special scheme for the relief of destitution. They allocated £275,000 for public utility schemes that would provide employment for unemployed men, and an additional £100,000 for emergency relief. Some of these funds were earmarked for the southern and western seaboards that had experienced a failure of the fishing industry and potato crops in the early 1920s.[11] Another series of emergency measures was introduced in 1944 to try to deal with the conditions of poverty and distress that were by-products of the Second World War. These measures included food allowances, in the form of bread, butter, and milk, to those families who received home assistance and widows' and orphans' pensions; special grants to local authorities to provide assistance in kind to recipients of home assistance; and low-cost footwear to the children of parents on low incomes or in receipt of any form of public assistance.[12]

Housing

Poor housing was an aspect of poverty that raised significant concern right into the 1950s. The task of providing a sufficient stock of comfortable, healthy, affordable homes for poor and working-class families was one of the most challenging problems to face successive governments in the first half of the twentieth century. Census, newspaper, and ISPCC data indicate that into the 1950s overcrowding, evictions, and substandard housing were fairly common; social commentators periodically warned that poor housing jeopardized the health and well-being of children and may also have contributed to juvenile delinquency and petty crime. The housing problem was three-fold: a shortage of suitable accommodation for working-class families who could afford reasonable rents; the squalid and overcrowded living conditions of the poorest families, in slums, tenements, and condemned cottages, who could afford no better; and homelessness brought about in part by insecure lease arrangements and evictions. These conditions continued into the 1950s, and they were significant factors in committals to industrial schools.[13]

The problems of overcrowding, squalid housing, and evictions appear frequently enough in a variety of sources to suggest several conclusions: that a significant segment of the population experienced these conditions at some point in their lives; that these conditions were dangerous and even deadly on occasion; that overcrowding and evictions in some cases contributed to the break-up of families; and, finally, that these conditions were not confined only to the poorest or most marginalized families. Working-class families in general, even those that were relatively well off, were affected by the shortage of affordable housing.[14] Newspaper and ISPCC case files are full of accounts of families living in squalid conditions "unfit for human habitation." Many families were utterly destitute and incapable of improving their circumstances without the financial assistance of family, friends, or public assistance authorities. Other families spent years waiting for a corporation or council house to become available, and in the meantime had to take whatever accommodation they could get. Other working-class families could afford modest rents but could not find safe and healthy accommodation, or faced discrimination from landlords who did not want to rent to families with children. Being able to afford accommodation was no guarantee that a family would actually be able to secure it.

The housing problem was not an exclusively urban one. The reports of the ISPCC provide insight into the nature and extent of the housing problem throughout the country. Parents often appealed to the ISPCC for help in securing better accommodation for their families, and the ISPCC occasionally intervened with local authorities on behalf of "worthy" families. Of the roughly four hundred ISPCC case files surveyed, approximately fifty were explicitly concerned with poor housing. But housing conditions were mentioned in many others, even if it was not what brought the family to the notice of the ISPCC in the first place. In 1954 the ISPCC was called to a house in Wexford town where they found a woman living in a single room with her six children who ranged from two months to nine years:

> I visited as a result of a complaint. The mother and her six children were present. The father was at his work. This family are living in an upstairs room in the home of a [relative]. The mother is allowed to do the cooking downstairs in the kitchen, but the children are not allowed to use the kitchen except when [relative] is out, which is not very often, otherwise they have to stay in the room or get out on the streets. The twins have never been taken downstairs yet. It is a bad case of overcrowding and is bad for the children's health. Woman is doing her best under difficult circumstances.[15]

This was a clear case in which whatever neglect the children suffered stemmed solely from the family's difficulty in securing adequate housing, and not from any shortcomings on the part of the parents. With the ISPCC inspector's help the family moved into their own cottage a month after this initial report was made, and the ISPCC subsequently closed the case as "satisfactory."

A much more severe case was documented in an ISPCC case from 1956. In April 1956 an ISPCC inspector visited a family in Wexford town consisting of parents and their five children ranging in age from one to sixteen years. The inspector was shocked by what he discovered:

> I called at the request of [mother]. [She] stated, "I have asked you to call as I have heard that your Society might help me in getting a house. We have lived here thirteen years. The house is infested with rats. For the last two years it has been terrible. I have killed twenty rats in one day, inside the house. I am afraid the rats will eat one of my children when they are sleeping at night." All the floor boards are eaten away with the rats. There is a partly open sewerage outside the front door. The rats come up from there and eat their way into the house. Advised woman never to leave the baby alone for a moment. Told her I would write to the housing officer.[16]

This family had already endured these living conditions for more than two years before appealing to the ISPCC for help. It was another four months before the family's application for a council cottage was approved. The two cases here had "happy endings" in the sense that the families involved eventually moved into more sanitary and healthy accommodation. But not all families were so lucky, especially in urban areas like Dublin where accommodation was in short supply and families had to take whatever they could get, even if it meant living in rat-infested basements.

The *Irish Workers' Voice* newspaper championed the cause of safe and affordable housing in the 1940s and 1950s. Admittedly the newspaper's bias was in favor of working families and critical of government inaction, but the conditions described in this newspaper were echoed in other sources, so there likely is some truth in their reports. A 1949 newspaper article analyzed an informal survey conducted by one of its reporters:

> Investigating slum conditions in Dublin I visited the tenement house in Pearse Street, the tenants of which were saved from eviction a couple of months ago by the swift intervention of the Irish Workers' League. The three largest families expect to move into Corporation houses very shortly. The remaining tenants, though somewhat relieved to be left in the house instead of being evicted as they had anticipated some time ago, are not at all happy at having to live still in the same wretched conditions.
>
> This house has no backyard and the one lavatory is at the top of the house. When choked as it frequently is, being used by so many people, its contents are exuded down through the whole place. The children, I found, are the worst affected by these conditions. There being no back yard they have nowhere to play except in the small airless rooms, the gloomy evil-smelling stairs and the open streets outside, which are constantly beset by traffic dangers.
>
> In other tenement houses in the vicinity I found rooms where water from the lavatory cistern overhead seeped down through the ceiling, and rooms with large rat holes eaten into the floor and walls. In some cases the sewers run through the halls and quite frequently they overflow and send their contents around the hallway and into the rooms. I noticed several bulging front walls which threatened to collapse any minute.[17]

The *Workers' Voice* continued to comment on urban squalor in subsequent months and years (in November 1949, for example, they reported on "36 persons in rat pit"). But they also reported on conditions outside of Dublin city, in villages like Maynooth and Blackrock. The tone of their reporting suggests that they believed the government was not doing enough to provide adequate housing for Ireland's poor, and their reporting was intended to keep pressure on the government to do better. (There is no evidence, however, to suggest that their reporting was in any way effective in compelling the government to act.)

The housing problem was so severe that in the late 1930s the government initiated an investigation of the housing conditions of the working class in Dublin. The resulting report, published in 1943, noted that the housing problem was not of recent origin and, indeed, that it already had been the subject of extensive enquiry:

> Few social problems have been subjected to such thorough examination during the last century and a half by Royal commissions, Departmental Committees, Inspectors, Corporation Surveys, Social Service organisations and philanthropists. The more noteworthy were the Royal Sanitary Commission 1879–80, the Royal Commission on the Housing of the Working Classes 1885 (each of which devoted special attention to Dublin City); the Departmental Committee on Dublin Housing Conditions 1913–14; the Chief Engineering Inspector (Mr. P.C. Cowan's) Report 1918; the official decennial Census Reports since 1821,

and the several less systematic unofficial attempts to enumerate and classify the population of the City which were made between the years 1798 and 1821.[18]

The report noted that an increasing number of families lived in overcrowded tenement houses. In 1879, for example, there were nearly 10,000 houses categorized as "tenements" in Dublin, and each tenement was home to an average of 12 people. By 1938 the number of tenements had dropped to just over 6,000, and the average number of people living in each tenement had risen to 17.7. Furthermore, 70 per cent of the people surveyed by the inquiry lived in one-room flats.[19] These statistics point to a serious overcrowding problem that was compounded by the absence or inadequacy of sanitary, sewage, and garbage disposal facilities. The inquiry concluded with recommendations as to slum clearance and the building of 20,000 affordable houses and flats to accommodate the city's working-class families.

In addition to causing misery for countless working-class children, overcrowding, substandard housing, homelessness, and evictions contributed to industrial school committals. In a case that came before the Dublin Children's Court in 1945 the ISPCC sought the committal of four children on the grounds that the parents could not exercise proper guardianship. The father had been ordered to evacuate his Defence Forces quarters but could not find any other accommodation. In commenting on the dilemma, the district justice noted: "The Corporation authorities sometimes complain when I send children away to schools, because of the extra burden placed on taxpayers; yet here is a case where if a house could be found for this man, there would be no need to send his boys away."[20] The district justice appealed to the Dublin Corporation to provide accommodation for the family, but the corporation claimed their hands were tied: "The position in connection with these emergency cases is becoming more serious every day, and the requirements in such cases are getting beyond our resources … In these circumstances the justice will, I am sure, appreciate our difficulties and the impossibility of providing relief for the family."[21] The ISPCC inspector had also attempted to secure housing for the family, to no avail, because landlords were reluctant to rent to families with children. Three of the children were committed to an industrial school while the parents and baby became casuals at St Kevin's Institution.[22]

In another case from 1945 the ISPCC applied for the committal of five children of a family that had been evicted from their home for nonpayment of rent. The family became casuals at St Kevin's, which meant that they could only enter the institution at 6p.m. and had to leave each morning at 8a.m. The mother spent her days wandering the city streets with her five children in tow. All five children eventually were committed to industrial schools.[23] While in the first case the shortage of housing, and a reluctance on the part of landlords to rent to families with children, was the root cause of the family's circumstances, in the second case the eviction and subsequent homelessness were symptomatic of the profound cycle of poverty in which this family appeared to be trapped.

In 1946 the ISPCC applied for the committal of six children after the family was evicted from their home and camped out on the side of the road at Ballymun, north of Dublin: "whatever household goods the family possessed were on the roadside. Some of the family slept on a bed there covered with a tin roof. The younger children slept in a wardrobe and one of them in a pram. They took such food as they got off a table on the roadside."[24] The father had been temporarily unemployed but at the time of the court proceedings was working and able to support his family, but he could not find accommodation for them. The ISPCC inspector tried to place the children with relatives temporarily, and the case was adjourned for two weeks. When the case again came before the court the ISPCC inspector informed the district justice that relatives had taken in the parents and two of the children. The four remaining children were committed to Goldenbridge industrial school.[25] Again, here is a case where the committal of the children probably could have been prevented had the family been able to secure suitable and affordable accommodation.

A case from 1949 was, according to the district court justice, "the worst that had ever come before [him]."[26] The ISPCC applied for the committal of five children because of the family's hazardous living conditions, which consisted of an old storeroom at the back of a house in North Great George's Street that had been condemned by public health authorities. The storeroom had no light, no windows, and no ventilation. The father had applied for a corporation house fifteen months previously but, according to the Corporation's housing spokesman, "there were many deserving cases on the waiting list and [he] did not think that this case would receive priority."[27] The case was adjourned for a week while the ISPCC made one final appeal to the Corporation, without success. Two of the children were sent to industrial schools while the other three remained with their parents as casuals at St Kevin's.[28]

Although housing conditions began to improve by the late 1950s, there continued to be a link between evictions and committals to industrial schools. In 1956 a father applied to have his four children committed to an industrial school after the family was evicted from their flat in Keogh Square (which, interestingly, was located directly across the street from Goldenbridge Industrial School). The father was unemployed and unable to pay any rent. When the district justice adjourned the case for a week to allow investigations to be made, the father asked what he was supposed to do with the children in the meantime. The district justice recommended that the family go to St Kevin's as casuals.[29] In a similar case, also from 1956, a father applied to have his five children committed to industrial schools because they were about to be evicted from their corporation house. The father planned to look for work in England, and to send for the children once he and his wife got settled there. The case was adjourned for a week so that industrial school vacancies could be found for the children.[30]

The housing conditions that prevailed into the 1950s were part of a broader pattern of poverty that affected the lives of countless working-class children and their families. Some working-class children lived, on a daily basis, in tiny, unventilated, rat-infested hovels that afforded no privacy and no sanitary facilities. Other children became casuals with their families at St Kevin's and other public institutions. And untold hundreds, if not thousands, of children were consigned to industrial schools because of dangerous living conditions, evictions, and homelessness. In spite of the conditions that were publicized regularly in ISPCC reports and newspaper articles, and in spite of surveys that revealed the devastating effects of overcrowded and substandard housing, successive governments did little to increase the stock of affordable, safe, healthy accommodation.

Diet and nutrition

There is evidence to suggest that, at least into the 1950s, the diet and nutrition of the average poor or working-class family was substandard. Food shortages and rationing during the Second World War made it even more difficult for poor families to feed their children. A number of nutritional surveys published in the 1940s revealed the connection between hunger and malnutrition on the one hand, and income and family size on the other. This material supports the view that some families were too poor to purchase sufficient quantities of food for their children. The reports of county medical officers give some insight into the extent of malnutrition, although the information included in those reports, and indeed the availability of the reports themselves, is uneven at best.

In 1943 Dr Charles Clancy Gore conducted a survey of nutritional standards amongst one hundred working-class Dublin families, comprising 684 men, women, and children. His goal was to assess the extent of malnutrition in working-class families and to gauge the links between family size, poverty, and malnutrition.[31] Gore's survey was modelled after a study that had been conducted a year earlier by the British Medical Association (BMA), which costed out a minimum diet for working-class people. This diet, which included moderate amounts of meat, dairy products, and fruits and vegetables, cost 14s 1d per week sterling. Comparing this standard with the actual incomes of survey participants, Gore found that 61 per cent of survey participants, and 71 per cent of children, lived in households with income levels well below the threshold for an adequate, nutritious diet.

The size of the family, more than anything else, determined whether a household had an income sufficient to provide an adequate, nutritious diet. Not surprisingly, larger families were more likely to fall below their minimum income threshold than smaller families. More than half of survey participants spent less 7s per week on food, an amount that was half of the minimum amount specified by the BMA. Only twelve survey participants spent an adequate sum per week on food according to BMA standards. Gore also found that larger families, and families with less income to spend on food, tended to spend most of their available food budget on bread, which was inexpensive and filling but had little nutritional value. Meanwhile, respondents spent little or none of their food budget on meat, dairy products, fruits and vegetables. Overall Gore concluded:

> the standard of living of these families is obviously low. This may be due entirely to prevailing war conditions, causing the very marked increase in the cost of living. In peace time it is probably that the smaller families would have adequate incomes. At the moment it is possible, only for these smaller families to maintain with difficulty a reasonable standard of living. It is, however, absolutely impossible for the larger families to provide adequately for themselves, at present.[32]

In other words, wartime austerity may have made it difficult for a larger number of families to provide a basic adequate diet. But for large families, wartime austerity only compounded their already subsistence circumstances.

The Department of Health undertook a survey in 1946 of the food habits of families across the socio-economic spectrum. Families around the country were included in the survey but the primary focus was Dublin and former congested districts in rural Mayo, Donegal, and Kerry.[33] The survey was not concerned with the question of malnutrition but, rather, evaluated what families ate, how much money they spent per week on food, and the correlation between income and food expenditure and food habits. The survey's findings reinforced the findings of earlier studies, particularly in its conclusion that the quality and quantity of food improved as income increased, and deteriorated as family size increased.

The survey examined the food habits of "slum families," "artisan dwellers," and "middle-class families," and assessed what families ate for breakfast, dinner, and tea. The findings were presented by age, so it is possible to know, for example, what children typically ate based on family incomes. The survey categorized two types of meals, the "bread and spread" and the cooked meal. The "bread and spread" consisted of tea or a milk-based drink, bread and a butter or jam spread. The cooked meal consisted of fish, meat, or eggs and may also have included potatoes and vegetables or a pudding. Perhaps the survey's most striking finding was that 44 per cent of children in slum families ate only "bread and spread" meals; this figure declined to 36 per cent of children in "artisan families," and 18 per cent in "middle-class families." The survey found that intakes of dairy products were insufficient in all income groups, although these deficiencies were most pronounced in slum families. The survey also noted a marked lack of variety in the diet available to slum families.[34]

Another source of information on dietary standards amongst children are the reports of the county medical officers, although they are uneven in availability, coverage, and findings. According to the Offaly county medical officer's report for 1945 only one out of over 1,200 children inspected under the school medical inspection scheme were malnourished, while in 1934 in Dublin over 6 per cent of inspected children showed signs of malnutrition.[35] In North Tipperary in 1940 over 11 per cent of children were found to be suffering from malnutrition.[36] These wide variations could be the result of timing – the high rate in North Tipperary occurred at the height of wartime rationing and food shortages, although one would expect that the rate in Offaly would be higher given the accumulative effects of wartime shortages. But the Offaly county medical officer also pointed out that the school medical inspection relied on the cooperation of parents: "all children present in school at time of inspection, with occasional exceptions, presented themselves for medical examination. These exceptions are not infrequently children who are dirty, ill-kept and neglected, obviously in need of medical attention which is withheld due to the intervention of parents who apparently have little interest in the welfare of their children."[37] (In other words, parents of children who were malnourished and ill-kempt may have deliberately kept them home from school on the days that inspections were scheduled to occur.) In spite of the wide discrepancies, hunger and malnutrition were fairly widespread amongst poor families at least into the 1950s. The biographical and autobiographic accounts of working-class Irish childhood reinforce that view.[38] Many of the authors recall that bread, butter or dripping, and tea or cocoa were staples in their diet, and that meat and fresh fruits and vegetables were rare treats.

There is no direct evidence linking malnutrition and poor diets to industrial school committals. However, malnutrition was probably but one of a number of symptoms of poverty and poor living conditions that characterized the lives of poor children generally, and that contributed to the committal to industrial schools of children whose only "crime" was that their parents were poor. There is a certain irony in the fact that, on the one hand,

Catholic rhetoric insisted on abundant fertility, which translated into large families, at the same time that a number of official surveys clearly revealed the link between large families and poverty. The larger the family, the more likely it was that the children of the family would experience poverty, poor living conditions, and malnutrition as part of their daily lives.

Public assistance and the poor and neglected child

When the Irish Free State came into existence in 1922 the British poor law system, based on parishes and workhouses, was still in effect. One of the first initiatives of the new Irish government was a reorganization of the poor law system based on Ireland's economic, social, and moral circumstances. Under the Local Government (Temporary Provisions) Act (1923), boards of guardians, relics of the British poor law, were abolished and their functions transferred to county boards of health and public assistance.[39] Many workhouses were closed and others were re-named county homes; each of the twenty-six counties had at least one board of health and public assistance and at least one county home.[40] In addition, the act provided for outdoor relief (called home assistance) for families with at least one child, although decisions about who was to be relieved, and how much relief would be granted, were left to the discretion of individual boards. The first report issued by the Department of Local Government and Public Health, covering the period 1922 to 1925, outlined the main features of the new system:

> the abolition of the existing system under which the poor were relieved in Workhouses established in each Poor Law Union; the centralization of the administration under one authority in each county; the establishment in each county of central institutions in which the poor of the county could be relieved; enabling all poor persons requiring relief to be relieved either in or out of the central institution as might be thought advisable.[41]

The Commission for the Relief of the Sick and Destitute Poor, appointed in 1925, investigated the living conditions of the poor as a result of the new scheme and reported their findings in the 1927 *Report of the Commission for the Relief of the Sick and Destitute Poor*.

The Commission found that although outdoor relief was an improvement over the previous British poor law, the system had two main flaws: the paltry amount of relief offered, particularly to widows and to able-bodied men with families, and the fact that the county homes had, in effect, become "catch-all" institutions that took no account of the specific needs or backgrounds of the inmates.[42] This was particularly true for children: county homes were neither designed nor intended to provide for the long-term needs of children, as they increasingly began to do. Until the 1930s, the cash assistance provided by the boards of health and public assistance was the only financial assistance, besides Old Age Pensions, available to people who could not, for whatever reason, provide for themselves and their families. A series of legislative measures in the 1930s and 1940s, including the introduction of unemployment assistance, widow's and orphan's pension, and the children's allowance, would expand the safety net somewhat, but a large number of people continued to live on the margins of subsistence at least into the 1950s.[43]

One significant flaw in the new scheme of public assistance was that each board of health and public assistance had almost complete discretion to determine both who to relieve and how much relief to give. Legislation outlined the general categories of persons who legally could be relieved through home assistance, but the amounts granted, and the eligibility criteria, varied from one county to the next, based on little more than the whim of the local authorities in charge at any given time. In fact, the regulations governing home assistance did not compel the boards of health and public assistance to grant cash assistance; they were also authorized to provide assistance in kind, and to require some kind of labor in return for assistance: "Where a Board of Health allows Home Assistance to any able-bodied person, the Board of Health may, at their discretion, grant such assistance in articles of food, fuel or in other articles of absolute necessity and require such person as a condition of the granting of such assistance to perform such suitable task or work as the Board may determine so long as such person shall continue to receive Home Assistance."[44] The Offaly board of health and public assistance habitually refused requests for assistance, or discontinued assistance, in cases where able-bodied men refused to engage in labor provided by the board.[45]

Admittedly, local authorities were constrained by two realities: they had only a finite amount of money with which to grant relief, and they feared a backlash from ratepayers if they were seen to be rewarding sexual immorality, vice, idleness, and other "moral" failings. The Wicklow board of health and public assistance frequently articulated frustration at both the limited amount of funds at their disposal, and prevailing economic conditions that put constant strain on their resources. In 1923 a health inspector reported:

> The number of applications for Emergency Help had been again enormously high. Almost every day she had received piles of applications for Home Help from different parts of the District, most of the applicants stating they and their families were on the verge of starvation, the cause of their destitution being unemployment. She dealt with the various cases as well as she could, refusing to issue Orders to a number of the applicants, whether justified or not she could

not say. The abnormal conditions existing at present in the District made the issuing of Emergency home help a tremendous responsibility. The average expenditure of Emergency Help for the past month was £14 a week, and if given to all who applied it would certainly be double that amount.[46]

In 1940 the health inspectors were still complaining about both the economic conditions that strained their meager resources, and the anomalies of the relief scheme that kept even the "deserving poor" living on the edge of utter destitution: "The administration of Home Help is becoming more complicated and difficult each year. The Assistance Officers are obliged to spend most of their time investigating applications and dealing with the cases of the able-bodied unemployed. The old people who are destitute and delicate and also widows and orphans are deprived of the small additional allowances they so badly need."[47] The boards of health and public assistance were limited in the assistance they could give not only by their own financial constraints, but also by the failure of the central government to take action to ameliorate bad economic conditions. As a result, tens of thousands of children grew up in destitution and deprivation; in such an environment, children likely were compelled to go out and work at early ages so that they could contribute to the family income. This meant, in effect, that their future opportunities were limited and they began the cycle of poverty and deprivation again as adults with families of their own. These conditions also contributed to committals of children to industrial schools.

Financial constraints aside, the boards of public assistance often displayed a mean spiritedness that may seem staggering to modern sensibilities. The following case, from 1926 Wicklow, illustrated the judgmental attitude that underpinned many boards:

> The Superintendent Assistance Officer reported that she had visited [a man] for the purpose of asking him to refund a sum of £3 provisional assistance given him last year. She saw the man's wife who assured her it was absolutely useless to ask them to pay back the relief as they were in dire distress and poverty and unable to provide themselves and their children with the bare necessaries of life. The husband, it was stated, only got work on odd days, and they were often dependent on charity of the neighbours to save them from starvation. They had no stock or crops, except a pony and a few drills of late potatoes.[48]

The board continued to insist that the man repay the provisional assistance in spite of the fact that their own home assistance officer found that "the whole place presented an appearance of poverty and misery."[49] The Dublin board was even stingier in its relief efforts, especially when it came to financing medical or therapeutic care for the children of the poor who had medical, physical, or mental disabilities.[50]

The most extensive insight into how local authorities made decisions about the distribution of home assistance comes from board of public assistance minutes and ISPCC case files; from these one can evaluate the impact that decisions had on the lives of poor children. Most applications for home assistance were straightforward, and assistance was given if the local authorities believed the family was "worthy" (in other words, that the husband, if unemployed, made a concerted effort to find work, and that the parents provided for their children in ways that coincided with middle-class standards of respectability). But the cases where there were questions of "immorality," "idleness" or parental neglect illustrate the way the boards conceived of their responsibility, and the way they judged who deserved relief and who did not. Often, somewhat nebulous "moral" concerns outweighed the best interests of children in the decision-making process and, indeed, children were deemed worthy or unworthy not according to their own needs, but according to subjective evaluations of their parents' characters and behavior.

A case from 1930 Offaly illustrates the financial concerns that were ever-present in the minds of some boards of public assistance. A man applied for home assistance because he was unable, due to illness, to work. His wife was dead and he was struggling to keep his home and children together: "There was no food in the house and the circumstances in general were very bad; [the man] had 6 children to maintain all of whom are poorly clothed."[51] The man was given provisional assistance until his circumstances could be investigated further. The board ultimately decided that the children should be boarded out or sent to industrial schools because they did not believe the man was capable of caring for them properly. However, they wanted an appraisal of the man's 30-acre farm before deciding the children's fate. They planned to use the appraisal to determine how much money the man should contribute to maintain his children in the industrial school.[52] Unfortunately the man's voice is not recorded at all in the board's records, so his feelings on the situation are impossible to discern. But in this instance it is clear that while some concern was expressed for the well-being of the children, the main concern was who ultimately should pay for their care.

Two similar cases from 1938 Offaly reveal the seeming randomness of board decisions when it came to granting home assistance. In July 1938 a man applied for home assistance following the death of his wife: "From [applicant] stating that his wife died a short time ago leaving him with three small children, the eldest being 3 years, and the youngest 6 weeks. As the children cannot be left alone, it is impossible for him to go to work, and he would be grateful if the Board would grant him home assistance."[53] In this instance a decision was deferred until the assistance officer could "investigate and report" on the man's circumstances. Two weeks later another widower appeared before the board requesting assistance: "[Applicant] is a widower with three children, and is in receipt of 10/6 per week Military Service Pension. He stated that due to the fact that he was granted this pension he is debarred from signing at the Unemployment Exchange with the result that he is unable to obtain work."[54] The board decided immediately to grant this man 6s per week until he was able to secure a steady job and someone to help him with the children. In an interesting postscript, the man mentioned in the first case again appeared in the records of the Offaly board in October 1938, at which time it was reported that he would be granted temporary assistance, for a period of two weeks, provided he returned to work.[55] It is impossible to get inside the collective mind of the board to determine why they hesitated in giving relief in the first case, when they had no hesitation whatsoever in the second case, even though the second widower had other sources of income. It could be that the board believed the children in the first case were simply too young to be cared for by their father, and that they would be better off in a foster home or institution. The impact of this seeming randomness on the lives of the children involved cannot be measured, but it is not unreasonable to conclude that the reluctance or inability of boards of health and public assistance to help in these circumstances likely spelled the break-up of many homes and the committal of countless children to industrial schools.

Two cases from the late 1950s further underscore the seeming randomness of the way home assistance was granted, and suggest that little had changed from the 1930s to the 1950s in the way local authorities dealt with home assistance. In a case from 1959 Wexford a woman requested the ISPCC's help in applying for home assistance after her husband was convicted of indecent assault on a niece and imprisoned. The husband's imprisonment left the family with only £6 per month children's allowance (which was only slightly less than the monthly income in the above case). The ISPCC inspector took a great interest in this case and "lobbied" the local authorities on the family's behalf: "I went to the assistance officer who assisted her and will continue to do so until her husband returns. Advised woman in the interest of children."[56] This case is interesting because one might assume that this family would not be regarded as "worthy" of assistance because of the nature of the husband's crime. But the ISPCC inspector kept in close contact with the family over the span of four months, and she even managed to secure an increase in the original home assistance grant. In this instance the ISPCC inspector and the local authorities appear to have believed that the husband's criminality should not "taint" the rest of the family. This seeming generosity was not evident in another case, from late 1950s Mayo.

This case, that spanned the years 1957 to 1962, illustrates the difficulties faced by poor families, particularly when confronted with both unexpected unemployment or illness, and unwillingness on the part of local authorities to provide assistance. An ISPCC inspector first visited the family in July 1957 at the mother's request. The inspector reported that:

> I called to the home and woman informed me she was very short of cash and food for the family. When questioned as to the lack of food in the home when man was working, woman stated man is a Council worker on the roads, and due to the inclement weather the previous week he was off work a few days. She requested I would recommend her for home assistance for this week only. I gave her a note to the local A/P.[57]

At the time of the inspector's visit the woman was six months pregnant. The inspector conducted a series of visits, but beyond commenting on the woman's apparently inferior housekeeping skills (which were perhaps not surprising given that she already had seven children under nine years of age to care for, and was expecting her eighth child) it does not appear that the ISPCC took concrete action to help the family. It also is not clear that the local authorities provided assistance to the family – there is no indication to that effect in the ISPCC case files.

The ISPCC inspector returned to the house less than a month after the original complaint was closed. The woman again asked for the ISPCC's help because she could not make ends meet on her husband's wages. (Although the husband was working steadily and earning good wages, the family had accumulated rent arrears in excess of £20 and had ten mouths to feed.) The ISPCC inspector suggested committing the children to industrial schools, which the mother resisted.[58] The ISPCC inspector interrogated the mother and father about their finances, and it is clear that the inspector believed the family's circumstances were the result, not of insufficient wages or too many mouths to feed, but of poor planning and housekeeping by the mother. After a series of inspection visits the case was closed, again with no specific action taken to help improve the family's circumstances.

The ISPCC was again called to the house in June 1958, this time because the woman wanted the ISPCC's assistance in having two of her younger children placed in industrial schools. It appears that the woman's health had deteriorated since giving birth in October 1957, and her husband was not able to care properly for the younger children. The children were not, in the end, committed to industrial schools, because the ISPCC inspector recommended that the mother try to place the children with relatives.[59] (Given the inspector's earlier recommendations, this outcome is somewhat puzzling.) The ISPCC was again called to this house in December 1962 after the family's fortunes had taken another turn for the worse. The mother died some time in 1961 or 1962 and the father, who was in ill health himself, could not care for the children. He requested the ISPCC's assistance in keeping his family together because he did not want them sent to industrial schools.[60] There is no record in the ISPCC inspection report of the children having been committed to industrial schools, which suggests that the family made do with their own resources. But there is no logical reason that this family should have been denied assistance given their financial circumstances and the ill health of both parents.

Based on an analysis of roughly four hundred ISPCC case files, the conditions in which this family lived were not unique or extraordinary. The family, consisting of two parents and eight young children, lived in a three-roomed cottage; they faced periodic unemployment, illness, and injury, which had a negative impact on their quality of life as well as the constant threat or possibility of having their children taken from them and sent to industrial schools. They also endured the regular censure and scrutiny of ISPCC inspectors, who tended to be judgmental and to evaluate their behaviors, housekeeping and parenting skills from the perspective of middle-class prosperity and comfort rather than from the perspective of working-class poverty and deprivation. It is likely that even a modest amount of home assistance, combined with more consistent medical care, would have enhanced this family's, and especially the children's, quality of life significantly.

A case from 1958 Wexford further illustrates the censure and scrutiny that working-class families faced when they sought help from the ISPCC or the local authorities. A woman asked for the ISPCC"s help because she was having trouble making ends meet on 35s per week home assistance. Her husband was ill and unable to work, and his insurance stamps had run out (which meant he was no longer entitled to unemployment assistance). Beyond recommending that the woman contact the Society of St Vincent de Paul, a charitable agency, for clothing, the ISPCC took no action to assist the family. In fact, it seems that the ISPCC inspector believed that, although the financial resources available to this family were exceedingly low, the mother was not doing all she could to make the family comfortable and happy: "The children are very poorly clad. The bed clothes are bad. The house is very badly kept. Man looks poorly, but woman should do much better."[61] The case was closed shortly after the inspector's first visit to the house, and it is possible that the ISPCC inspector did not believe the woman tried hard enough to meet her family's needs on the meager resources available to her. In this case it seems that the ISPCC's "moral sensibilities" took precedence over what was best for the children in determining the outcome of the case.

It is clear that local authorities were compelled to make difficult decisions with regard to home assistance, given that financial pressures (and their own moral sensibilities) precluded them from meeting all requests for assistance. However, an examination of the cases that appear in board of public assistance minutes or ISPCC case files suggests that the selection process was somewhat arbitrary or random. One local authority balked at offering assistance to a widower that would have enabled him to keep his family together, while another readily offered assistance to a woman whose husband had been imprisoned on a sexual assault conviction. A variety of factors influenced the decision-making process, and often what was best for children was low on the list of priorities. As a result, many poor families were broken up when children were sent to industrial schools for no reason other than that their parents could not support them. Countless other children lived in squalid, overcrowded and substandard housing, suffered hunger, malnutrition, and deprivation and likely repeated the cycle of poverty when they married and had families of their own.

The state and 'defaulting parents'

One issue that has not been addressed by historians, and that was not acknowledged or addressed by successive Irish governments, was the "defaulting parent," or the parent who abandoned his or her (usually his) children and failed to provide for them. This problem contributed significantly to child poverty and the committal of children to industrial schools. In the typical scenario, a man migrated to England to find employment, leaving behind a wife and children and promises to send money home weekly. Within a few months the family stopped hearing from him, and the weekly or bi-weekly telegrams ceased. Two sources, local authority records and the case files of the ISPCC, provide insight into links between defaulting or deserting parents and childhood poverty and neglect. Local authorities tended to concern themselves with defaulting parents only insofar as the failure to provide forced the abandoned spouse to apply for home assistance. Local authorities often were reluctant to grant relief in these cases because they recognized the difficulty of recouping their expenditures from the defaulting spouse/parent. They were not concerned, as a rule, with the impact of the failure to provide on the health and well-being of children. They also appear not to have been overly concerned with preserving the integrity of the family, as they were often quick to recommend the committal of children to industrial schools rather than granting home assistance to keep the family together.

A case from 1925 Cork illustrates the attitude of that local authority when it came to providing home assistance in cases of desertion. The case involved the mother of three children who ranged in age from four to eight years: "Her husband has deserted her, and the children are very badly looked after. She is not making any effort to maintain them and is depending completely on the Home Assistance she is in receipt of. The children are not being sent to school."[62] The parish priest became involved in the case, suggesting that the mother was not conducting her home "as a decent home should be," and that the children would be better off in an industrial school.[63] The outcome of this case is, unfortunately, not indicated in the minutes. However, the boards of health and public assistance tended towards parsimony when it came to both home assistance and maintaining children in industrial schools in cases where parents were not in a position to contribute to their children's maintenance. It is therefore more likely than not that the children were not sent to an industrial school, but also that the amount of home assistance was reduced, rather than increased, because of the mother's perceived moral failings.[64]

The boards also tended to be stingy if they believed that there was no chance of recouping outlays of home assistance even after the deserting spouse/parent had been traced. The following case from 1935 County Wicklow is fairly typical in this regard: "[A woman applied] for home assistance for herself and two children, stating that she has been deserted by her husband who has gone to England, and that she is in very poor circumstances. Order – That [woman] be granted temporary assistance, and in the meantime that the NSPCC be notified with a view to discovering the whereabouts of her husband."[65] When the board realized that they likely would not recoup their costs in this case they ceased home assistance payments. In a similar case from 1939, a woman requested that the provisional assistance being paid by the board be made permanent because her husband had deserted her and their six children, leaving them destitute. The board did not make the assistance permanent but they did order that proceedings be taken against the husband so they could recoup the cost of the assistance already paid.[66]

While local authorities could be reluctant to grant home assistance unconditionally in cases of deserting or defaulting parents, they were willing to pay to have defaulting spouses returned to Ireland for prosecution, as evidenced by the following case from 1937 Wicklow: "The Superintendent Home Assistance Officer reported that [man] went to England last September. His wife and two children are on home assistance ever since. She has sworn information to have him arrested, but the Guards will not take action unless the Board agree to pay the cost of bringing [him] back. The board decided to defray the cost of bringing [man] back in order that proceedings may be instituted."[67] It is not clear whether prosecuting a defaulting parent helped to improve the family's quality of life. What is clear, however, are board of public assistance priorities: they were willing to pay to return a defaulting parent to Ireland for prosecution but they often were reluctant to provide assistance to the families of such defaulters.

The problem of defaulting parents can be seen even more explicitly in the records of the ISPCC. The founding mission of the ISPCC was to protect children from ill-treatment and neglect; in Ireland, however, ISPCC inspectors spent a significant percentage of their time trying to trace defaulting parents, often in an effort to prevent children from being sent to industrial school on the grounds of parental poverty. Of the nearly four hundred ISPCC cases that were examined here forty, or 10 per cent, specifically mentioned failure to provide as the reason for ISPCC intervention. This may seem like a paltry number, but failure to provide was a factor in perhaps another 25–30 per cent of cases even if it was not the primary issue or symptom.[68]

A case from 1957 Cork is unusual in the sense that both parents had deserted their child in St Finbarr's hospital: "It appears that the parents are living apart in England … It is further stated that there is 3 other children of the family in homes in London … I am to request that [the child's mother] be seen and asked if she has any account of her husband and what are her future plans about the child."[69] The family abandoned the child, aged five years, because, when they made the decision to migrate, he was ill in hospital. The parents made no arrangements to send for the child once he recovered, and clearly they were not all that concerned about the fate of this child or their three others who ended up in institutions in London. The child was committed to an industrial school in Cork and likely lost all contact with his parents and siblings in England.

Another case from 1957 Cork is noteworthy because not only was the mother the deserting parent, which was not the norm, but it also reflected the widespread belief that men should not have the sole care and custody of their daughters. In this case three children (two boys, aged two and three years, and a 14-year-old girl) had already been committed to industrial schools, leaving two girls, aged twelve and six, at home. The mother abandoned the family, leaving the father to care for the children. The father contacted the ISPCC for assistance and the ISPCC recommended that the children be committed to industrial schools.[70] It was not unusual, in these kinds of cases, that some children in a family were committed to industrial schools while others were allowed to remain at home. It was also not unusual that children were dealt with at different times and in different ways. Sometimes parents committed some of their children in the hopes of keeping the rest of the family together. More importantly, it was not unusual for ISPCC inspectors, parish priests, and others to strongly encourage men to commit their daughters to industrial schools when their wives died or deserted the family.[71] Although never explicitly stated, the belief that men should not have custody of their daughters in the absence of wives had less to do with their supposed deficits in childcare and more to do with an inherent suspicion (or perhaps fear) of deviant or perverted working-class male sexuality.

The defaulting or deserting parent, although often overlooked in social histories of twentieth-century Ireland, was a significant factor in the poverty endured by working-class families at least into the middle decades of the twentieth century. The defaulting parent may have been a distinctly Irish phenomenon, given prevailing economic conditions: many men and women viewed temporary or permanent migration to Britain as a solution to unemployment and poverty at home. Some men and women took their responsibilities to their families seriously and sent money home regularly. But many others saw migration as an opportunity to shirk their responsibilities entirely. Perhaps they intended to desert their families from the start, or perhaps they went with the best of intentions but were "seduced" by the temptations of the big city. Indeed, for some men and women, migrating to Britain may have provided an "out" from an unhappy marriage in an era before divorce was available to Irish couples. Whatever the reason, the seemingly common practice of desertion was but another factor that shaped the experiences and life chances of poor Irish children.

Legitimate children in state care: industrial schools

The Department of Education, in their annual reports, published statistics on the number of children committed to industrial schools on an annual basis, grounds of committal, the number of children discharged from schools each year, and where those children went on release (i.e. back to their families, to employment, to further their education, to other institutions, etc.) Unfortunately these statistics do not distinguish between legitimate and illegitimate children. However, anecdotal evidence provided by district justice minute books, newspaper accounts of committal proceedings, ISPCC case files, and the records of county boards of health and public assistance, suggest that the majority of children committed to industrial schools in any given year were legitimate children. They were committed, by and large, because their parents could not afford to care for them or because their parents neglected them according to the standards of the middle-class court system and middle-class ISPCC inspectors (typically the neglect could be traced directly to poverty rather than malice).

Many of the children confined to industrial schools ended up there after neighbors, friends, or parish priests complained to the local branch of the ISPCC that they were neglected or abused by their parents.[72] In many cases – it is impossible to know how many – neighbors complained not because the children were being abused or neglected but because they objected to the parents' lifestyle or to the standards of hygiene and cleanliness maintained in the home.[73] Many families could have done a better job caring for their children if they had fewer children and a steady and secure source of employment that paid a living wage (or, in the absence of this, a more consistent and effective scheme of public assistance). Church and state conspired to promote high fertility through legislation and through rhetoric that condemned those who sought to "artificially" limit the size of their families.[74] At the same time, however, it was becoming increasingly clear that prevailing economic realities did not allow the average family to support more than two or three children with any degree of comfort.

The legal system for committing children to industrial schools was sufficiently vague that any "concerned party," such as an ISPCC inspector, probation officer, or school attendance officer, could bring a child into court and request a committal order.[75] District justices often were only too willing to grant committal orders, with little investigation into family circumstances and background and few efforts to help needy families in ways that did not involve sending children to industrial schools. According to the 1925–27 Department of Education report, more children were confined to industrial schools in Ireland than in England and Wales combined, an extraordinary statistic given the vast differences in population size.[76] The same report acknowledged that English poor law institutions housed more children than similar Irish institutions, not unsurprising given prevailing demographic trends in each country. But this difference may also suggest that divergent philosophies underpinned the treatment of needy children: poor law institutions were, in theory, voluntary and temporary stopgaps for families experiencing occasional or seasonal destitution, unemployment, or illness. On the other hand, confinement to industrial schools represented a permanent, often irrevocable separation of parent and child. The British government had begun to use alternative methods to deal with poor or neglected children at the same time that enthusiasm for institutionalization was increasing, rather than decreasing, in Ireland. Statistical evidence shows that, into the 1950s, roughly one in ten children who left industrial schools annually returned to their parents' custody, while the remainder went directly into employment secured for them by the school's resident manager, or into other institutions such as magdalen asylums, county homes, or institutions for "mental defectives."[77]

Perhaps one of the most striking aspects of state provision for children in the mid-twentieth-century was that, in any given year, 8,000 to 10,000 children were institutionalized, at public expense, in industrial schools, certified schools, extern institutions, and private (although predominantly religious-run) orphanages, all of them technically under the oversight of the Departments of Education and Health.[78] Another 1,500–2,000 children were boarded out, making for a total of 9,500–12,000 children in care annually. While it is impossible to compare Ireland's rate of institutionalization with figures elsewhere in Europe, it does seem that Irish rates were exceedingly high, underscoring both the preference for institutionalization on the part of local authorities, and the ease with which local authorities and district court justices stripped allegedly unfit parents of the custody of their children and, therefore, their parental rights.[79]

While poverty was the predominant factor in the committal of children to industrial schools, the question remains as to why official policy preferred to remove children from the care of their parents rather than providing assistance to keep families together. The answer lies in part in the fact that, when the Irish Free State came into existence, a vast and extensive religiously-run system existed to provide for "problem" children, and it was convenient and cost-effective from all perspectives to allow the system to continue. It could only survive, however, if it retained a guaranteed number of children at public expense. Taking children away from poor, neglectful, or abusive parents thus served financial, social, and political ends: it provided a steady infusion of cash into the church's mammoth network of convents, agencies, and institutions; it relieved families of the burden of caring for more children than their meager resources would allow; and it relieved the state of responsibility for developing a secular, state-run system that was cost-effective but that put the needs of children and their parents above political expediency.[80]

Conclusion

In theory, legitimate children enjoyed a more stable and prosperous existence in post-independence Ireland because they were not subjected to the same negative attitudes and stereotypes as illegitimate children. However, legitimate children could also experience a precarious existence for a variety of reasons. Social and economic conditions were such that many families lived in endemic and relentless poverty, experienced homelessness, evictions, and substandard housing, and probably did not have a sufficient income to provide a balanced and nutritious diet. This meant that children experienced hunger and malnutrition that affected their health and physical development; it probably contributed to early school leaving so that children could go to work and contribute to the family economy; and it resulted in the committal of tens of thousands of children to industrial schools. The case files of the ISPCC, combined with the reports of the boards of health and public assistance and newspaper accounts, reveal that it was not uncommon for parents, particularly fathers, to abandon their families and fail to provide for them. This, in turn, resulted in either children living on the margins of subsistence or in the break-up of families as children were committed to industrial schools. The local authorities, who were responsible for relieving poverty and destitution, were often stingy and mean-spirited in dispensing relief and this, too, resulted in children living in poverty or being committed to industrial schools. All in all, the life of the average poor legitimate children does not appear to have been all that much better than the life of the illegitimate child. It is clear that Irish society did not value child life to the extent that they professed to, and lacking either statutory or constitutional rights, children had no one to speak or advocate on their behalf.

Notes

1 The Fianna Fáil government returned to power in the 1957 Election commissioned a survey on economic development and later that year introduced the Programme for Economic Expansion, the first such program of its kind. See Patrick Lynch, "The Irish Free State and the Republic of Ireland, 1921–66," in *The course of Irish history*, ed. T.W. Moody and F.X. Martin (Cork: Mercier Press, 1987), pp. 336–7. See also Terence Brown, *Ireland: A social and cultural history, 1922 to the present.* (Ithaca, NY: Cornell University Press, 1985), pp. 185–204; Fergal Tobin, *The best of decades: Ireland in the 1960s* (Dublin: Gill and MacMillan, 1996); J.J. Lee, *Ireland 1912–1985: Politics and society* (Cambridge: Cambridge University Press, 1989), pp. 341–59; Diarmuid Ferriter, *The transformation of Ireland* (Woodstock, NY: Overlook Press, 2005), pp. 541–3.

2 John P. Dunne, "Poverty problems for a patriot parliament," *Journal of the Statistical and Social Enquiry Society of Ireland*, 14 (1922), p. 190.

3 *Report of the Commission on the Relief of the Sick and Destitute Poor, Including the Insane Poor* (Dublin: Stationery Office, 1927), p. iii.

4 *Report of the Commission on the Relief of the Sick and Destitute Poor*, p. 56.

5 *Evening Herald* (3 January 1930), p. 1.

6 *The Standard* (3 April 1936), p. 4.

7 *The Standard* (5 May 1939), p. 10.

8 T.W.T. Dillon, "The social services in Eire," *Studies*, 34 (September 1945), p. 327. See also Charles Clancy Gore, "Nutritional standards of some working-

class families in Dublin, 1943," *Journal of the Statistical and Social Inquiry Society of Ireland*, 17 (1943–44), p. 247 and T.W.T. Dillon, M.D., "Slum clearance past and future," *Studies*, 34 (September 1945), pp. 13–20.

9   Dillon, "The social services in Eire," p. 327.

10   ISPCC, *Annual report of the Dublin branch 1944–45*, p. 3.

11   Department of Local Government and Public Health *Annual Report 1922–25*, pp. 141–2.

12   National Archives of Ireland (hereafter NAI), Department of the Taoiseach S13438A, Memorandum from Social Welfare to Government, Public Assistance Footwear Scheme, 25 June 1953.

13   For a discussion of the housing problem in Dublin in the nineteenth and early twentieth centuries see Jacinta Prunty, *Dublin slums 1800–1925: A study in urban geography* (Dublin: Irish Academic Press, 1998). The Housing Acts 1925–30 provided for a scheme of government grants for the building of houses and flats for the working classes, and it gave local authorities discretion to undertake building projects. To qualify for grants the houses and flats had to be of a minimum size and square footage.

14   See Ferriter, *Transformation of Ireland*, pp. 394–6.

15   ISPCC case files, Wexford, 5 March 1954.

16   ISPCC case files, Wexford, 21 April 1956.

17   *Workers Voice* (July 1949), pp. 3–4.

18   *Report of the inquiry into the housing of the working classes in the city of Dublin, 1939–1943* (Dublin: Stationery Office, 1943), p. 15.

19   *Report of inquiry into the housing of the working classes*, p. 17.

20   *Evening Herald* (27 October 1945), p. 1.

21   *Evening Herald* (31 October 1941), p. 1.

22   St Kevin's was one of a number of institutions in Dublin that functioned in a manner similar to the county homes. In addition to the sick and destitute, St Kevin's had a "casual ward" that allowed people to seek shelter in the evening, but casuals had to leave the institution during the day.

23   *Evening Herald* (12 December 1945), p. 1; (19 December 1945), p. 2.

24   *Evening Mail* (21 November 1946), p. 4.

25   *Evening Mail* (5 December 1946), p. 6.

26   *Evening Mail* (16 February 1949), p. 5.

27   *Evening Mail* (16 February 1949), p. 5.

28   *Evening Mail* (23 February 1949), p. 6.

29   *Evening Mail* (28 November 1956), p. 6.

30   *Evening Mail* (12 December 1956), p. 8.

31   Charles Clancy Gore, "Nutritional standards of some working class families in Dublin," *Journal of the Statistical and Social Inquiry Society of Ireland*, 17 (1943–44), p. 242.

32   Gore, "Nutritional standards of some working class families," p. 253.

33   Congested districts were those in parts of western Ireland (particularly County Mayo) covered by the authority of the Congested Districts Board. Although generally sparsely inhabited, these regions were defined as "overcrowded" because more people lived there than could make a living there.

34   Department of Health, *National nutrition survey* (Dublin: Government Stationery Office, 1948).

35   *Report of the Offaly County medical officer*, 1945, p. 35; Department of Local

Government and Public Health, *Annual Report 1933–34*, p. 77.

36 *Offaly Chronicle* (4 July 1940), p. 2.

37 *Report of the Offaly County medical officer*, 1947, p. 41.

38 See, for example, Angeline Blain Kearns, *Stealing sunlight: Growing up in Irishtown* (Dublin: A.A. Farmar, 2000); Evelyn Doyle, *Evelyn: A true story* (London: Orion, 2002); Frank O'Connor, *An only child* (Belfast: Blackstaff, 1993); Christy Kenneally, *Maura's boy: A Cork childhood* (Cork: Mercier Press, 1996); Sean Maher, *The road to God knows where: A memoir of travelling boyhood* (Dublin: Veritas, 1998).

39 Each county had its own board of health and public assistance; some of the larger counties, including Dublin, had at least two boards.

40 Some counties, like Tipperary, and urban areas such as Cork and Dublin, had several local authorities and several local authority institutions.

41 Department of Local Government and Public Health, *Annual Report 1922–1925*. (Dublin: Stationery Office, 1925), pp. 52–3.

42 *Report of the Commission for the Relief of the Sick and Destitute Poor*, p. 56.

43 Unemployment relief, introduced in 1933, was a contributory scheme that employed workers paid into, to see themselves through temporary periods of unemployment. Women were not, generally, eligible for this assistance. Widow's and orphan's pension, introduced in 1935, provided relief to widows with at least one child, and was intended to prevent widows from having to go out to work to support their children. Children's allowances, introduced in 1944, were not means-tested or contributory. The allowance, the amount of which increased periodically, was paid to families on behalf of the third and each subsequent child (families with one or two children received no allowance).

44 Offaly board of health and public assistance minutes, 25 March 1930.

45 See, for example, the case from 1933 when the Offaly board of health and public assistance directed the home assistance officer to discontinue relief to an able-bodied man who refused to work on a children's playground in return for his relief. Offaly board of health and public assistance minutes, 11 April 1933.

46 Wicklow board of health and public assistance minutes, 22 January 1923.

47 Wicklow board of health and public assistance minutes, 11 March 1940.

48 Wicklow board of health and public assistance minutes, 31 May 1926.

49 Wicklow board of health and public assistance minutes, 31 May 1926.

50 See, for example, Dublin board of health and public assistance minutes, 21 October 1925; 14 April 1926; 22 January 1930; 18 February 1931; 16 March 1932; 27 April 1932; 13 September 1933. One striking case was that of Peter Purdue, two of whose children were sent to the Deaf and Dumb Institute in Cabra, north Dublin. For a period of two years, from 1931 to 1933, Purdue was engaged in a battle with the Dublin board of health and public assistance over who should pay to maintain the children in the institution. Purdue claimed that he did not have the money to support the children, while the board insisted that he pay at least a nominal amount. There are at least four entries in the minute books in which the board threatened to return his children to Purdue unless he contributed to their upkeep in the institution.

51 Offaly board of health and public assistance minutes, 21 January 1930.

52 Offaly board of health and public assistance minutes, 22 February 1930.

53 Offaly board of health and public assistance minutes, 12 July 1938.

54 Offaly board of health and public assistance minutes, 26 July 1938.

55 Offaly board of health and public assistance minutes, 25 October 1938.

56 ISPCC case files, Wexford, 21 November 1959.

57 ISPCC case files, Mayo, 9 July 1957.

58 ISPCC case files, Mayo, 15 January 1958.

59 ISPCC case files, Mayo, 16 June 1958.

60 ISPCC case files, Mayo, 6 December 1962.

61 ISPCC case files, Wexford, 22 July 1958.

62 Offaly board of health and public assistance minutes, 10 March 1925.

63 Offaly board of health and public assistance minutes, 10 March 1925.

64 This conclusion is based on an exhaustive examination of the minutes for four boards of health and public assistance for the period 1925 to 1945.

65 Wicklow board of health and public assistance minutes, 25 June 1935; see also 26 July 1938.

66 Wicklow board of health and public assistance minutes, 28 February 1939.

67 Wicklow board of health and public assistance minutes, 14 December 1937.

68 The author examined approximately four hundred of several thousand case files in ISPCC possession. The files were chosen randomly, and are taken from all over the country, so there is no reason to assume that they are unrepresentative.

69 ISPCC case files, Cork, 25 June 1957.

70 ISPCC case files, Cork, 26 August 1957.

71 One high-profile case that clearly illustrated this point involved Desmond Doyle and his daughter Evelyn, as discussed in the Introduction.

72 According to ISPCC annual reports, only a fraction of cases came to the attention of the NSPCC through their own investigations. The majority of complaints came from "interested" third parties, including neighbors, schoolteachers, parish priests, and the gardaí. See *Annual reports of the Dublin branch* (Dublin: ISPCC, 1930–60).

73 Of the seven former inmates who participated in the first episode of RTÉ's *States of fear* series, four were sent to industrial schools, along with their brothers and sisters, because neighbors complained to the ISPCC after the parents separated, or when their widowed mother began dating another man. Two of the former inmates were sent to industrial schools after getting into trouble with the police, and only one was sent because she was illegitimate and her mother could not support her. *States of fear,* written and produced by Mary Raftery, Radio Telefís Éireann, RTÉ Dublin, 1999.

74 The Censorship of Publications Act (1929) and Criminal Law (Amendment) Act (1935) criminalized the advertisement and importation of birth control methods, which effectively put safe and effective methods of family limitation out of reach of most poor Irish women. In discussing adoption legislation in the early 1940s Archbishop John Charles McQuaid was adamant that only couples who could prove that they were not "artificially" limiting their families (in other words, using some form of contraception) would be eligible to adopt children. (See Dublin Diocesan Archives (hereafter DDA) Adoption Policy Files, 1950–52, Episcopal Committee Statement on Legal Adoption, January 1952.)

75 An examination of justice minute-books from several counties and from the Dublin Children's Court indicate that the ISPCC was the complainant in 51 per cent of cases in urban areas, and in 91 per cent of cases in rural areas; the police and school attendance officers were responsible for a further 17 per cent and 15 per cent of complaints respectively. The Children Act (1908) was the primary

legal mechanism for committing children to industrial schools. The grounds for committal were expanded and changed slightly with further Children Acts in 1929, 1941, 1949, and 1957.

76 Department of Education, *Annual report 1925–27* (Dublin: Government Stationery Office, 1927), p. 91.

77 Department of Education, *Annual reports.*

78 Figures are based on statistical information published in annual reports of the Departments of Health and Education.

79 The 1925–27 Department of Health *Annual Report* noted that Ireland's rate of institutionalization was higher than rates in England and Wales, Scotland, and Northern Ireland. But comparisons with Europe cannot be made because there are no comparable sets of statistics – at least none that the author has been able to locate.

80 This steady infusion of cash did not enable the male and female religious to live extravagant lifestyles, as alleged by Mary Raftery, Eoin O'Sullivan, and others in the media. The costs of operating an institution (heating, maintenance, staffing, etc) remained essentially static no matter how many children were accommodated.

2

Cherished equally? "Outdoor" provision for illegitimate children

Introduction

As will be seen in later chapters, an examination of official attitudes and responses to infanticide reveals a remarkable degree of ambivalence among clerics, lawmakers, and judges, about their responsibility to protect illegitimate children from harm at the hands of their unwed mothers. But each group was ambivalent for slightly different reasons. The Catholic hierarchy paid lip service to Catholic "sanctity of life" doctrine while tacitly acknowledging that infanticide was inevitable in a country like Ireland, and that the life of an illegitimate child was not valued, by the state or by society, to the same degree that the life of a legitimate child was. The Catholic response to infanticide was primarily concerned with preserving the Catholic Church's moral authority and their hold over female sexuality; concerns about the fate of illegitimate children were secondary at best. Lawmakers also paid lip-service to their responsibility to protect illegitimate children although they, too, were preoccupied by more practical concerns, such as the cost of caring for children, and their desire to be seen as compassionate, in keeping with similar legislation elsewhere in Europe. And the court's ambivalence stemmed from the fact that they had a duty, in theory, to uphold the "sanctity of life" on the one hand, while confronting, on almost a daily basis, the lack of respect that actually existed in Irish society for the lives of illegitimate children.

This ambivalence carried over into the legislative and social policy arenas, where the rights of illegitimate children were murky at best. The Proclamation of the Easter Rising, and the Democratic Programme of the

First Dáil, vowed to both "cherish all the children of the nation equally," and to provide all children with the basic necessities of life.[1] In spite of this, children generally were disregarded in twentieth-century Irish society, and no child was more disregarded, in policy and practice, than the illegitimate child. Many illegitimate children were consigned to an institutional existence, or to an uncertain and often abusive or exploitative fostering arrangement, because their mothers could not or would not care for them. The arrangements made by the local authorities to care for illegitimate children often had the effect of irrevocably breaking the bonds between children and their biological families, leaving the children with no safety net when, in their teenage years, they were pushed into self-sufficiency. The practices adopted by local authorities typically emphasized the fact that illegitimate children were "unwanted," not necessarily by their mothers (although sometimes that was the case) but certainly by a society reluctant to accept the financial burden of their maintenance and fearful of their alleged potential for juvenile delinquency and anti-social behavior.

This chapter argues that the Catholic doctrine of the sanctity of human, and especially child, life, and the value that early nationalist lawmakers placed on child life, bore no resemblance to the way that government and society dealt with illegitimate children in the twentieth century. Lawmakers did not always regard children as future citizens to be valued and molded, but often as dangerous and burdensome populations to be confined, regulated, and controlled. The state, with the assistance and cooperation of the local authorities, religious orders, and Catholic philanthropic organizations, used institutionalization, boarding-out, and overseas adoption as the most effective and inexpensive means of controlling potentially deviant, immoral and delinquent illegitimate children.[2] But this chapter also seeks to set the record straight with regard to illegitimate children being raised in their own homes and families. Church and state unquestionably conspired to limit the services available to unmarried mothers and their children, and while there was a general social censure of unwed motherhood and illegitimacy, nonetheless thousands of unmarried mothers kept their children, loved them, and raised them as best they could. ISPCC case files, newspaper accounts of industrial school committal proceedings, and boards of health and public assistance minutes all point to the almost heroic efforts some women made, sometimes with the help of family and friends and sometimes entirely on their own, to keep their children. Popular wisdom has tended to suggest that all illegitimate children were shunted into institutions or sent overseas for adoption, but this simply was not the case.[3]

The illegitimate child at home

The received wisdom in twentieth-century Irish history is that all unmarried mothers were shunted into institutions – either magdalen asylums or mother and baby homes – and their babies taken from them and sent to institutions themselves, boarded out in foster homes in Ireland, or sent to the United States for adoption.[4] This perception is far from accurate, however. Statistics exist for the number of children who were born outside of marriage in each year of the twentieth century, but no firm statistics document how many of those children remained with their families versus becoming entangled in the bureaucratic system. Limited records survive for three mother and baby homes that maintained unmarried mothers and their children at the expense of local authorities, and these records, although scant, suggest that a significant number of children left these institutions with their mothers:

Table 1

	SHH[a]	SRA[b]	MH[c]
1938			
Taken by mother	20	47	51
Boarded out	24	20	10
Died	30	54	3
1939			
Taken by mother	28	66	40
Boarded out	27	13	8
Died	38	27	5
1940			
Taken by mother	30	73	38
Boarded out	11	8	26
Died	17	19	13

[a] Sacred Heart Home, Bessboro, Co. Cork.
[b] Sean Ross Abbey, Roscrea, Co. Tipperary.
[c] Manor House, Castlepollard, Co. Westmeath.

Statistics for the children's home at Pelletstown, Co. Dublin, and Tuam, Co. Galway tell a similar story. In 1941, a total of 218 children from Pelletstown were "placed at nurse, adopted, or sent to other institutions,"

28 were boarded out by the local authorities, and 99 were taken by their mothers; 14 children were placed at nurse, etc. from the children's home in Tuam, while 23 were boarded out and the remaining 53 sent home with their mothers.[5] Admittedly some of the mothers who took their children with them made private fostering arrangements for them, and it would be virtually impossible to trace such children.

It also should be noted that illegitimate children born in county homes and maternity hospitals were as likely to go home with their mothers as they were to be boarded out, sent to institutions, or sent overseas for adoption. Statistics on the number of able-bodied women and children receiving home assistance further elucidates this point. The number of illegitimate children in receipt of home assistance rose steadily from a low of 499 in 1932 to a high of more than 1,500 in 1945. Meanwhile, the number of legitimate children in receipt of home assistance declined steadily, from a high of 16,199 in 1934 to a low of 7,515 in 1939; in 1945 there were 8,683 legitimate children in receipt of home assistance.[6] The rate of births of illegitimate children rose steadily from 1932 to 1945 – in 1932 there were 1,819 illegitimate births, representing 3.2 per cent of all births, and in 1945 there were 2,590, representing 3.9 per cent of all births; it is possible that the increase in the number of illegitimate children in receipt of home assistance was merely a reflection of the increase in illegitimate births.[7] It is also possible that some local authorities looked favorably on granting unmarried mothers and their children home assistance, which may have enabled them to keep their children rather than relinquishing custody to local authorities or industrial schools.[8] While statistics exist on the number of children boarded out each year by the local authorities in each county, they are virtually useless here because they do not distinguish between legitimate and illegitimate children; neither do statistics on children committed to industrial schools.

Given the patchy nature of statistical data it is not possible to make definitive statements about the number of illegitimate children who remained with their mothers or other family members, versus those who were institutionalized, boarded out by local authorities, or placed at nurse by their mothers or private agencies. But the sketchy statistical evidence at least raises the distinct possibility that more illegitimate children went home with their families than had previously been assumed. The records of the ISPCC, combined with the records of the county boards of health and public assistance, attest to the fact that many illegitimate children were raised in "normal" home and family environments. These sources also provide some insight into the conditions in which illegitimate children lived in their homes and families. In all likelihood the majority of these children were treated no differently than children who were born into "respectable" poor families. Perhaps the main difference was that illegitimate children were more likely than their legitimate counterparts to live in abject poverty, primarily because of their limited access, due to financial constraints and inherent bias, to educational, apprenticeship, and employment opportunities.

One issue that faced unwed mothers who kept their children was what would happen to those children when they married, especially when their spouses were not the fathers of their children. By the end of the twentieth century blended families with step-parents and half-siblings had become almost as commonplace as "traditional" families. But in mid-twentieth-century Ireland the most common blended families were those created by the marriage of widows and widowers. Men taking on the financial and emotional responsibility of parenting illegitimate children were problematic from a number of perspectives, and the tensions that arose in families over this issue often left the children themselves in a precarious position. In the absence of statistics it is impossible to know how typical this scenario was, although anecdotal evidence suggests that it was fairly common.[9] In some cases, illegitimate children were accepted by their stepfathers and treated like all the other children in the family. Such cases, because they were not problematic, did not come to the notice of the ISPCC and therefore few if any records even note their existence.

But in other cases illegitimate children were "cast off" by mothers wishing to marry; extended family members only took in these children grudgingly, or they ended up in state care. It was not unusual, for example, for illegitimate children to live with grandparents, aunts and uncles, or other extended family members even though their own mothers were married and had families with their new husbands. An early example of this scenario comes from the Wicklow board of health and public assistance minutes from 1923: "The boy ... proposed to be boarded out ... was the illegitimate child of [mother], recently married to a man ... residing at Raheengrainey. This [man] had been allowed into a cottage rented by [his] uncle who flatly refused to allow [his] wife's illegitimate child in. This child had until then been reared with the mother's sister amidst a houseful of the latter's children and was very sadly neglected."[10] The ISPCC visited a home in County Wexford following a complaint from neighbors about the behavior of a 15-year-old boy. His grandmother raised the boy because his mother did not want him: "I visited as a result of a complaint. This boy has been before the court for stealing stuff from a hotel yard. He has been brought up by his grandmother. His mother was married about three months ago ... She does not appear to want him. The grandmother allows him to do as he wishes. His uncle … a farm labourer, takes no interest in him. The grandmother is an easy going woman."[11] In this case the child likely ended up with his grandmother and uncle by default, and no one showed any degree of concern for him.

When extended family members died or no longer were willing or able to look after illegitimate children, mothers were either forced to make alternative arrangements for them or, more commonly, reluctantly bring the children into their new families. This scenario was clearly illustrated in a case from 1958 Wexford, when the ISPCC was called by a neighbor to investigate allegations that an illegitimate child was being singled out for neglect and abuse by her mother and stepfather:

> I visited as a result of a complaint. It is alleged that the parents take very little interest in their children or home. [Stepfather] is not the father of [the girl] and it is said that both the mother and man do not treat her well. The child lived with the maternal grandmother until about eight months ago when the grandmother died. Her own mother then took her. [The mother] denied there was any difference between the children. [The girl] is very pale but appears to be hardy. She has a burn on her right wrist. The mother said she put her hand on the hot stove.[12]

The ISPCC inspector conducted a series of supervisory visits over the course of three months and closed the case in November 1958, after concluding that the situation had improved significantly.

The ISPCC was called out to the same family a year later in response to further complaints: "I visited as a result of a complaint … It is alleged that the mother ill-treats this child and treats her badly. Woman denied beating the child and told me that [the child] was wild and fond of telling lies. She alleges that the granny had spoiled the child. I saw no marks on the child."[13] Again the ISPCC inspector conducted a series of supervisory visits, and again the case was closed in August 1960. The ISPCC was called out yet again in March 1961:

> I visited as a result of a phone message … stating that this child was being beaten and ill-treated by the mother, and asked that I visit this [morning]. [The mother] was at home. Man was at work. Woman denied that she ill-treated her illegitimate child at any time and could give no reason why people would allege such things. She gave me permission to see and talk to her child in the presence of a nun. I met [the nun] and the sister who teaches [the child]. The teacher never found any trace of beatings on the child who answered all my questions and did not give me the impression of being cowed. I arranged to have the child examined by the school medical officer today. [The child] is not [her stepfather's] daughter.[14]

This last case was closed in August 1961, and there do not appear to be any additional reports on this child or family. It is difficult to believe that neighbors would complain, on three separate occasions, about the child's treatment if, in fact, she was not being mistreated.

As bad as conditions were for some illegitimate children in their own homes, ISPCC case files also attest to mothers who struggled to raise their children in a "normal" family environment. In October 1958 the county medical officer in County Galway solicited the help of the ISPCC in effecting the discharge of a six-year old illegitimate child from the county hospital. The child had been admitted to the hospital two years previously for an unidentified illness (given the duration of treatment it is possible that he was being treated for turberculosis), but had been "fit for discharge" for over a year. The CMO hoped that the ISPCC could persuade the mother to take her child, or to make alternative arrangements for him. The child's mother explained that she was anxious to take the child, and that her husband was willing to take the child, but they did not have suitable accommodation to meet the needs of their growing family. The family obtained a county council house in Castlebar, Co. Mayo, and the boy was removed from the hospital and reunited with his family in December 1959.[15]

In 1950 a 5-year-old child, who had been boarded out in Wexford town, was returned to his mother, then living and working in London. The mother sought the ISPCC's help in transferring the child to London and paying the cost of his travel.[16] The child had originally been placed in a private arrangement and his mother paid a weekly sum towards his maintenance. It seems that she intended the arrangement to be temporary, until she could find work in London and save enough money to be able to support herself and her son. The NSPCC in London advised the ISPCC that they did not think the mother could care for the child given that she also had three young children already living with her. Ultimately, however, the child was returned to his mother and presumably lived a "normal" life with his family.

The ISPCC, by its nature, dealt with families at times of crisis and dysfunction. It is not surprising, then, that ISPCC case files document a grim and dreary existence for Ireland's poorest children. And the lives of some illegitimate children were particularly grim and dreary. They could be shunned and mistreated by their families and communities. Their mothers often had few employment prospects and likely lived on the margins of society, relying on the largesse of family and friends or, in rare circumstances, home assistance. ISPCC inspectors could be intemperate in their criticism of the men and women who came under their notice, often describing poor mothers and fathers as "lazy" and "useless." They were even more strident in their condemnation of unmarried mothers, and it is clear they assumed that the poor circumstances in which illegitimate children lived were due in large part to the moral intransigence of their mothers. There is no reason to believe that the views of ISPCC inspectors differed from "respectable" Irish society as a whole. These attitudes inevitably shaped the experiences, and quality of life, of many illegitimate children.

Many ISPCC inspectors were particularly critical of women who had more than one illegitimate child, and they were often reluctant to help such women. This attitude was abundantly evident in a 1957 case from Co. Wexford: "I visited as a result of a complaint. The mother gave birth to her third illegitimate child a week ago. The baby was very weak and small. The mother refused to go into Hospital and it was feared the baby would die. I visited this a.m. thinking the mother and baby was still at home only to find that they went into hospital yesterday. The mother is of a low mentality and cares very little for her children."[17] This family had just over £1 per month with which to feed, clothe, and house five people. There is no question that the mother's "moral intransigence" had an impact on her children's quality of life, because she had to support three children on children's allowances and meager home assistance, and because people who might otherwise have been charitably-minded would not be inclined to help a woman with three illegitimate children. But the fact that the ISPCC readily dismissed this woman as a moral reprobate made the lives of her children that much more difficult; their well-being was all but lost in the ISPCC's strident value judgments.

Another ISPCC inspector was similarly contemptuous of an unmarried mother with three children in 1960 Wexford: "I visited as a result of a complaint. It is alleged that this unmarried mother pays very little attention to her children or home. Her eldest [daughters] are working. She gets their wages but wastes it. The youngest child is poorly clad and unwashed. The home leaves much to be desired. Some slates have been blown off with the storm and the rain comes in through the upstairs room. Told woman I would see the housing officer."[18] In spite of the fact that the house was in very bad repair, and that the mother had only £1 per week with which to house, feed, clothe, and educate her children, no action was taken to improve the family's material circumstances. The ISPCC inspector likely believed the mother wasted her children's wages and thus was not worthy of assistance. In refusing to aid the mother, however, the ISPCC also refused to help her children.

A case from 1953 Wexford reinforces the judgmental attitude evident in ISPCC reports. The ISPCC was summoned to the house of an unmarried mother living with her 4-month-old child, her mother, and her married sister; on arrival the inspector found the child to be "undernourished and sickly."[19] According to the report: "The mother lives in with the maternal grandmother. There is another married sister staying in the home, and it is alleged that the house is visited by strange men. The maternal grandfather is living apart from his wife … and again it is alleged that his wife and two daughters ran him away. The mother of this child is a lazy useless young woman and does not seem to take much interest in her child. She spends her evenings and nights walking the streets of Gorey."[20] In branding the mother as "lazy" and "useless," and assuming that the women of the house drove their men away, the ISPCC inspector decided that the family was not worthy of help and took no action to help the child even though he appeared to be "undernourished and sickly."

Statistics document the number of illegitimate children born in a given year but not the number of children who were raised in their own homes by their own families. The available data on mother and baby homes show that a substantial percentage of women took their children home with them and intended at least to try to care for them. In many respects the children who were cared for by their own families likely had the same kinds of experiences as other children of their age and socioeconomic background. But they also faced challenges that other children might not have faced. In some cases children were "hidden away" by families who were ashamed of them. In others, illegitimate children were either rejected or marginalized by stepfathers who resented the burden of providing for other men's children. Additionally, available evidence suggests that some mothers eventually gave up and had their children committed to industrial schools. They may have given up because of destitution, because of the rejection of family and friends, or simply because they no longer wished to be saddled with the burden of caring for a child.

Boarding out

The boarding-out scheme was first introduced in Ireland under the Irish Poor Law Amendment Act (1862); this act allowed local authorities to board out with local families children who otherwise would be maintained in workhouses.[21] The plan was rooted less in a growing awareness of the benefits of family, rather than institutional, rearing for children than in the desire to clear workhouses of children (based on the belief that workhouses were little more than training camps for juvenile delinquents) and reduce the overall cost of caring for illegitimate children. The boarding-out system was re-affirmed by the Irish Free State under the 1924 County Boards of Health (Assistance) Order, which represented an extensive overhaul of the Irish poor law system, and the Public Assistance Act (1939). In the absence of statistical data it is impossible to say definitively that the majority of children who came into the boarding-out system were illegitimate. However, the reports of Department of Health inspectors suggest that this was the case. The majority of these children likely were born in county homes, the children's homes in Tuam, Co. Galway or Pelletstown (Dublin), or one of the handful of mother and baby homes throughout the country that were approved for the reception of local authority cases.[22] Parental consent was necessary, technically, to board out children, although such consent was easily dispensed with if the mother could not be traced or was deemed to be "unfit." In the overwhelming majority of cases, local authorities were responsible for the entire cost of caring for children, although a small percentage of unmarried mothers made modest contributions toward the maintenance of their children.

From 1922 responsibility for overall administration of the boarding-out system fell to the Irish Department of Local Government and Public Health (renamed the Department of Health in 1947). There was no immediately discernible shift in policy at this time, although as the years went by Department of Health inspectors of boarded-out children increasingly voiced the view that boarding out was preferable to an institutional existence. This was particularly true for illegitimate children who otherwise would have no hope, and thus no experience, of a "normal" family life. Indeed, this view was articulated by the Department of Health's inspector of boarded-out children in their very first report, published in 1925:

> It is believed that the successful upbringing of the children would best be achieved by having the children individually cared for in the families of the respectable poor. The requirements of home life supply the means of cultivating natural affections, self-reliance and the perception of the duties of everyday life, which are invaluable towards the development of the children into normally minded adults. In the home life under the boarding-out system strong ties of affection spring up between the child and the members of the family with whom it lives. Where the homes of foster parents are situate in rural localities the children are reared in healthy surroundings and have opportunities of acquiring training and experience suitable to them in after life. It is not unfitting that they might for the most part become absorbed in the agricultural industry.[23]

Similar arguments were made repeatedly in reports submitted by the inspectors of boarded-out children to the Minister for Health – reports that were intended never to see the light of day. (It should be noted that in spite of their preference for boarding out over institutionalization, Department of Health inspectors did not intend that boarding out would facilitate upward social mobility. Rather, it showed poor children their place in the social hierarchy, and helped keep them there.)

Various politicians echoed the views of the Department of Health inspectors, although their concerns were of a more practical nature. In the debate on the Children Bill of 1940, T.D. Allen voiced his belief that local authorities often showed preference for institutional care rather than boarding-out for the children in their charge, and that in the long run this policy was not cost-effective:

> According to the local taxation accounts, local authorities contributed, in the year 1938–39, £39,000 for boarded-out children and children at nurse. In the same year, they contributed £54,000 odd for children in reformatory and industrial schools. The vast majority of children comprised in these categories are similar in type. My objection to committing to industrial schools is that, when the time comes for these children to leave the schools, they are very often waifs and strays and do not fit into the community. Many of them will never fit into rural life. If those children … were taken in hand and boarded-out amongst the rural community … they would cost no more than they do under the present system and they would fit into the life of the community later on and be good citizens.[24]

For this politician, as for many others, the main concerns were pragmatic. They advocated the cheapest method of care, but they were also concerned that illegitimate children grow up to "fit in" and be "good citizens" – in other words, that they do not descend into delinquency and crime and become even heavier burdens on state resources. But while Department of Health inspectors mentioned the importance of boarded-out children "fitting in," they were concerned primarily with the children's physical and emotional well-being.

The boarding-out system was overseen at the central government level by the Department of Health, which had overall responsibility for establishing the regulations under which the system was administered, and conducting annual inspections of all of the children boarded out throughout the country. The day-to-day administration of the boarding-out system fell to local authorities at the county level; they were expected to implement Department of Health regulations and to conduct monthly inspections of boarded-out children under their care, but otherwise they had a fair degree of latitude in how the boarding-out scheme operated in their districts.[25] As a result, the amounts paid to foster parents varied from one county to another, as did the inspectional regime. The task of inspecting boarded-out children fell, depending on the local authority, to home assistance officers, public health nurses, or infant life protection visitors. But available evidence suggests that, no matter who conducted the inspections, in most counties the inspectors failed in their duties. Inspections typically were carried out sporadically or not at all, were cursory in nature and as a result hundreds, and perhaps even thousands, of children fell through the cracks. In some cases it took inspectors years to discover that a boarded-out child had died or been sent by the foster parents to an industrial school. (Foster parents did not have the legal authority to seek the committal of foster children, but this did not prevent some of them from doing so.)

Department of Health regulations required that children who came under the care of local authorities and were deemed "suitable" be boarded out rather than sent to industrial schools or other institutions. However, the records of the various local authorities indicate that only a fraction of the children who were "suitable" were, in fact, boarded out; the remainder were maintained, at the expense of local authorities, in county homes, industrial schools, and other institutions. The local authorities often argued that they simply could not procure enough foster homes to accommodate all of the children who came into their care. In reality, however, local authorities preferred to spend the extra money maintaining children in industrial schools because, although it cost more in financial terms, it cost far less in terms of human resources. It was easier to send children to industrial schools than to expend the time and energy necessary to solicit applications, inspect potential foster parents and foster homes, and keep regular tabs on boarded-out children. It is clear that some of the men and women responsible for conducting the inspections of foster homes found the duty onerous and burdensome, and often shirked their responsibilities even as they reported that they had conducted the required inspections.[26] As a result, hundreds if not thousands of children died, were sent to industrial schools, or were exploited, neglected, or abused by their foster parents. In short, although the boarding-out system under Irish administration was motivated, in part, by the desire to raise "unwanted" children in as normal a family environment as possible, the way the system was administered was guided more by the narrow agendas and self-interests of local authorities and home assistance officers than by the interests of the children themselves.

The tendency of many local authorities to opt for institutionalization rather than boarding out often caused friction between themselves and the Department of Health, to the point that successive Ministers for Health were compelled to remind the local authorities of their duties along the lines of the following entry from the Wicklow board of health and public assistance minutes:

Read circular letter dated 2nd September, 1924, from Local Government Department, impressing on Boards of Health the advisability of boarding out in suitable homes in the rural districts such children as were being maintained in County Homes and were proper cases for boarding out. Suggestions as to suitability of homes should be sought from Assistance Officers and others likely to have useful sources of information. The appointment of a Ladies Committee to act in conjunction with the Board and its Assistance Officers might also be of advantage. It could be arranged, if so desired, that a Lady Inspector with specialist knowledge and experience would be available to attend meetings and to afford advice or assistance.[27]

These kinds of reminders were issued repeatedly by the Department of Health in the 1920s, 1930s, and 1940s, and typically were met with the same defeatist response on the part of the local authorities: that in spite of their best efforts they simply could not secure a sufficient supply of good foster homes for all of the children in their care. The following plea, from the Leitrim superintendent assistance officer (SAO), is fairly typical in this regard: "The difficulty we are confronted with is that there are no suitable people prepared to board out children. Repeated advertisements have been inserted in the local press for foster parents but except for some applications for children of 10 to 12 years the response is negligible."[28] This entry appeared in the 1946 minutes, and it is possible that wartime austerity made local authorities' efforts to secure good foster homes more difficult. But similar disclaimers were made, throughout the country and throughout the 1920s, 1930s, and 1940s, suggesting a more endemic pattern of apathy and indifference on the part of local authorities.

There is, however, some grain of truth to local authority claims about the difficulty of securing suitable foster homes. Evidence suggests that some foster parents (it is impossible to know how many) accepted foster children solely for the maintenance grants that were paid to them by the local authorities, or for the work the children could do. They requested older children who would be "useful" around the house, rather than younger children who required more care and supervision. But it is also true that the local authorities, and particularly the home assistance officers, resented the burden that boarding-out placed on them. Although it was cheaper, financially, to maintain local authority children in foster homes than in industrial schools, in the long run many local authorities believed that the cost was much higher, in terms of both financial and human resources, because of the inspectional responsibilities that went along with the boarding-out system. Many local authorities were unwilling or unable to pay qualified people to carry out the inspectional regimes that were required of them by law. Children, and especially illegitimate children, were not a political or economic priority for them.

The failure of local authorities to carry out their responsibilities to boarded-out children came under public scrutiny in the mid-1940s, after a foster mother in County Westmeath was convicted of assaulting and ill-treating a boarded-out child in her care and fined £10.[29] The case was publicized in the national media and prompted a scathing editorial in the local newspaper, the *Westmeath Examiner*, as a result of which the Westmeath County Council launched an investigation into the matter. The newspaper editorial was critical of both the county council's investigation, and of the way the local authorities carried out their responsibilities: "The report of the Committee of Inquiry into the treatment of boarded-out children will be submitted to the County Council at its next meeting on Monday week. It exonerates all the officials concerned in the sad case … At the same time there is a tacit admission that supervision of the homes to which these children are entrusted is not as frequent and strict as it ought to be."[30] The editorial recommended both the appointment of women as visiting officers, and an increase in the maintenance allowance paid to foster parents, which the editorial called "ridiculously inadequate for the proper maintenance of a child."[31] The editorial concluded with a stern reminder to local authorities of their responsibilities to boarded-out children: "The Council has a responsibility which it cannot shift entirely to its officials. Its members are the guardians of these little ones. This … case has done useful service on concentrating attention on the duties of those who are to look after children who are deprived of the advantage of parents and who are entitled to a fair start in life."[32] This was one of the rare occasions when public commentary cast an unfavorable light on the boarding-out system, but this negative attention appears to have had little effect on how the system was administered.

One might assume that the children under local authority care who were "lucky enough" to be boarded out rather than sent to industrial schools enjoyed a more stable and "normal" existence than those reared in industrial schools. The reports of the inspectors of boarded-out children indicate that some boarded-out children did become fully integrated into their foster families, and continued to be part of those families even after the boarding-out allowance ended when children reached fifteen years of age. But there is ample evidence to suggest that a significant number of boarded-out children were, at a minimum exploited, and sometimes neglected and abused as well. This stemmed in part from the poor inspectional regime in many counties, but also from the fact that many foster families took in boarded-out children solely for the maintenance grants, or because the children would be useful to them in some tangible way. In effect, many foster families viewed boarded-out children as little more than unpaid servants and not as vulnerable children who needed love and guidance to usher them into healthy, stable adulthood.

A case from 1944 clearly illustrates the exploitation that some children experienced in foster homes: "On the day of inspection this child had five teeth extracted at school and had been sent home early as the day was extremely cold. Despite this however his foster mother had no scruples about sending him on a message to a shop at a considerable distance from his foster home, where I found him later in the evening. He was small and thin, was poorly clad, and looked cold and pale. I do not think that this child is well or kindly treated."[33] It is surprising that the inspector did not recommend removing this child to a new foster home. But given the treatment described in the inspection report, it is unlikely that this child had a stable and happy future to look forward to.

The primary safeguard against exploitation, neglect, and abuse – the inspectional regime – often failed to protect children because of the haphazard way in which it was carried out. In her report on children boarded-out in County Leitrim, the Department of Health inspector noted: "There is every reason to believe that the assistance officers' visits of inspection to the foster homes are extremely irregular. The condition of many of the homes is ample proof that the foster parents do not anticipate or expect regular visits of inspection."[34] It is clear from the Department of Health inspector's observation that foster parents not anticipating visits from assistance officers was an ongoing problem and not one of recent origin. An even more strident criticism was made of the inspectional regime in Co. Longford: "The Assistance Officers are extremely careless in the matter of regular inspections, in many cases only visiting the children once or twice a year. It should be noted that the regulations stipulate that the children should be visited monthly, and a serious view should be taken of laxity in this respect."[35] Although Department of Health inspectors repeatedly highlighted the lax inspectional regimes conducted at the local level, the Department of Health did little to hold local authorities accountable, or to improve the overall administration of the boarding-out system.

Miss Kennedy O'Byrne, another Department of Health inspector, voiced her concerns about the inspectional regime in many counties. She suggested, however, that it was not the fault of individual assistance officers but, rather, was a systemic shortcoming that could only be fixed with a complete overhaul of the system:

> In my opinion the time has come to make a radical change in the whole system of supervising boarded-out children. The duty of this supervision is at present largely in the hands of the Assistance Officers, mostly elderly men, who have innumerable other duties heaped upon them especially since the emergency [the Second World War]. Under the circumstances it is impossible for these Officers to make more than a hurried and superficial monthly visit to those boarded-out children. Even with the very best intentions it is in my opinion impossible for the Assistance Officers to make the right kind of inspection, which is essentially a woman's job: viz, examination of the child's person, hair, clothing, bedding and general circumstances, combined with a certain intuition to discern whether the child is not below par in health and not unduly suppressed.[36]

In short, Kennedy O'Byrne assumed that only a woman could do the job of inspecting boarded-out children effectively; since the majority of assistance officers were men, it seems that the local authorities did not share her views and concerns.

The effects of sub-par inspectional practices are evident throughout Department of Health inspectors' reports. Miss Clandillon, a Department of Health inspector, reported on a 10-year-old girl who was in the care of a foster parent in County Wexford. In this report, dated March 1951, Miss Clandillon stated: "I found a marked lack of affection for the child in this home and too great a stress was laid on her usefulness … This child has a sister, aged seven, who is at present in an institution, and for whom she appears to have a great affection. I consider it would benefit both of these little girls if a foster home could be found for them where they could live together."[37] Three years later Miss Clandillon again reported on this girl, who was still in the same foster home: "At my last inspection I recommended the removal of this child. There appeared to be a marked lack of affection for her and too much stress was laid on her usefulness. I now find that the foster mother is not anxious to keep the child, and I suggested to the Children's Officer that a home might be sought for her in Wexford where she could attend a secondary or vocational school."[38] By the time of this last report the child was approaching the age at which local authorities ceased to pay boarding-out allowances (which may have been the reason the foster mother no longer wished to keep the child). The paper trail on this child ended with the 1954 report; it is possible that the child was sent to an industrial school so that she might learn a "useful" skill. The implication of the inspector's reports was that the inspectors failed in their duties, and as a result this child's future prospects were more limited than they might have been had the local authorities heeded the Department of Health inspector's advice earlier on.

Another shortcoming of the boarding-out system was that it was driven, in large measure, by purely mercenary or pragmatic concerns on both sides. The local authorities were often more concerned with the financial bottom line than with what was in the best interests of children, and many foster parents were driven solely by what the foster child offered, in terms of the boarding-out allowances or their labor. In her report on boarded-out children in Kildare in 1950, Miss Clandillon gave the following assessment of a prospective foster family: "[This couple] gave as their reason for wanting a child that they needed help on the farm. They would not take a child under 9 years and would have preferred a boy of about 12. I would not recommend the home because the attitude of the proposed foster parents, the lack of suitable accommodation and because it appeared that any child placed in this home would be used as an unpaid help."[39] In her 1955 report Miss Clandillon reported on another foster home: "The foster mother … was anxious to know how soon the child could leave school and whether she would be permitted to keep him at home from time to time to help on the farm."[40] In another 1955 report Miss Clandillon noted that a boy had run away from his foster home because his foster mother overworked him. He returned to the home of his relatives, who took him to an industrial school in Tralee. The boy expressed the wish to stay in the industrial school rather than being forced to return to the foster home.[41] (It is noteworthy, in light of complaints by former industrial school residents, that this child preferred the institutional regime to the foster home that was, at least in theory, supposed to provide him with a normal family environment.)

An extreme example of foster children being exploited appeared in the 1957 report of the Donegal superintendent assistance officer in relation to two boys boarded-out on a farm. The inspector interviewed the foster parents and the boys as well as teachers and neighbors. The neighbors, who were somewhat reluctant to speak openly about the situation lest it cause tensions with the foster parents, nonetheless offered their assessment of the situation: "they had often heard the boys crying loudly and they often complained of being beaten. They did … state that these children were overworked, that they did all the work on the farm, plant all the potatoes and save the turf, milk, feed and look after cows, calves and hens and were not treated as children should be and both neighbours further said that the children should have been removed long ago."[42] Both neighbors reported that the foster mother's 56-year-old son was in poor health and did nothing around the farm, which suggests that the foster parents took in the two boys solely for their labor. (And the fact that the foster mother's son was 56 years of age suggests that she was probably well into her seventies, and well above the stipulated age for fostering children.) Although the Department of Health inspectors often recommended the removal of children from homes where they were being overworked or exploited, the available evidence suggests that their recommendations were not often heeded.

Concerns about boarded-out children being overworked was further reflected in concerns for their school attendance. The Department of Health inspectors of boarded-out children frequently voiced concerns about the poor school attendance records of many boarded-out children; they suspected that many boarded-out children were being kept home from school to work. Assistance officers responsible for inspecting boarded-out children were required to submit quarterly school attendance records, and it seems clear from these records that many foster children were kept out of school to work in various capacities for their foster parents. A case from County Offaly clearly illustrates official concern in this regard. In all cases where the department thought school absences to be excessive they requested a report from the relieving officer of the reasons for the absence, and if a child was absent for five days consecutively he demanded a medical certificate:

> The Minister for Local Government and Public Health has had before him Assistance Officer's Reports on boarded-out children, with school certificates for the month of February and he desires to be informed as to the nature of the illness which prevented [foster child], a boarded-out child with [foster mother] from attending school regularly during the month.
>
> The Home Assistance Officer was requested to procure the required Medical Certificate of the illness of [foster child]. This was done and was forwarded to the Department.[43]

Two years later the department was still concerned about the school attendance of this child and requested a report on the child's health:

> Letter from Local Government Department, dated 15/5/28, requesting to be informed of the opinion of the Tuberculosis Medical Officer as to [foster child] state of health immediately it is obtained.
>
> The Secretary reported that he had sent same on the 16th instant, the remarks of the T.M.O. being as follows:
>
> [Foster child], aged 12, is in a well nourished condition, well clad, and in 5th standard in school. He has no pulmonary trouble.[44]

There was no justification for keeping this child home from school, and a Department of Health official instructed the local authorities to report to the guards (gardaí, or police) if the child continued to be absent from school. A year later, in November 1929, the department was still demanding explanations from the local authorities about this child's school attendance:

> From the Local Government Department 11–12–29 pointing out that [foster child], boarded out with [foster mother] was absent from school on nine days in the month, and requesting to be furnished with a medical certificate as to the state of his health.
>
> The Assistance Officer stated that the Department's Inspector [Miss Litster] when on her last visit of inspection, had suggested that in future when this boy be kept from school a certain amount be deducted from the maintenance allowance, as she thought this would induce the foster parent to send the child to school regularly. Adding that a sum of 6/- had been deducted from [foster mother's] maintenance allowance, in the present instance.[45]

Although the amount of correspondence between the department and the Offaly board of health and public assistance regarding this particular child was unusual, and spanned nearly five years, the Department of Health's attention to the details outlined in board of public assistance minutes was not unusual. On the other hand, it is not unreasonable to wonder why this child was not removed from the foster home given the inspector's suspicions of foster parents' motives and actions.

In 1933 the Department of Health inspector clearly stated the department's views on the issue of school attendance: "From the Local

Government Department … in regard to [foster child] with [foster mother], Cloneyhurke, who was kept from school 6 days during the month of June to work, requesting that the boy be removed from his present foster home and boarded-out elsewhere. Stating that if parents require workmen they should employ them and not utilise the services of boarded-out children for whose maintenance they are paid."[46] As it happened this foster mother reported that the child had been kept home from school because he stepped on a nail and could not walk. However, the response of the Department of Health inspector suggests that there was, generally, good cause for concern.

School attendance continued to be a concern for the Department of Health into the 1940s and 1950s, and the fact that their inspectors repeatedly had to remind local authorities of regulations with regard to excessive absences suggests that the regulations were ignored with remarkable regularity. A letter from the Department of Health to the Cork board of health and public assistance in March 1939 inquired as to why no medical certificates were included with reports on one particular child, who had missed seven out of seventeen school days in one month.[47] In April 1940 another letter passed between the Department of Health and the Cork board of health and public assistance on this same issue: a boarded-out child had missed ten out of twenty school days in a month, and no medical certificates had been furnished.[48] And, again in July 1940 the Department of Health was still reminding the Cork board of health and public assistance about the need to submit medical certificates when boarded-out children missed four or more days of school. The fact that reminders were made with such frequency suggests that the local authority inspectors were not adequately monitoring the school attendance of boarded-out children.

If the life of many boarded-out children was tenuous during their "formative" years, their fate once they reached fifteen years of age – the age at which boarding-out allowances ceased – could be even more uncertain. The lucky minority of children were "adopted" by their foster families in the sense that the families kept them in spite of the fact that the boarding-out allowances ceased.[49] The following entry from a 1939 inspector's report illustrates this scenario:

> [Foster child] aged 15 years, boarded out with [foster mother], Loughley, Carrigaline. This child is well cared and happy. The foster home is a good one and the foster mother very attached to the girl. Her teacher informed me that she has great talent for needlework. The girl is anxious to go to the technical school in Passage West to be trained in needlework and domestic work. I suggest that the boarded-out period be extended for a further year to enable her to be so trained.[50]

In this instance the inspector recommended that the local authorities continue to pay a boarding-out allowance for an additional year so that the child could receive training that would enable her to support herself in the future. The board of public assistance refused, and the foster mother subsequently declined to keep the girl. A case from 1925 Wicklow had a much happier ending: "the child … boarded out with [foster mother], Ballycullen, would be 15 years old on 18th August next, and might be taken off the list of boarded-out children. [Foster mother], who was a small farmer in comfortable circumstances, wished to adopt the child, as she stated she would not part with her for the world. She loved her as one of her own and would provide for her in future. She asked that the usual outfit be provided the child."[51] This outcome was, unfortunately, the exception rather than the rule.

Of course, even when foster parents agreed to keep the children after they came of age, things could go horribly wrong. In 1935 a foster father asked the Offaly board of health and public assistance for permission to retain custody of a boarded-out girl when she reached 15 years of age, and the home assistance officer strongly recommended this course of action: "[Foster father's] wife died about six years ago, and the girl has become very attached to her foster parent. It is a first class home, and he would strongly recommend that [foster father's] application be granted. He would also mention that there is another girl in the house aged 18 years whom [foster father] adopted when she was a baby."[52] It was almost unheard of for an unmarried man to be allowed to foster children, especially girls, so this case is extraordinary for that reason alone. But at the same time that the home assistance office was enthusiastically endorsing this foster father, the foster father was charged with sexually assaulting the girl. Extraordinarily, the Minister for Health gave his sanction to the foster child being allowed to remain with this foster father more than two weeks after he had already been arrested and the girl sent to the Good Shepherd magdalen asylum in Limerick.

In the absence of statistics it is impossible to know what number of children continued to be part of their foster families after the boarding-out allowances ceased, and how many were literally pushed out into the world and made to fend for themselves once they reached fifteen years of age. It does seem, from inspection reports, that the children whose foster families refused to maintain them when the boarding-out allowances ceased posed a significant challenge and caused a great deal of worry for Department of Health inspectors. These inspectors were not always convinced that the local authorities did right by former boarded-out children once they came off the boarding-out rolls. In her 1941 inspection report, Department of

Health inspector Miss Murray noted the futility of boarding children out if their foster parents were only going to give them up once they reached the age of fifteen:

> there is on the whole a lack of those ties of affection between children and foster parents which is a feature of the boarding-out in other parts of the country. This is shown by the frequent refusal of foster parents to provide a home for the children after the age of 15 unless the Board continues to maintain them. Recently a girl of 15 was returned to the County Home by the foster parents when payments for maintenance ceased. Nothing is gained by rearing children in foster homes if they are returned to the County Home at the age of 15.[53]

The solution, according to Miss Murray, was to board children out at much earlier ages and impress on foster parents the extent of the commitment they were required to make. But the concerns expressed by Miss Murray reflected the fact that, for many foster parents, boarding out was nothing more than a financial arrangement.

The problem was exacerbated by the fact that while Department of Health inspectors regularly made recommendations like the one above, that local authorities continue to pay boarding-out allowances for an additional year so that a child might obtain further education or training, local authorities typically ignored these recommendations; most likely they did not want to set a precedent that ultimately would cost them money. But a bigger problem was that most foster parents were unwilling to accept responsibility for foster children once the boarding-out allowance ceased. The following case is fairly typical in this regard. A boy and his younger sister were placed in a foster home in County Meath when he was 13 years of age (their previous foster mother had died). The Department of Health inspector reported that: "[Foster child] who will be sixteen shortly has not been attending school regularly in recent months. The foster mother said she is not anxious to keep him and wants to have him placed in employment when he reaches sixteen years. She appears to have very little interest in him but seems to have some affection for the younger child."[54] The boy was not mentioned in subsequent reports, so his fate is not known. One can imagine, given the foster mother's attitude, that he was pushed out into the world with few practical or technical skills with which to support himself and no family or safety net to fall back on.

Even when employment and accommodation were secured for former boarded-out children, there is ample evidence that they were exploited, underpaid, and mistreated by their employers. In 1933 the Offaly board of health and public assistance secured employment for a 15-year-old boy, but the prospective employer refused to pay the boy the wages suggested by the local authorities:

From the Department of Local Government … in regard to the hiring-out of [foster child] with [employer] Cloneyquin, Portarlington, pointing out that the wage proposed to be paid to [foster child] namely £6 a year appears altogether too low, and to request that [employer] may be asked to provide the boy with clothes and boots in addition to paying him the wage in question. Mr. Buckley, Assistance Officer to whom this matter was referred, reported that he had called on [employer] and that he will not consent to pay the boy … £6 a year and supply him with clothes and boots, but that he will agree to pay him £5 per annum and supply him with clothes.[55]

After several months of negotiating with the employer, and shifting the boy from one employment situation to another, he was subsequently admitted to the county home because no other employment could be found for him. This probably began a cycle of sporadic unemployment punctuated by stints in the county home and perhaps, if the boy became desperate enough, even petty crime and imprisonment.

The case of a teenage girl was even more convoluted than the case cited above. When the girl reached fifteen years of age in 1923, her foster mother initially said she would keep the girl even without the boarding-out allowance; she then changed her mind, and the girl and another boarded-out child were moved to another foster home. Between September 1923 and January 1926 this girl was moved to three different foster homes and seven different employers:

When she was 15 years old the Assistance Officer got her a nice situation in Dublin, but when there about a month her employer wrote to say she was unsatisfactory and that she could not keep her. The Assistance Officer asked [employer], Bridge Street, Bri, to give her a trial; as the girl proved useless and unmanageable she also had to let her go. The Supt. Assistance Officer then got her into Baggot Street Convent to be trained for domestic service, but they refused to keep her. She then got her into an institution in Henrietta Street for training servants, and the Sisters there had now written that they could keep her no longer. The Nuns in Gloucester Street had taken her for a trial, but probably she would not be kept there either, and the Supt. Assistance Officer asked for directions as to what should be done. The girl had no home or relatives who would be responsible for her, and she was not eligible for admission to the County Home.[56]

The girl's fate from this point is unclear, and it is entirely possible that she ended up in a magdalen asylum or perhaps even a lunatic asylum given that she had no relatives and was apparently "difficult" to manage. It is likely that many formerly boarded-out children drifted from job to job, or from one institution to another, because they had no roots, no solid training or education, and no support network to sustain them in hard times.

The circumstances of younger children were not always any more secure than those of children who reached the age at which they came off the boarding-out rolls. Foster parents often returned the children entrusted to their care, for a variety of reasons, and this trend reinforces the ulterior motives that many foster parents had in taking on boarded-out children. Not a single report by the Department of Health inspectors was free of comments about neglectful or unsuitable foster homes. Children often were removed from foster homes because of the death of the foster parent, which stemmed from the fact that many local authorities were not all that discriminating in their selection of foster parents. (So, for example, it was not unusual for young children to be placed with elderly foster parents.) The Department of Health inspectors had to remind the local authorities repeatedly that children, especially very young children, should not be boarded out with elderly foster parents; these reminders usually went unheeded.

The age of foster parents was a constant source of worry for Department of Health inspectors. In her 1945 inspection report the Department of Health inspector made this point abundantly clear:

> A child should in no case be boarded out with an aged foster mother. There is naturally a great inclination to take this course in cases where a foster mother has already proved herself worthy by successfully rearing a number of boarded-out children, but nevertheless, it is a mistake. A child boarded out with an aged foster mother is likely to suffer neglect through the illness or feebleness of its guardian. Should the foster mother die while the child is young it entails a break with the child's life with consequent disturbance and upset.[57]

The possibility that boarded-out children would be neglected owing to the age of the foster mother was borne out time and again in the inspector's reports; the following example is typical in this regard: "This child is 5½ years of age and his foster mother is 77. It is inconceivable why the child was boarded out in this home. He was not clean, was very thin, and extremely small for his age."[58] Although this child clearly was neglected, this neglect stemmed not from malice or thoughtlessness, but from the inability of the foster mother, due to her age and infirmity, to care for such a young child. In spite of continued reminders from the Department of Health inspectors about the age of foster parents, however, it seems that local authorities were less concerned than they should have been with the age of the foster mothers, primarily because raising their standards would have meant they had to work twice as hard to find suitable foster homes for the children in their care.

Sometimes boarded-out children were returned because it was "inconvenient" for the foster parent to keep them, as was the case in the following example from 1957 Dublin: "A letter has been received from their foster mother stating that she is going on a visit to England during this month and requesting the Board to remove [the foster children] from her care."[59] Both of the girls were sent to industrial schools. In other cases children were returned because they did not "give satisfaction" to their foster parents, which often meant they were unable to do the kind of chores that the foster parents expected of them. Some foster parents appear to have taken children and sent them back to the local authorities with alarming frequency, and Department of Health inspectors generally did not recommend that such foster parents be removed from the list of approved homes. The following case from 1953 Co. Kildare was fairly typical in this regard: "[Foster mother] informed me that she intended to send these boys [aged five and ten years] back to the County Home. She appeared to have no affection whatever for them. She already had three other boys, one of whom had been taken by his mother … and the others sent back to the County Home."[60] Although Miss Clandillon recommended that these two boys be removed from this foster home, she did not suggest that the foster mother be stricken from the list of approved homes.

As previous examples suggest, some boarded-out children were neglected because of the age and infirmity of their foster parents. But age and infirmity were not the only causes of neglect. Department of Health inspectors of boarded-out children often expressed concern generally about the neglect of foster children, which is not surprising given that many of them likely were taken solely for economic reasons. Examples of neglect appeared frequently in the pages of the inspectors' reports on boarded-out children; the problem, however, was that the local authorities were slow to respond to allegations of neglect, in part because they had such difficulty procuring foster homes that they hung on to the homes they had, no matter how bad those homes might be. The case of two young girls boarded out in Leitrim in the 1940s illustrated this point: "Both these children were badly clad and were far from clean. Their school lunch was entirely inadequate. [One girl] was wearing sandals on the day of the inspection [4th October] and as the day was wet and she had to cross fields on her way to school, her feet were soaking. This foster home was commented on in last year's report but no improvement has taken place in the meantime."[61] This was but one of four instances of obvious neglect noted by the inspector in just this one report. Given the lax inspectional regime already alluded to, it is not surprising either that children were neglected, or that foster parents rarely were censured in any way for their treatment of the children in their care.

A case from 1943 Kerry clearly illustrates the extent to which foster children could be neglected and overlooked in their foster homes: "I found this child almost naked, the only clothing she had on when I saw her was a cotton frock although [the foster mother's] own two children were very well clad. The child did not seem happy and looked suppressed. I advise her removal to a more suitable foster home and foster mother."[62] There were two similar instances of neglect documented in this same report. In 1955 Miss Clandillon expressed concern about the fate of a seven-year-old child boarded out in County Cork:

> This little girl is very thin and appeared to be very nervous of strangers. I got the impression that there is not much affection or security for her in this home. [Foster mother's] sister, married brother and his wife and baby are all living in the home now and it is possible that the child will be relegated more and more to the background. I suggested that the home be carefully supervised and if it is thought that the child would receive more affection in another home that she should be removed.[63]

And in her 1953 report Miss Clandillon chronicled an extreme case of neglect involving seven children, all of whom were boarded out in the same home (which was against Department of Health regulations, but the local authorities appear not to have been concerned with that):

> The foster mother was not at home when I visited but I was told by the other children that the two [foster] children had been removed by their father earlier in the day. The bedding in the room they occupied was very dirty. The baby … was in a cot in the front bedroom. The child was blue with cold and did not appear to have had any attention for hours. The other four children looked healthy but the elder boy has severe strabismus and was not wearing glasses. I consider it very remiss of [foster mother] to go out leaving a child of eight years in charge of the home especially when a baby of only six months had been entrusted to her care.[64]

This foster mother clearly had more children in her care than she was capable of caring for, and the fact that so many children were in her home in the first place speaks to the haphazard administration of the system.

Another problem that often resulted in the neglect of boarded-out children was the tendency of some foster parents to spend maintenance allowances on themselves and their own families rather than on the boarded-out children in their care. Department of Health inspectors repeatedly raised this concern in their annual reports: "[Foster child] was at home from school at the time of my inspection. He looked thin and pale and had been vomiting for days. The foster mother had not had medical attention for him … I am not altogether satisfied with this foster mother's attitude towards the children. She remarked that she 'does not make much out of them' and that if she buys sufficient butter and milk for the children she will have nothing left out of the allowance."[65] Department of Health inspectors also suspected that foster parents did not use the twice-yearly clothing allowances solely for the use of the foster children in their care:

many foster parents, when confronted, could not account for how they had spent the money. The following entry from the Offaly board of health and public assistance minutes reflected these suspicions:

> There is still evidence that sufficient care is not taken to insure that the money allowed for clothing is spent exclusively for the benefit of the child. There is considerable reluctance on the part of some foster mothers to procure them for inspection, and many devises are resorted to, so as to escape compliance with the regulations. A number of bills examined by the inspector did not correspond with the articles of clothing, nor could some of the foster parents produce the items which appeared on the bills.[66]

In her 1955 inspection of children boarded-out in County Cork Miss Clandillon reported on a 14-year-old girl who obviously was neglected by her foster mother: "She told me also that [foster mother] did not buy clothes for her, and that the dress she was wearing had been given to her by a neighbour."[67] This foster mother clearly did not spend the twice-yearly clothing allowance on the child.

The reports submitted by Department of Health inspectors of boarded-out children document a litany of flaws in administration and inspection and, worse, a sustained pattern of exploitation, neglect, and indifference on the part of local authorities and many foster parents. But there were cases where foster parents literally were saviors for children who otherwise would have fallen through the cracks. For some children, the foster home provided the kind of loving and nurturing environment that their own families could not or would not provide. This is evident, for example, in the inspector's report of an 11-year-old boy who had been in the same foster home since he was four years old. The inspector was concerned that the boy had no supervision from the time he returned home from school until his foster parents returned home from work at 7p.m. But this concern aside, the boy was well treated by his foster parents:

> The boy brings a good lunch with him to school and on his return from school he goes into the house where a thermos flask of tea and some bread and butter have been left for him ... The boy appeared to me to be well clad, well cared and very happy ... he had a good substantial dinner with the family when they returned home ... Notwithstanding the apparent lack of supervision of this boy during his after school hours, I do not suggest changing him to another home as in the future he will probably have a chance of being trained as a gardener by his foster father.[68]

This child seems to have been treated just like the foster parents' own children, and his future seemed secure.

The depth of affection that foster parents could have for their boarded-out children is reflected in an ISPCC case from 1958 County Mayo. The foster mother sought the advice of the ISPCC because she feared her foster son was getting out of control:

> [Foster mother] stated she received [the child] 6 years ago when he was 6 years old, he was now 12. She was told he was an illegitimate child ... She said in general that the whole family had become very attached to [the child] but there were times when his behaviour was very annoying. He was very disobedient at times, was inclined to retort with cheeky answers and for no reason at all would start shouting and screaming outside the house and would not stop when told to do so. [Foster mother] said he was also very dirty in his habits and personal hygiene as he often dirtied his trousers ... [Foster mother] said that [the child] was being bullied at school and blamed for everything that happened. She was however quite convinced of his honesty ... and she also said that he was very truthful. Asked if she wanted [the child] removed she said no, not for the present. Perhaps if you give him a good talking to, making him realise that he could be taken away if he does not do what he is told, it may make him change for the better. I told her I would call back some day soon and have a talk with him after school was over.[69]

Although the ISPCC conducted a series of supervisory visits to the home, the child's behavior did not improve, but the foster mother continued to refuse to give the child up. While there was inevitably a measure of exploitation and abuse that boarded-out children suffered, and they in all likelihood suffered higher levels of abuse and exploitation because they literally had no one to advocate on their behalf, there were also cases where children were treated like the natural children of their foster parents, and even their troublesome behavior would not compel the foster parents to give them up. In this particular instance the foster mother appears to have had an unusual degree of empathy with the foster child, and recognized that his background had an impact on his behavior.

In spite of the "happy endings" occasionally documented in inspection reports, the experiences of boarded-out children generally were mixed. Many boarded-out children were abused, overworked, or neglected by foster parents who regarded them as little more than unpaid servants, and who agreed to accept them in the first place only for the boarding-out allowances and the work they could perform. Even in foster homes where children were not exploited or abused, they likely faced a sense of alienation or isolation because they were not fully integrated into their foster families and they knew they did not belong. Another significant issue for boarded-out children was the uncertainty of their futures. They faced instability, lack of training and educational opportunities, and the absence of a safety net or support network, all of which likely limited their future prospects.

Children at nurse

Children at nurse were children who were placed in foster homes under a private arrangement, either by unmarried mothers themselves, or by charitable or "adoption" societies such as St Patrick's Guild.[70] Typically these arrangements were of two types: those in which a one-time payment was made for the child and the foster parent agreed to keep the child indefinitely; or those in which a regular weekly or monthly fee was paid, and the foster parent agreed to keep the child only so long as the fee was paid. Even when charitable agencies, rather than mothers, made these arrangements, mothers were expected to make regular contributions to their children's upkeep. These arrangements, although made by private agencies or individuals, nonetheless were governed by the Children Act (1908). Women accepting children "for reward" (i.e. children at nurse) were obliged to notify local authorities within 48 hours. Failure to do so could result in prosecutions under the various Children Acts. The Children Acts also compelled local authorities to make the same monthly inspections of children at nurse as they made on boarded-out children, and Department of Health inspectors also made annual inspections. (These compulsory inspections ceased when a child at nurse reached the age of nine, however, and their fate beyond that point is anyone's guess.) The local authorities were required to post, in public venues throughout their districts, advertisements outlining the provisions of the Children Acts with regard to children at nurse. It is clear from available evidence, however, that the system of administration and inspection was even more haphazard and precarious than administration of the boarding-out scheme, and many children at nurse fell through the cracks or, worse, died because of the poor administrative and inspectional regimes.[71]

In the absence of firm statistics it is impossible to say with any clarity how many children were placed at nurse or what ultimately happened to them.[72] However, board of health and public assistance minutes, especially for Dublin, and the reports of Department of Health inspectors, indicate that these arrangements almost always broke down, mainly because mothers eventually stopped paying to maintain their children, at which point foster parents refused to keep the children. Children in these circumstances ended up in the care of local authorities and were boarded out or sent to industrial schools at local authority expense. Dublin, however, appears to have been a notable exception. The Dublin board of health and public assistance steadfastly refused to accept financial responsibility for children who were placed at nurse under private arrangement (they did, however, meet their statutory obligation to inspect the homes of such children). As a result, children placed at nurse in Dublin often ended up being committed to industrial schools by the courts once the financial arrangements fell through, because there were few other options to provide for them.[73]

In almost every inspection report Department of Health inspectors noted the inept way that the registration and inspection of children at nurse were carried out in each county. Miss Murray's report on children at nurse in Co. Longford in 1944 was typical:

> The Children Acts are not administered effectively, and no serious effort has ever been made to enforce the provisions of the Acts. The last notice in connection with the Acts was issued in October 1943 and took the form of a small advertisement in the local press; no posters have ever been issued. There are undoubtedly nurse children in the county who have not been registered, and until a more vigorous attempt is made to locate these children the Acts cannot be said to be properly administered.[74]

Miss Murray was still commenting, four years later, on the poor record of inspection of nurse children in Longford:

> There are now seven children registered as at nurse compared with three at the time of my last inspection. It is most unlikely that this figure represents the total number at nurse in the county and a determined effort should be made to locate all children who are covered by the provisions of the Children Acts. In addition to the issue of quarterly advertisements setting forth the regulations and the penalties for non-compliance, the help of the Assistance Officers, Medical Officers, District Nurses and the Garda should be enlisted … I am not satisfied that inspection of children registered under the Children Acts is either regular or thorough. All the county Public Health Schemes should be at the service of these children, particularly the Free Milk Scheme. On enquiry I was informed that none of the children now at nurse in the county are, or ever have been, in receipt of Free Milk. It is the duty of the Infant Life Protection Visitor (in this case the Assistance Officer) to inform foster mothers of the various Public Health Schemes in operation, and to advise them to take advantage of all available services.[75]

Not only were local authorities remiss in carrying out their inspectional duties, but they also failed to inform the foster mothers of other schemes of assistance for which they might have been eligible, and that might have improved the quality of life of the children in their care.

Miss Clandillon offered a similar indictment of the system of inspecting children at nurse in Co. Limerick: "There appears to be an extraordinary lack of interest in the welfare of nurse children in Limerick City area and no effort seems to be made to have them registered. In two of the four homes on the register there was also an unregistered child; I can only conclude from this fact that even these four homes are not inspected by the Infant Life Protection Visitor."[76] Reports for Cork were equally bleak: "On the returns for 31st March 1949 there were only seven children registered under the Children Acts … The work of inspection has been left to the Assistance Officers and I understand that the County Manager made an order recently appointing them Infant Life Protection Visitors. I fear that this arrangement will effect no improvement in the inspection of the children nor in the keeping of the registers."[77] Part of the problem, as Miss Clandillon acknowledged, was that there were several charitable agencies in Limerick all trying to care for more children than they knew what to do with. They were not as discriminating in their selection of homes as they should have been, and generally there was a disregard for the law amongst these charitable agencies and amongst the women who agreed to take children for reward. There can be little doubt, in these circumstances, that a significant number of children got lost in the system.

Miss Litster was so concerned with the way the Children Acts were administered in the 1940s that she circulated a memorandum within the Department of Health outlining her concerns: "The administration of the Children Acts throughout the country gives cause for grave uneasiness. The acts, except in a few areas, are administered in a haphazard manner. There are two main causes for this: the apathy of the majority of the Local Authorities, many of whom are also practically ignorant of the provisions of the Acts and of the duties devolving on them under the Acts; the method of inspection generally in use."[78] Miss Litster pointed out that while a handful of counties appointed designated infant life protection visitors or public health nurses whose sole responsibility was the administration of the Children Acts, most counties relied on assistance officers – the same, typically male, officers who dispensed home assistance and administered the boarding-out system. Miss Litster articulated in the clearest terms her frustration with this system: "The sole reason for their appointment … would appear to be that as Assistance Officers, they cover a district and are in touch with the people living in it. It would provide as good an argument for appointing the district postman. It is futile to expect that inspections will be properly carried out in such circumstances."[79] Most local authorities assigned inspectional duties on the basis of expediency and frugality rather than on the basis of who was best equipped to perform the tasks involved.

In spite of the frequent and alarmist nature of Department of Health inspectors' warnings about flaws in the system, there is no evidence of improvement into the 1950s. Many local authorities excused their poor performance on the grounds that the "emergency" (rationing, travel restrictions, etc) during the Second World War made it impossible for them to discharge their duties efficiently. But the systemic nature of the failure existed well before the war started, and it was highlighted again, in most damning fashion, by Miss Clandillon in 1959, when no such excuse could be offered:

> I wish to draw attention, as a matter of urgency, to the serious position which has developed in North Cork with regard to the inspection of boarded-out children and nurse children ... The nurse children were not visited except when the S.A.O. [superintendent assistance officer] wished to check on the children of over nine years in an effort to amend the returns for the half-year ended 31/3/59. The half-yearly returns are never forthcoming when required. One foster mother told me she had not had any inspections since my own last visit in June, 1957. No effort is made to keep the registers of boarded-out and nurse children up to date. In fact, the whole picture is one of neglect and indifference.[80]

Given that complaints about the system of inspection were made consistently throughout the 1930s, 1940s, and into the 1950s, it is unlikely that it ever improved significantly, and that by 1959 bad conditions had reached a crisis point. Only in Dublin city is there evidence of a concerted effort to administer the system efficiently, and to prosecute those who violated the law.[81]

Department of Health inspectors were right to be concerned given the seemingly high mortality rate amongst children at nurse. Children at nurse were particularly vulnerable to extreme neglect, and thus to premature death, because there was no incentive on the part of foster mothers to care for them. In fact there was a disincentive, particularly if the foster parent received a lump sum rather than monthly payments. In 1924 the Dublin board of health and public assistance expressed outrage that St Patrick's Guild, a private Catholic adoption society," placed a child in a home where two children had already died: "[Infant Life Protection Visitor] reports that [foster mother] ... has been given care of an infant ... 5 months [St Patrick's Guild], although two children in her care died recently in Cork street, all given out by [St Patrick's Guild]. This is contrary to directions of Local Government Board's Circular to Rescue Societies."[82] The death of children placed at nurse continued to be a problem in the 1930s, 1940s and 1950s. In her 1950 report Miss Clandillon blamed the poor inspectional regime for the death of a three-week-old infant in December of 1949:

> The foster parents of an unregistered infant ... were prosecuted recently for neglecting the child to such an extent that it died. This baby was born in the County Home, Killarney, on 3rd December 1949, was discharged on 16th December ... the child was taken to a wretched home in Killarney and was readmitted on the 28th of the same month to the County Home where it died the following day.[83]

Two children died in Wexford in 1939, but because of poor inspectional practices, the Department of Health was not notified for more than two years: "A register of infants at nurse under the Children Acts 1908–1934 is kept by the Secretary of the Board but it is not written up to date and no entries are made as to deaths, removals or so-called adoptions. I found that the lists supplied to me contained the names of two children who had died."[84] It is entirely possible, and indeed likely, that more nurse children died than Department of Health officials were aware of, given shoddy administration and the fact that not all foster parents registered the nurse children in their care.

No countrywide statistics exist for the number of deaths of children at nurse, so it is impossible to make definitive statements about how many nurse children died annually. Anecdotal evidence, however, suggests that it was a significant problem. The Dublin board of health and public assistance minutes indicate that, in the 1920s and 1930s, at least one nurse child died every month while in the care of a foster parent.[85] The reports of inspection of children at nurse in the North Riding district of Tipperary noted that five nurse children died between 1948 and 1953. Admittedly these statistics are sketchy, and on the surface five children in as many years may not seem extraordinary. But when one considers that typically there were less than ten children registered at nurse in any given county, this statistic becomes somewhat more sinister and meaningful.

Conclusion

The state, under the auspices of the local authorities, became responsible for thousands of illegitimate children annually for a variety of reasons. Some children came into their care because their mothers and extended families abandoned them, while others were relinquished by mothers who could not provide for them. Healthy children who could not, for whatever reason, be cared for by their own mothers and families were supposed to be boarded out in suitable working-class foster homes. However, because of a lackadaisical attitude on the part of local authorities, combined with a reluctance on the part of many working-class families to foster children for anything other than monetary gain, many of the children who could and should have been boarded out ended up spending significant portions of their childhood in mother and baby homes, county homes, and industrial schools. Others endured fostering arrangements that could be neglectful, abusive, and exploitative. Available evidence also suggests that a significant number of illegitimate children were raised with their own families, and they likely had experiences that differed little from working-class children who were born to married parents.

What becomes clear from an examination of both the provisions that were made to care for illegitimate children who could not be cared for by their own families, and the administration of the various schemes, was that practical and financial expediencies often took precedence over the welfare of the children themselves. Local authorities, who were responsible for funding and inspecting the children in their care, were primarily concerned with keeping costs down. On the surface this would have meant boarding children out with suitable working-class families rather than maintaining them in institutions. In reality, however, many local authorities found the inspectional responsibilities imposed on them to be onerous and burdensome, and they often preferred to maintain children in institutions simply to spare themselves the cost, in financial and human terms, of ensuring that all of the children in their care were well treated and being suitably prepared to provide for themselves eventually. This attitude is most clearly evident in the way the inspections of boarded-out and nurse children were actually carried out. These inspections were supposed to be carried out on a monthly basis by individuals designated by the local authorities. In reality, however, inspections were carried out haphazardly and were cursory at best. Children got lost in the system – it is impossible to know how many children suffered this fate or what ultimately became of them.

It is also clear that the various parties who were responsible for administering the system of care, and providing for children in care, were not on the same page in terms of priorities and expectations. The Department of Health held overall responsibility for children who came into state care, and their inspectors did their best to advocate for children who had no one else to advocate for them. But the inspectors' recommendations and views were often overshadowed by the local authorities, who were concerned only with how much money they spent providing for children in care, and industrial school resident managers, who were spurred by both financial and moral considerations to lobby for institutional (and specifically industrial school) care. Anecdotal evidence suggests that some children literally became pawns in the conflict between and amongst the Department of Health, the local authorities, and the resident managers, and that each party was more concerned with advancing its own agenda than with ensuring the health and well-being of the children who, for a variety of reasons, did not enjoy the love, care, and protection of biological families.

Notes

1   *Minutes of Proceedings of the First Parliament of the Republic of Ireland 1919–1922* (Dublin: Stationery Office, 1921), vol. 1 (29 January 1919), cols 23–4.
2   Children maintained by the local authorities were provided for entirely out of

the "rates" or local taxes. The one exception to this rule was illegitimate children maintained in industrial schools. Some of these children were committed by the courts and were paid for by equal contributions from both central and local authority funds. Other children were maintained in industrial schools solely at the discretion, and expense, of local authorities.

3   This view is evident in Mary Raftery and Eoin O'Sullivan, *Suffer the little children: The inside story of Ireland's industrial schools* (Dublin: New Island Books, 1999); Mike Milotte, *Banished babies: the secret history of Ireland's baby export business* (Dublin: New Island Books, 1997); and June Goulding, *The light in the window* (Dublin: Poolbeg, 1998). It is also evident in scholarly works such as James Smith, *Ireland's magdalen laundries and the nation's architecture of containment* (Notre Dame, IN: University of Notre Dame Press, 2007); and Maria Luddy, "Moral rescue and unmarried motherhood in Ireland in the 1920s," *Women's Studies*, 30 (2001), pp. 797–817.

4   See Diarmuid Ferriter, *The transformation of Ireland* (Woodstock, NY: Overlook Press, 2005); Maria Luddy, *Prostitution and Irish society, 1800–1940* (Cambridge: Cambridge University Press, 2007); and James Smith, *Ireland's magdalen laundries*.

5   Department of Local Government and Public Health, *Annual Reports* (Dublin: Stationery Office, 1939, 1940, 1941). These reports did not provide mortality rates for the Dublin and Galway institutions.

6   Department of Local Government and Public Health, *Annual Reports*.

7   Department of Health, *Quarterly report on births, deaths, and marriages.* (Dublin: Stationery Office, 1932, 1945).

8   Although legislation related to home assistance did not explicitly include or exclude unmarried mothers, most local authorities operated on the general principle that unmarried mothers should not be given home assistance. However, statistics show that many unwed mothers were successful in securing home assistance for themselves and their children, although it is likely that their applications were judged far more harshly than were the applications of married couples with families.

9   References to this type of scenario are found in a variety of sources, including ISPCC case files, Department of Health and Department of Education files, and local authority files, and span the years from the 1920s to the 1960s; this suggests that it was more common than might be expected.

10   Wicklow board of health and public assistance minutes, 3 December 1923.

11   ISPCC case files, Wexford, 23 May 1960.

12   ISPCC case files, Wexford, 9 June 1958.

13   ISPCC case files, Wexford, 24 November 1959.

14   ISPCC case files, Wexford, 16 March 1961.

15   ISPCC case files, Mayo, 15 October 1958.

16   ISPCC case files, Wexford, 12 June 1950.

17   ISPCC case files, Wexford, 18 July 1957.

18   ISPCC case files, Wexford, 18 March 1960.

19   ISPCC case files, Wexford, 6 October 1953.

20   ISPCC case files, Wexford, 6 October 1953.

21   For a discussion of the development of Ireland's boarding-out system see Joseph Robins, *The lost children: A study of charity children in Ireland 1700–1900* (Dublin: Institute of Public Administration, 1980), pp. 272–84.

22 The various Public Assistance Acts empowered local authorities to pay to maintain individuals in institutions, called extern institutions, if the kind of care required could not be provided in the county homes. Some examples of extern institutions were the mother and baby homes referred to above, institutions in Dublin catering specifically for physically and mentally disabled children, and a handful of orphanages that catered for children from "respectable" families whose parents had died.

23 Department of Local Government and Public Health, *Annual Report 1922–1925*, pp. 65–6.

24 *Debates of Dáil Éireann*, vol. 11 (11 December 1940), col. 1128.

25 Because responsibilities for the boarding-out system were split, to some extent, between the Department of Health at the local level, and local authorities at the county level, there also were two layers of inspection. Local authority inspectors were obliged to conduct monthly inspections of the children in their locality; there were, at any given time, three Department of Health inspectors, each responsible for conducting annual inspections of all boarded-out children in a particular geographic region.

26 This conclusion is based on an analysis of hundreds of Department of Health inspectors' reports on boarded-out children, along with the minutes from four boards of health and public assistance.

27 Wicklow board of health and public assistance *Minutes*, 22 November 1924.

28 NAI, Department of Health A30/139, letter from SAO Mahon to Minister for Health, 21 November 1946.

29 NAI, Department of Health A30/139, clipping from *Irish Independent*, 29 March 1945.

30 NAI, Department of Health A30/139, "Boarded-out children," *Westmeath Examiner*, 28 April 1945.

31 NAI, Department of Health A30/139, "Boarded-out children," *Westmeath Examiner*, 28 April 1945.

32 NAI, Department of Health A30/139, "Boarded-out children," *Westmeath examiner*, 28 April 1945.

33 NAI, Department of Health A19/105, Mary Murray's report on boarded-out children in County Longford, 21 December 1944.

34 NAI, Department of Health A16/25, report of inspector of boarded-out children, 6 November 1947.

35 NAI, Department of Health A19/105, Mary Murray's report on boarded-out children in County Longford, 21 December 1944.

36 NAI, Department of Health Augusta McCabe box 2, report of children boarded out in County Kerry, 18 August 1943.

37 NAI, Department of Health Augusta McCabe box 8, reports of inspector of boarded-out children, Wexford, 8 March 1951.

38 NAI, Department of Health Augusta McCabe box 8, reports of inspector of boarded-out children, Wexford, 8 May 1954.

39 NAI, Department of Health Augusta McCabe box 7, Miss Clandillon's report on prospective foster parents. NAI Department of Health Augusta McCabe box 9, reports of inspector of boarded-out children, Waterford, 11 October 1949 and 25 February 1954.

40 NAI, Department of Health Augusta McCabe box 7, reports by Miss Clandillon on children boarded and nursed out, Kildare 1950–59.

41 NAI, Department of Health Augusta McCabe box 8, reports of Miss Clandillon on children boarded out in Kerry 1955.

42 NAI, Department of Health A8/290 vol. 2, report of SAO B. Griffin, 13 June 1957.

43 Offaly board of health and public assistance minutes, 27 April 1926.

44 Offaly board of health and public assistance minutes, 22 May 1928.

45 Offaly board of health and public assistance minutes, 21 January 1930.

46 Offaly board of health and public assistance minutes, 8 August 1933.

47 Cork board of health and public assistance minutes, 13 March 1939.

48 Cork board of health and public assistance minutes, 22 April 1940.

49 Boarded-out children could not be legally adopted once they reached the age at which maintenance grants ceased, because adoption legislation was not introduced in Ireland until 1952.

50 NAI, Department of Health A5/79, report on boarded-out children in Cork South, 23 October 1939.

51 Wicklow board of health and public assistance minutes, 27 July 1925.

52 Offaly board of health and public assistance minutes 26 March 1935.

53 Offaly board of health and public assistance minutes 13 September 1941.

54 NAI, Department of Health Augusta McCabe box 7, Miss Clandillon's report on boarded-out and nurse children, Kildare 1953.

55 Offaly board of health and public assistance minutes, 12 September 1933.

56 Wicklow board of health and public assistance minutes, 25 January 1926.

57 NAI, Department of Health Augusta McCabe box 2, annual report of boarded-out children for the year ending 31 March 1945.

58 NAI, Department of Health A16/25, report of inspector of boarded-out children, 6 November 1947.

59 NAI, Department of Health A8/290 vol. 2, letter from Dublin board of assistance to Department of Health, 10 July 1957.

60 NAI, Department of Health Augusta McCabe box 7, reports by Miss Clandillon on children boarded and nursed out, Kildare 1953.

61 NAI, Department of Health A16/25 report of inspector of boarded-out children, 6 November 1947.

62 NAI, Department of Health Augusta McCabe box 2, report of children boarded-out in County Kerry, 18 August 1943.

63 NAI, Department of Health Augusta McCabe box 8, Miss Clandillon's report on boarded-out children, 25 February 1955.

64 NAI, Department of Health Augusta McCabe box 8, Miss Clandillon's report of boarded-out children, 8 May 1954.

65 NAI, Department of Health Augusta McCabe box 8, Miss Clandillon's report of boarded-out children, 21 April 1953.

66 Offaly board of health and public assistance minutes, 21 September 1941.

67 NAI, Department of Health Augusta McCabe box 8, Miss Clandillon's report on boarded-out children, 6 October 1955.

68 NAI, Department of Health A5/79, report on boarded-out children, Cork South, 1939.

69 ISPCC case files, Mayo, 26 November 1958.

70 Adoption societies were charitable organizations, typically operated under the auspices of a religious order, that assisted unmarried mothers in securing private fostering arrangements for their children. The mothers were expected to

contribute a weekly, monthly, or annual sum for their children's maintenance and, if they could not afford the full amount, the adoption society might make up the difference. St Patrick's Guild and the Catholic Protection and Rescue Society in Dublin were two of the more well-known and active societies. Others included St Anne's in Cork, St Mura's in Co. Donegal, and St Attracta's in Sligo.

71 The Dublin board of health and public assistance reports for 19 August 1924 noted that four unregistered children had been placed in a single home by the Catholic Protection and Rescue Society. By the time these children came to the attention of local authorities in Dublin one of them had already died. A report from December 1924 noted that the Catholic Protection and Rescue Society had placed two children in a foster home despite the fact that two nursed children had already died in that home. A similar report was made in June 1929, when the Dublin board of health and public assistance discovered that a 2-week-old child had been placed, by the Catholic Protection and Rescue Society, in a home where just weeks earlier a 7-week-old child had died. The Dublin board of health and public assistance minutes are full of similar examples.

72 Department of Local Government and Public Health annual reports provided annual statistics for children in care in four categories: boarded-out, hired out, maintained in county homes, and maintained in other institutions. Some statistics are included in individual inspection reports, and in occasional entries in board of health and public assistance minutes, but these statistics are piecemeal and somewhat random. Additionally, available evidence suggests that regulations governing children at nurse were not followed, rendering somewhat dubious the accuracy of any statistics that do exist.

73 See, for example, Dublin board of health and public assistance minutes, 27 August 1924; 3 June 1925; 9 January 1929; 20 February 1929; 25 January 1933.

74 NAI, Department of Health A19/105, Miss Murray's report on boarded-out children in County Longford, 21 December 1944.

75 NAI, Department of Health A19/105, Miss Murray's report on boarded-out children in County Longford, 25 February 1948. Under the free milk scheme families in receipt of home assistance were entitled to daily milk rations. Similar schemes administered by various local authorities also provided footwear and turf. Foster parents were also entitled to avail of these programs on behalf of the children in their care.

76 NAI, Department of Health Augusta McCabe box 8, reports of inspector of boarded-out children, Limerick, 19 February 1949.

77 NAI, Department of Health Augusta McCabe box 8, Miss Clandillon's report on boarded-out children, 29 March 1950.

78 NAI, Department of Health Augusta McCabe box 3, internal Department of Health memorandum, 23 September 1946.

79 NAI, Department of Health Augusta McCabe box 3, internal Department of Health memorandum, 23 September 1946.

80 NAI, Department of Health Augusta McCabe box 7, letter to Mr. Hargadon, Department of Health, from Miss Clandillon, 3 November 1959.

81 The Dublin board of health and public assistance minutes are full of letters and instructions from the local authorities to the various adoption societies, suggesting that a fairly diligent inspectional regime existed in Dublin.

82 Dublin board of health and public assistance minutes, 17 December 1924.

83 NAI, Department of Health Augusta McCabe box 8, Miss Clandillon's report on

boarded-out children, 29 March 1950.

84 NAI, Department of Health A31/37, extract from Miss Kennedy O'Byrne's report, 1938–39.

85 This conclusion is based on an examination of the Dublin board of health and public assistance minutes for the period 1923 to 1934, after which point these records were no longer available.

3

Cherished equally?
Institutional provision for
illegitimate children

Introduction

Chapter 2 examined state provision for illegitimate children in other than institutional settings. Many illegitimate children remained with their mothers or extended families and were raised in ways similar to other children of their social class. Others were raised in foster homes where they were, at best, treated like the biological children of their foster parents and, at worst, ignored, neglected, exploited, and abused. As Chapter 2 demonstrated, often there was a gap between what Department of Health inspectors thought was best for children, and what local authorities were willing or able to do for the children in their care. While Department of Health inspectors argued that a good (albeit class-appropriate) foster family was preferable to an institutional upbringing, it was also cheaper, which should have made local authorities happy since they were responsible for financing the care arrangements. But the boarding-out system required a significant expenditure of human energy, and available evidence suggests that many local authorities were unwilling to expend the effort necessary to administer the system efficiently and in the best interests of the children involved. They preferred instead to maintain children in a host of "poor law" institutions where they could, in effect, shift responsibility onto the shoulders of the religious orders who ran them.[1]

Examining policy and practice related to illegitimate children illustrates the range of options available to those individuals and agencies who were responsible for them, and in the available data there are occasional, tantalizing insights into what life might have been like for the tens of thousands of children who got caught up in "the system." But the existing official data gives little insight into the first-hand experiences of illegitimate children, or what ultimately became of them once they came out of the system. The first-hand experiences of illegitimate children are among the most difficult to uncover, not only because of the secrecy that often attached to illegitimacy, but also because their voices generally are absent from the official sources that chronicled their existence.

Institutionalization

The only alternative to a potentially insecure or exploitative boarding-out arrangement, an equally insecure nurse arrangement, or overseas adoption (see Chapter 4) was confinement in one of a number of institutions that existed around the country specifically to care for children whose parents could not or would not care for them.[2] Many illegitimate children began their institutional lives at birth, in mother and baby homes overseen by religious orders, or county homes that were part of the state's network of poor relief institutions.[3] Unmarried mothers who were maintained in mother and baby homes at local authority expense, and who did not wish to keep their children, were expected to remain in the homes for two years. During this time they worked to earn their keep and cared for their children while arrangements were made to board their children out or send them overseas for adoption. Women who could afford to pay a boarding-out allowance or adoption fee, or who planned to keep their children, remained in the homes for a few months. Available evidence suggests that, contrary to long-held beliefs and assumptions, many unmarried mothers left these institutions in a matter of months, and many also took their children with them.

Mother and baby homes

Most mother and baby homes operated privately, outside of any system of state regulation and control, although several of these, including the Sacred Heart Homes in Bessboro, Co. Cork, Roscrea in Co. Tipperary, and Castlepollard, Co. Westmeath, qualified under the various Public Assistance Acts as extern institutions and thus received capitation grants for the women and children in their care.[4] Local authorities in Dublin and Galway maintained auxiliary homes at Pelletstown and Tuam, respectively, specifically for unmarried mothers and their children. These institutions were funded entirely out of local rates, but day-to-day administration was left to religious orders.[5]

Unmarried mothers gave birth in mother and baby homes, rather than county homes, in those counties that provided such institutions. The rationale behind this separate accommodation was twofold: protecting unmarried mothers who had "fallen" for the first time from being drawn into prostitution by more "hardened" cases; and ensuring that "respectable" poor women did not have to share maternity wards in county homes with unmarried mothers. Most mother and baby homes operated on a common plan: women were expected to remain in the homes for two years to care for their children and earn their keep; at the end of two years they were allowed to leave, and their children were boarded-out, sent to other institutions, or sent abroad for adoption. However, unmarried mothers who made the choice to take their children with them were allowed to leave the institution after just a few months – once they had sufficiently recovered from their confinement and made plans for themselves and their children.[6] Critics of the mother and baby home system point to the two-year period of confinement as particularly punitive. What they fail to acknowledge, however, is that once that two-year period ended, women were allowed to walk away from their children free and clear – they had no further emotional or financial obligations towards the children. In fact, when the Department of Health was contemplating opening a mother and baby home in Dunboyne, Co. Meath in 1954 they expressed the view that women who left their children behind should be expected to contribute towards their maintenance.[7]

While Department of Health inspectors regularly commented on the fact that children were retained in these homes for far too long, and encouraged local authorities to step up their efforts to secure suitable foster homes, the conditions of overcrowding, and the tendency to maintain children in mother and baby homes until they were old enough to be sent to industrial schools, were the norm.[8] This trend was due both to reluctance on the part of local authorities to expend energy in securing good foster homes when institutionalization provided such an easy and painless alternative, and to a resistance on the part of religious orders to a boarding-out system that diverted precious financial resources from institutions to foster homes.[9] What was best for the children involved typically was secondary to more pragmatic concerns.

Related to overcrowding was the fact that almost all of these institutions had, at various points in their histories, alarmingly high rates of infant mortality. This might lead one to question not just the kind of pre-natal care availed of by unmarried mothers, but also conditions in the institutions themselves. In 1926 the Dublin board of health and public assistance made note of the conditions in Pelletstown: "Commissioners take a very serious view of the number of deaths during the week and require a detailed report from Doctor dealing with same. It has also been brought to the Commissioners' notice that babies leaving Pelletstown to be placed at nurse often present a delicate and even starved appearance."[10] The annual report of the Department of Local Government and Public Health reported on the number of deaths of infants in institutions versus the number of admissions; in Bessboro, Roscrea, Castlepollard, and Pelletstown, one-third or more of children admitted each year died.[11] An undated report on conditions in mother and baby homes for the quarter ending 31 March 1943 noted a high mortality rate in the mother and baby home at Bessboro:

> Deaths among infants in the Bessboro Institution were found some time ago to be attaining a very high proportion and the matter was taken up with the authorities. Various excuses were given, eg malnutrition, skin diseases, etc. The Department's view was that the position was at least partially attributable to overcrowding. These provide a further incentive to speeding up the boarding-out of children over two. Where overcrowding has been reduced it is observed that the death rate also falls.[12]

Infant mortality clearly was a significant problem in mother and baby homes, and one that was attributed to a variety of circumstances. It is not unreasonable to conclude that many mothers were relieved of the burden of caring for an illegitimate child simply by virtue of their premature death in these institutions.

While legislation clearly laid out inspectional responsibilities in relation to local authority children boarded-out, at nurse, or maintained in industrial schools, there was no such clear-cut statutory responsibility in relation to mother and baby or county homes. But a handful of inspection reports that have survived in Department of Health files suggest that some Department of Health inspectors extended their concern to local authority children in these institutions, even if they were not legally obliged to do so. In her report on children maintained in the Sean Ross Abbey, in Roscrea, Co. Tipperary, Department of Health inspector Miss Litster noted that at the end of September 1944 there were 118 babies maintained at local authority expense. The report also noted that the mothers were required to remain in the institutions until their children were boarded out, and that because of backlogs in boarding children out, some mothers remained for four or more years.[13] (If the mothers were willing to take their children with them they could have been discharged sooner.)

The situation at Sean Ross Abbey was so dire by the end of 1945 that the Sisters of the Sacred Hearts of Jesus and Mary (the religious order that administered the institution) closed it to new admissions. The Department of Health sent a letter to the Kildare County Council expressing alarm at the large number of their children who were maintained in Sean Ross Abbey:

"It is … essential that the public assistance authorities will at once take energetic steps with a view to boarding out these children … The Parliamentary Secretary will now expect to be informed fully within the next fortnight of the action taken by the County Manager to ensure that the children in this institution who are suitable for boarding out are placed without delay in approved foster homes."[14] The superintendent assistance officer (SAO) of the Kildare County Council responded by essentially throwing up his hands and insisting that he simply could not find enough foster homes for all the children who needed them, and his parting salvo underscored his diligence and sincerity: "I would like to point out that unless a home is suitable in every way I will not take the responsibility of recommending it."[15] Co. Kildare did not have a designated local authority children's home, so presumably they had no choice but to send their children to an appropriate institution in another county. In a later letter, the Kildare SAO repeated his claim that he could not find suitable foster homes, but he also expressed the view that, in general, illegitimate children should not be boarded out at all: "I may mention that personally I am of the opinion that if the family of the girl are in a position to take the child it should not be boarded out, as to do so is unfair to others who are keeping and maintaining illegitimate children without any help from public funds."[16] In all likelihood the SAO was merely trying to rationalize or justify his and his council's failure to fulfil their legal responsibilities to the children in their care.

County homes

Only a handful of counties had mother and baby homes or children's homes specifically designated to provide for illegitimate children. Some local authorities, like Kildare in the example cited above, sent their illegitimate children to institutions in other counties. But most local authorities simply used their county homes as "dumping grounds" for illegitimate children who could not be dealt with in other ways. In theory county homes were intended to serve as temporary refuges for children in very specific circumstances; they were agents of poor relief and, as such, accepted children, along with their families, who were destitute or in need of medical care that they could not afford. County homes also served as "way stations" for children who were waiting to be boarded out or sent to industrial schools. County homes were not equipped to provide for the long-term needs of children, because they were never intended to house them long-term. In fact, however, county homes accommodated, on a long-term basis, scores of "problematic" children from a variety of backgrounds and circumstances.

Two of Miss Litster's reports on children in county homes have survived in Department of Health files, one from 1947 and another from

1948.[17] For the most part these reports are little more than lists of the names, ages, and status (i.e. legitimate vs. illegitimate) of children maintained in individual county homes, with little insight offered into why illegitimate children were maintained in county homes rather than being boarded out or placed in industrial schools. There are, however, tantalizing glimpses into the conditions under which some of these children came into county homes in the first place. The 1947 report noted "there are 22 children listed as 'deserted'. Their mothers, on leaving the County Home, placed some of these at nurse. Either the mothers ceased to pay for their maintenance when the children were brought back as deserted, or they were neglected and brought in by the Infant Life Protection Visitor. Others were left behind in the County Home by their mothers who escaped from the County Home."[18] This report suggests that some illegitimate children ended up in county homes by default after their mothers intentionally abandoned them.

Miss Litster went on to report that nine unmarried mothers escaped from the county home between the end of March 1946 and the time of her report in July 1947.[19] The problem for the local authorities in these instances was that if a mother could not be traced, the legal status of the child was somewhat tenuous. Legally, parental consent was required before local authorities could board-out children or send them to industrial schools. It therefore should have been difficult, legally, for local authorities to send to industrial schools children for whom parental consent could not be obtained. Some of these children may have remained in the county homes until their mothers came for them, which did occasionally happen, or until they reached the age at which they could be sent out for training or employment. But in all likelihood most were boarded-out or sent to industrial schools without the required parental consent. Contemporary critics of the industrial school system and state provision for vulnerable and marginalized children likely would be quick to point to this trend as evidence that local authorities transgressed the rights of unmarried mothers and their children in their haste to rid themselves of the burden of providing for the children in their care. And there were cases where this undoubtedly happened. But there were also cases where mothers, by fleeing and abandoning their children, willingly abdicated their rights as well as their responsibilities. In these cases mothers were just as responsible as local authorities, if not more so, for whatever plight subsequently befell their children.

The Dublin board of health and public assistance minutes give the clear impression that many children ended up in the county home because they had been removed from unsuitable homes where they had been placed under private arrangements:

Admission Board Clerk returns the names of seven children admitted to the Union since 1.4.1925, all nursed out from St. Patrick's Guild of Rescue, and for whom no payment has been received. He further states that nurse mothers with children from this Society have latterly endeavoured to have healthy children admitted to the Union as they plead poverty and state they cannot maintain the children on the small adoption fee, sometimes as small as £5, paid them by Miss Cruice. We direct the attention of the Ministry to the practice of this society accepting rewards for the care of children and then ridding themselves of all responsibility by dumping the children in the workhouse. Understand that this society (Miss Cruice) is drawing a government subsidy in respect of this work.[20]

The board's contention that St Patrick's Guild received a "government subsidy" for their work is somewhat dubious, given that there were no subsidies for which this program was eligible. But the bigger issue, that plagued local authorities throughout the country throughout the middle decades of the twentieth century, was what to do with children who were placed at nurse and then given up by their foster mothers, particularly in cases where their biological mothers ceased paying for their care and effectively abandoned them. Local authorities ended up taking many of these children into care because no one else wanted to assume responsibility for them.

Industrial schools

Many of the children maintained in mother and baby homes and county homes eventually found their way into one of Ireland's fifty-two industrial schools. Some of these children were committed through the courts, which meant that responsibility for maintaining them was split equally between local authorities and the Department of Education.[21] The administrators of mother and baby homes had the option of seeking court committals for the children in their care, but that same option was not available to the local authorities. (In other words, local authorities could not seek court committals for the children in their care.) However, local authorities could send children to industrial schools as "local authority children," but such children were maintained entirely out of local authority funds rather than splitting the cost equally with the Department of Education.[22] Although the cost of maintaining children in industrial schools was higher than the cost of boarding them out, there were payoffs: local authorities were relieved of inspectional responsibilities and they were relieved of the responsibility of providing for the children's futures when they reached fifteen years of age (the age at which they were removed from the rolls of boarded-out children). Children who were committed to industrial schools by the courts remained there until their sixteenth birthdays, and industrial school resident managers were responsible for finding employment and accommodation for children on their release, and for after-care.

As illustrated in Chapter 2, Department of Health officials consistently expressed a preference for boarding out illegitimate children rather than sending them to industrial schools. But communications between the Department's inspector of children, Alice Litster, and various local authorities make clear that most local authorities did not share this view. This resulted in a friction that underscored conflicting agendas and philosophies between and amongst the Department of Health, who oversaw the system, local authorities who funded it, the inspectors who inspected it, and industrial school resident managers. The inspectors of boarded-out children, employed by the Department of Health, were most concerned with the best interests of children in state care. Annual reports, as well as reports on individual children, often were painstaking in their detail of the circumstances in which boarded-out children lived and in their calls for greater oversight and inspection of the boarding-out system. Alice Litster, the Department of Health inspector who authored many of the Department's reports from the 1930s to the 1950s, often criticized local authorities' half-hearted efforts to board out children who would benefit from a stable family environment:

> Children are still being maintained in institutions who might profitably be dealt with otherwise. Although county councils are represented in court cases of proposals to commit children to industrial schools in practice, except in the case of Dublin ... applications for the committal of children to industrial schools are not opposed. It appears to be an extremely casual manner of treating the question of the disposal of a child's whole life, that a county council should not make an effort to discover in what manner the child's best interests will best be secured, whether by committal to an institution, by boarding-out if the child can be dealt with under the boarding out system, or if the family of which the child is a unit cannot be kept together by means of home assistance.[23]

This excerpt from a 1936 report illustrates the haphazard way that local authorities carried out their responsibilities to the children in their care. No mechanism appears to have existed, in any county, through which each child's case could be evaluated on an individual basis.

The absence of such a mechanism may have been due in part to the state of knowledge about childcare, child psychology, and child development in Ireland at the time. Evidence clearly indicates that local authorities were concerned primarily with the cost of caring for children; the welfare of the children themselves was of secondary importance (it might even be safe to say that it was of no importance at all). While local authorities acknowledged that boarding-out was the least expensive alternative, they also faced difficulty in securing suitable foster homes, primarily because maintenance rates were inadequate and because it was virtually impossible to ensure that families who applied to foster children were motivated by benevolent rather than mercenary impulses. Some local authorities faced considerable pressure from resident managers of industrial schools to maintain children in institutions, and only rarely did they attempt to buck that pressure. Some industrial school resident managers firmly believed that institutions like theirs were preferable to boarding out, and they occasionally made their views known to the Department of Health. Two specific examples provide insight into the sometimes tense relations between and among local authorities, the Department of Health, and some industrial school resident managers over how local authority children should be dealt with.

The first case involved a young boy who had been removed from an unsuitable foster home and placed, temporarily, in St Joseph's Industrial School in Tralee, Co. Kerry (a Christian Brothers school). While the inspector of boarded-out children ordered that the child be removed from the school as soon as a suitable foster home became available, the resident manager of the school pressed the local authorities to leave the child, based on "my knowledge of boarded-out children (of whom not a few have been sent here from conditions similar to those under which [the child] was living). I am convinced they receive a much better training and education in Industrial Schools than they can possibly obtain in the average country home which receives them."[24] The second case also involved the removal of children from St Joseph's; in this instance the resident manager protested against the planned boarding-out of three young boys in 1950. He went so far as to arrive unannounced at Department of Health offices in Dublin to present his case directly to the Minister for Health. The resident manager's objection stemmed from his assumption that the children were better off in an industrial school than in a foster home, and in light of the "care that has been given them and the [reorganization] of the school that took place to facilitate them – they were so young. I am appalled at the arbitrary manner in which exchanges were made and the removals effected."[25] The fate of these boys is not known, but the files documenting their removal from St Joseph's contain no orders for the transfer of the boys from St Joseph's to a foster home, so it is likely that they remained in the institution until the age of sixteen.

The resistance to boarding-out on the part of resident managers can be traced to their conviction, explicitly stated by the resident manager of St Joseph's and reinforced in letters that passed regularly between other resident managers and the Department of Health, that the industrial school was a more suitable environment for a "certain class of children" than the "average country home." Implicit in this conviction was the view that members of male and female religious orders were more suitable substitute parents than actual parents or foster parents, particularly in the moral training of children whose moral fiber was weakened by illegitimacy, poverty, or family dysfunction. But another source of this resistance was an economic reality: state-funded capitation grants were by no means generous, and resident managers needed to keep their schools full, and state capitation grants flowing, to ensure that income and expenditure balanced at the end of the fiscal year. The cost of running an industrial school remained essentially static whatever the number of children maintained. The request for certification under the 1939 Public Assistance Act, made by the resident manager of St Dominick's School, Waterford, was typical in its concern for financial matters: "The position is this – we have a splendidly appointed Industrial school here, which has been modernized recently at very great expense. Our numbers are gone down very much and there seems to be no prospect of getting children committed by the court. We only got two new pupils since last January, and twenty-two girls left school, their period of detention having expired."[26] Although money, rather than the best interests of the children in their care, seems to have underpinned some resident managers' ambivalence toward the boarding-out of children, the rather lackadaisical attitude of most local authorities suggests that, when it came to illegitimate and vulnerable children, they trod the path of least resistance. It was easier to bow to the pressure of the most outspoken resident managers than to buck the tide and formulate a consistent and coherent policy on caring for children for whom the only alternative to their own or a foster home was institutionalization.

Although the Departments of Education and Health shared responsibility for funding industrial schools, and for establishing guidelines and ensuring that those guidelines were implemented, the actual running of the schools was left to resident managers, all of whom were members of male or female Catholic religious orders. The extent to which individual resident managers operated virtually autonomously in the industrial school system is reflected in the inspectional regime carried out by the Departments of Health and Education, as opposed to the scrutiny that foster parents often encountered at the hands of Department of Health inspectors.[27] Admittedly, the system of inspecting boarded-out children had its shortcomings, and Department of Health inspectors often complained that monthly inspections did not occur frequently enough and that their recommendations were ignored. But when Department of Health inspectors conducted their annual inspections they examined the homes and the children, and it was not unusual for them to speak with the children, and with neighbors and teachers, and to inquire about their education, general health, clothing, and sleeping arrangements.

On the other hand, Department of Health inspections of local authority children maintained in industrial schools appear to have occurred infrequently, and with a marked lack of detail on the part of the inspectors.[28] Inspectors' reports were general in nature and said little about the physical and emotional condition of children beyond vague assertions that they "appeared well cared [for]."[29] Indeed, even Miss Litster, whose reports on boarded-out children were thorough and indicated a significant degree of concern for their welfare, was vague and circumspect in her reports on schools that applied for certification under the 1939 Public Assistance Act.[30] The Department of Health approved virtually all applications for certification, which often comprised little more than a sentence or two and which received a formulaic reply similar to that issued to St Joseph's in Dundalk:

> The above industrial school is situated in the town of Dundalk. It is certified for 80 children between the ages of 2 and 16; the accommodation limit is 100, and at present there are 76 children in residence. The dormitories are bright and airy and not overcrowded. There is an infirmary with 8 beds and one of the Sisters is a qualified nurse. The children are taught the standard national school subjects until they are 14, after which they are trained in household management. They would get posts as domestic servants, and the Sisters keep in touch with them as much as possible. The school appears to be suitable for the reception of children from the Public Assistance authorities, provided that the accommodation limit of 100 is not exceeded.[31]

Perhaps it is not surprising, given the sheer number of schools and children involved, that an application for certification as an institution suitable for the reception of local authority children received such cursory consideration, particularly if it was already a certified industrial school. At the same time, there appears to have been reluctance on the part of local authorities and Departments of Health and Education staff to interfere to any significant degree in the running of industrial schools. While children occasionally were removed from foster parents who were found to be neglectful or abusive, there is no documented evidence that children were removed from industrial schools for similar reasons, although first-hand accounts of former inmates, and sealed Department of Education files, suggest that neglect and abuse were common in some schools (or at least not completely unheard of).[32]

The commonly-held view about illegitimate children in twentieth-century Ireland is that they all were sent overseas for adoption or, more commonly, hidden away in a network of institutions where they remained, for the most part, until they reached their sixteenth birthdays. But as was shown in Chapter 2, this scenario was but one small part of a much bigger and more complex picture than has yet been realized. It is true that illegitimate children got caught up in the institutional quagmire as frequently as their legitimate peers, but their experiences may have had more deleterious effects long-term. Some children were born in mother and baby homes or county homes and remained there until they were old enough to be sent to industrial schools. Others experienced a revolving door at county homes: they were boarded out, returned to the county home for whatever reason, boarded out again, and returned to the county home in a cycle that only ended when they were sent to industrial schools or when they reached the age of sixteen years and were pushed out into the world to fend for themselves.

Surviving Department of Health files suggest that there was tension between and among Department of Health inspectors, local authorities, and industrial school resident managers over the fate of illegitimate children who came into the care of local authorities. One source of tension was the conflicting agendas of the parties involved. Department of Health inspectors were concerned primarily with the best interests of the children themselves. On the other hand, local authorities and industrial school resident managers were driven by more pragmatic, financial or economic concerns. A second source of tension was the conflict between Department of Health inspectors' preference for boarding-out over institutionalization, versus the local authorities' tendency to take the path of least resistance. A third complication was the insistence, on the part of some resident managers, that industrial schools were superior to foster homes to give a "certain class of children" the tools they needed to live respectable and upstanding working-class lives. What is missing is, of course, the perspective of the children themselves.

Media and autobiographi cal accounts of institutional life

Two of the most readily accessible first-hand sources of insight into the plight of children who were institutionalized are published autobiographies and television documentaries featuring former residents of institutions. A 1996 documentary, *Dear daughter*, that aired on RTÉ, first raised contemporary public awareness of the "secret" of Ireland's industrial school system. The documentary chronicled Christina Buckley's search for her Nigerian father and Irish mother. Buckley was committed to Goldenbridge Industrial School in 1952 after her mother gave birth outside marriage. In Buckley's case her illegitimate birth may have been compounded by the fact that her father was black, a Nigerian student who had come to Ireland to study medicine. Although Buckley's documentary focused primarily on her search for her parents, and her mixed feelings about them, there was also an undercurrent of anger at the institutional regime that she endured, and the female religious who allegedly perpetrated that regime. Although there was significant public outcry in the days immediately following the airing of *Dear daughter*, the outcry soon died down, perhaps because many people could not identify with Buckley's experience given that she was mixed-race.

Another set of documentaries, *States of fear*, aired on RTÉ in April 1999 and were much more effective at mobilizing a sustained public outrage over the alleged abuses of the industrial school system.[33] The documentary was followed up later that year with the sensationalist and poorly researched book *Suffer the little children*.[34] Both the documentary and book were guided by an explicitly anti-Catholic Church agenda that led the author to make serious but largely unsubstantiated allegations against various religious orders, supposedly on the basis of "evidence" found in these files (but never produced by O'Sullivan). These two sources, combined with autobiographical accounts and Department of Health inspection reports, raise vital questions not just about how the state conceived of its responsibility to some of Ireland's most needy and marginalized children, but also the nature of memory and the pitfalls of autobiographical and oral sources.

An example of Raftery and O'Sullivan's shoddy research can be found in allegations they made about Father Flanagan's visit to Ireland and his commentary on Ireland's industrial schools. They allege that when Father Flanagan visited Ireland in 1946 he made a scathing indictment of Ireland's industrial schools, calling the system "a disgrace to the nation." According to Raftery and O'Sullivan, Flanagan's "unprecedented criticism" came as a shock to Irish officials who were not used to hearing such criticism. A recent article by Daire Keogh, however, offers insight into the Father Flanagan case that entirely undermines Raftery and O'Sullivan's interpretation. While in Ireland Father Flanagan was given a copy of a pamphlet, *I did penal servitude*, documenting appalling conditions in Ireland's prison system. It was the prison system, and not the industrial school, that Flanagan called "a disgrace to the nation." Indeed Flanagan seems to have been somewhat complimentary on those parts of the industrial school system that he observed: "It had been a good fortune to visit Artane and he could not speak in too high terms of the great work being done there by the good Brothers ... Those little fellows receive a magnificent training; they are beautiful children and they cannot go wrong because they feel they belong somewhere and that is so important."[35]

In the days and weeks following the first episode of *States of Fear*, ordinary Irish people reacted to the documentary's allegations with a mix of outrage, compassion, and disbelief. Those who hailed the disintegration of the Catholic Church's power and influence pointed to the allegations of severe physical and sexual abuse raised in the documentary as "proof" that the church exploited its influence and position of power at the expense of the most innocent and defenseless of people: children with no voice and no parents to protect them. At the other end of the spectrum, staunch Catholics insisted that the Departments of Education and Health were entirely at fault because they forced the church to maintain thousands of "unwanted" children on shoestring budgets with no training and minimal oversight. The media-driven debate deteriorated into a "church-versus-state" polemic in which the real issues were clouded if not lost altogether.

Admittedly, evidence suggests that individual industrial schools "lobbied" to have children sent to them in an effort to keep capitation grants flowing, and local authorities bowed to pressure to maintain children in institutions rather than foster families. In this sense, religious orders did help to fuel and perpetuate the system. But many of the children committed by the courts to industrial schools first came to official notice because someone in the local community – neighbor, parish priest, or teacher – complained to the gardaí or the local branch of the Irish Society for the Prevention of Cruelty to Children (ISPCC) about alleged parental neglect or abuse, or because parents themselves approached the ISPCC for help in committing their children to industrial schools. The state's reluctance to take responsibility for illegitimate and needy children was mirrored by a similar reluctance within families and communities to accept "deviance" in their midst, or to fully embrace the principles of compassion, loyalty, and mutual responsibility that defined the Catholic-Christian faith. The industrial school system flourished not only because it suited the political, economic, and social agendas of church and state, but also because ordinary women and men supported it to relieve themselves of responsibility for caring for vulnerable, burdensome, or deviant individuals, and to protect their status and reputation in the community.

Children who were "unwanted" in the first half of the twentieth century are now being used as pawns (some actively, some more reluctantly) in a battle between the "liberal" forces who wish to see the Catholic Church in Ireland brought to its knees, and the "conservative" forces who refuse to hear a bad word said about the Catholic Church and its humanitarian and charitable initiatives. Somewhere in the middle of all the invective, and of all the heartbreaking, if sometimes unbelievable, allegations made by critics of the industrial school system, is the "truth" or perhaps more accurately the "reality" of the situation. In fact, children probably were mistreated to some extent in state-run institutions; they unquestionably were exploited and perhaps even neglected in foster homes; they were sent overseas in questionable and perhaps even unconstitutional and illegal adoptions; and overall they probably did not fare as well as many of their "legitimate" counterparts in the "battle of life." Unquestionably church and state must share a good deal of responsibility for the fate of illegitimate children (the state in particular, since they had legal and constitutional duties to safeguard the rights and interests of children who had no one else to do so). But there is a greater responsibility that has not yet been acknowledged in any of the discussions, debates, documentaries, and publications, and that is the responsibility of parents, extended families, and communities. One gets the sense, in reading between the lines of the narratives of former industrial school inmates particularly, that there is an undercurrent of unspoken anger directed not at the religious orders or the state, but at their own parents who consigned them to such a fate in the first place. It is easier to blame the people who were most immediately on the scene, and much harder to blame those who were supposed to provide love and care and security but who, ultimately, abdicated their responsibilities in a most profound way.

The first-hand accounts of illegitimate childhood are admittedly sparse. This may be the function of the shame and secrecy that surrounded illegitimacy in the twentieth century, or it may be a function of the fact that illegitimate children, because they were "unwanted" at least in the official rhetoric of the twentieth century, do not as adults feel that their lives are worthy of recording. Whatever the reason, the autobiographical accounts are disproportionately weighted towards institutionalization. Two sources of autobiographical narratives are the *States of Fear* documentary and Raftery and O'Sullivan's *Suffer the little children*. These sources must be used with care, however, because they are pieces of sensationalist journalism rather than scrupulously researched scholarly works. It is likely that the snippets of autobiography included in *Suffer the little children* were chosen with great care, and only those were used that supported the authors' polemic account of industrial schools in Ireland. For example, Betty was committed to a Sisters of Mercy industrial school in Tralee, Co. Kerry, in 1951: she was two years old at the time, and the reason for her committal was that her mother was unmarried, destitute, and unable to support her.

Betty documents an institutional existence punctuated by a regime of violence and abuse that got so bad that she claims to have set herself on fire when she was thirteen years old.[36] She further alleges that as a result of this suicide attempt she was transferred from the care of the Sisters of Mercy to a magdalen asylum run by the Sisters of Charity in Cork. What is interesting and somewhat curious about Betty's account is that Betty's own mother had spent some time in the same industrial school as a child, after the death of her mother. Furthermore, Betty's grandfather visited her periodically, while her mother only visited her every couple of years. It is not inappropriate to question why, if conditions in the industrial school were so bad, Betty's mother would consign her child to the same fate that she herself had suffered as a child and why Betty never told her grandfather about the abuse, or why her grandfather did not notice the debilitating effects of Betty's alleged suicide attempt. In short, while it is not the intention to question the validity of Betty's perspective, it is entirely appropriate to question why Betty's family, who apparently had not abandoned Betty entirely, did not do more to protect her if, in fact, she was being mistreated. It also is appropriate to note the absence of substantiating evidence: doctor's reports or medical records, or the corroborating testimony of girls who were in the industrial school at the same time as Betty. Autobiographical accounts are not unproblematic, and they should not be taken as "gospel truth," as they have been in recent years (at least by the media and some scholars).

Catherine was committed to an industrial school in 1937, at the age of six months, because her mother had been abandoned by her father and rejected by her family because she had a child outside of marriage. Catherine recalled that her mother visited her once each year, and that her mother had remarried and begun a whole new family by the time Catherine was five years old. Catherine alleged that she was singled out for abuse and neglect by the nuns because she was illegitimate; she never told her mother about the treatment she received because she feared she would get even worse after her mother left.[37] What is interesting about Catherine's case is that, even though her mother eventually married and had other children, Catherine was left in the industrial school. This appears to have been a fairly common phenomenon in relation to illegitimate children, and one can only conclude that the institutionalization or boarding-out of these children was a function not of poverty but of attitude. The mothers in these cases went on to have families and "normal" lives, but still chose to leave their illegitimate children in the care of the state. This suggests that the illegitimate children were not welcome in their new families, perhaps because their new husbands did not want the responsibility of financially supporting other men's children.

Mary's story is also fairly typical with regard to the experiences of illegitimate children in twentieth-century Ireland. Mary recalled: "I never knew my mother. She never visited and I have no memory of her. It never really occurred to me that people would love children. We never experienced it – never had hugs or kisses or anything like that. It just never arose."[38] Mary was moved from one institution to another, including the mental hospital at Grangegorman, before she finally escaped the system. It is likely that the treatment Mary received in the industrial school was little different from what the other girls, legitimate or illegitimate, experienced. But Mary's experience was set apart by the fact that she never knew her mother and thus never knew the love of family. Many illegitimate children who were consigned to industrial schools were similarly abandoned by their families, and when they were released from the industrial schools they floated from one job to another, and perhaps even from one institution to another, because they had no family and no safety net to support them through hard times.

The story of Elizabeth provides another valuable glimpse into how illegitimate children were regarded and treated in twentieth-century Ireland. Elizabeth was the product of an affair between her mother, a widow, and a married man. Although Elizabeth's mother had seven children, Elizabeth was singled out within her own home because of her illegitimate status. For the first seven years of her life Elizabeth was locked away in a room in her mother's house, and eventually she was brought by her mother to an industrial school: "I suppose it was the disgrace of having me, and her a widow for years. I think that's why I was kept hidden. When I was seven, I remember I got a little pink flowery dress, and a black car came for me and took me away. I never went back to that house again."[39] Elizabeth recalled that although her mother visited her once a month, she never felt that her mother loved or cared for her; in fact, Elizabeth believed her mother only came to the school to pay the Sisters the monthly maintenance fee (Elizabeth was not committed to the industrial school by the courts, and thus her mother would have been responsible for paying for her support). As an adult Elizabeth had no contact with her mother and her siblings, and on the one occasion that she tried to contact them she was told to stay away. Elizabeth was sent to an industrial school and effectively banished from the family because of her illegitimate status, while her seven siblings were allowed to remain at home with their mother and were raised in a normal family environment. Her mother's desire for respectability and acceptance in the community may have outweighed her maternal instincts or her love and affection for her child.

Although Angela was an illegitimate child she was not "unwanted" – her mother tried for more than two years to keep and support her daughter. However, people in her community believed that Angela's mother was unfit, primarily because she was an unwed mother, and Angela was committed to an industrial school: "My mother wanted to keep me, but the courts wouldn't let her. Apparently there had been a number of complaints about her in the town – I suppose they said that she shouldn't be allowed to keep a baby since she wasn't married."[40] Although the grounds on which Angela was committed by the courts are unclear, what is clear is that her mother continued to care for her throughout her time in the industrial school: "My mother came to visit me every third Sunday, which was visiting day. She never stopped caring about me."[41] This is a case where a parent's love for her child was interfered with, by a combination of nosy neighbors, ISPCC inspectors, district court justices, and religious orders, who thought they knew what was best for the child, and who assumed that Angela's mother was an unfit parent because she was unmarried and thus morally tainted.

Mary Phil Drennan, a former resident of the Sisters of Mercy industrial school in Cobh, Co. Cork, is one of a handful of people to have written a book about their experiences as illegitimate children in industrial schools. Drennan was sent to the industrial school at the age of eight months, after spending the first eight months of her life with her mother in a Legion of Mary hostel in Cork. Drennan's mother may have been a prostitute: "They [the nuns] said she had been 'working on the quays with the sailors' and was picked up when they saw her with a baby under her arm."[42] Drennan's mother only visited her sporadically while she was in the industrial school – not more than once every three or four years. When Drennan was eleven her mother married but she did not petition to have Drennan returned to her. Drennan's story is interesting for several reasons. First, Drennan's mother was a Protestant, but Drennan was baptized as a Catholic at the time of her birth – it is likely that members of the Legion of Mary who "rescued" Drennan's mother from her life of prostitution encouraged her to have the child baptized as a Catholic so that she could be sent to an industrial school (under law, schools were sectarian, and a Catholic school could not accept a Protestant child). The second interesting aspect of Drennan's story is that her mother had been married ten years before Drennan was born, and she had another daughter named Phyllis. Drennan's mother left her husband and Phyllis was sent to live with her maternal grandparents. However, when Drennan was born the maternal grandparents did not want her – perhaps because she was illegitimate. It was only in adulthood that Mary Phil Drennan discovered these "secrets" of her mother's past, and while her book is in part a diatribe against her institutional existence, one also gets the sense that she is angry with her mother and her extended family for denying her a normal family life solely because she was born outside of marriage.

It is not possible, on the basis of the sparse evidence included in these first-hand accounts, to draw any definitive conclusions about what life was like for illegitimate children in Ireland, or why they ended up in industrial schools. However, the stories presented here reinforce the impressions one gets from more "official" sources, and they offer insight into at least one facet of the life of illegitimate children: that of institutionalization. More specifically, each of these personal accounts gives insight into the different scenarios that resulted in the committal of illegitimate children to industrial schools. In some cases children were taken away from mothers who clearly cared for them, either because the mothers were desperately poor and could not provide for them, or because ISPCC inspectors and district court justices did not believe that unmarried mothers were "morally fit" to raise their own children. Other children spent their entire childhoods in industrial schools in spite of the fact that their mothers eventually went on to marry and have other children. In these cases, the children were denied a normal family life either because their mothers refused to admit their past to their new families, or because their new husbands did not want to be saddled with children that were not their own. And less common, but no less significant, were the children who were sent to industrial schools because their married or widowed mothers had affairs and ended up pregnant. In almost all of these cases it was individual families making decisions, based on their personal aspirations to respectability or a normal life for themselves, about whether the children would be rejected or accepted; in many cases it appears that they chose to reject their children to save themselves.

Factors leading to institutionalization

Most of the first-hand accounts written by adults who were born outside of marriage focus almost exclusively on the institutional phase of their lives. These accounts offer little insight into the conditions that they lived in that led to their institutionalization in the first place. This could be because those who have written such accounts have a specific agenda that emphasizes their institutionalization and underscores their victimization. Or perhaps they simply did not know why they were committed. Newspaper accounts of court cases in which children were committed to industrial schools offer insight into the conditions under which illegitimate children lived prior to being committed, but they also give insight into the lengths that some unmarried mothers went to try to keep their children, against the objections of the middle-class establishment.

Newspaper coverage of committal cases suggests that a good many illegitimate children committed to industrial schools came from mother and baby homes. On one day in 1945, at the Roscrea district court, three children were committed to industrial schools from the Sean Ross Abbey, the mother and baby home in Co. Tipperary:

> The Justice inquired what the mothers intended doing when the children were committed. One told the Justice she was going to work at £2 per month; and

the others said they were "getting jobs." The Justice said if such applications were going to be coming before him in numbers he would be very hesitant about making orders unless he ordered that contributions be paid by the mothers towards the children's maintenance ... the Justice ordered that the mother who had got a job should pay 1s. per week and said he could not make any order against the others, but hoped applications would be made at the proper time. All the children were committed.[43]

Although this anecdote is qualitative rather than quantitative in nature, it does illustrate the fate of many illegitimate children whose mothers could not or would not care for them, as well as the financial burden that was placed on the state, local authorities, and religious orders.

The large numbers of children being committed to industrial schools from mother and baby homes appears to have been such an extensive problem in Dublin that it elicited comment from an ISPCC inspector in 1945: "'We have a problem as regards these unwanted children, but we are not facing up to it. We have hundreds of these children.' So said Mrs. H. Clarke, NSPCC Inspector, today at the Metropolitan Children's Court before Justice O'Farrell, when she was applying for committals to industrial schools of a number of children."[44] The district justice in Castlepollard made an even stronger statement about the number of illegitimate children being sent to industrial schools from Manor House, the mother and baby home at Castlepollard, Co. Westmeath:

"This is a horrible state of affairs. They come in here and throw their responsibilities on to the rates. It is a pity I could not get a few of them in here and I would send them off to Mountjoy for cruelty," said District Justice Beatty, at Castlepollard, when he had before him an application to commit two children from the Manor House, Castlepollard, to Industrial Schools. Mr. J.R. Downes, solicitor for Westmeath Co. Council, said it was very difficult to place these children in Westmeath with foster parents. Inspector Glennon, NSPCC, said he had made inquiries and could not trace the mothers of these children. They had gone away.[45]

Many illegitimate children were committed to industrial schools from mother and baby homes at very young ages, and they likely had little or no contact with their families as they grew older.

Not all illegitimate children were committed to industrial schools within a few months of their birth. Newspaper accounts documented two cases in which illegitimate children came before the courts for committal to industrial schools after being locked away in their homes for a number of years. In one case, from 1948 Dublin, a child had been hidden away by her grandmother after the death of her mother:

A very small girl with a pale face was carried into the Children's Court, Dublin, today, by Mrs. H. Clarke, NSPCC, who with inspector D. O'Connor, NSPCC, applied to have her committed to a State industrial school. Mrs. Clarke told District Justice McCarthy that the girl had been kept in one room all her life, and as far as she knew no one had ever taken her outside in the air. She was four years of age, and could talk intelligently, but was not able to walk. Mrs. Clarke added that the child's mother died last January and since then she had been looked after by her grandmother. The grandmother appeared in Court. When asked by the Justice why the girl had been kept indoors she could offer no explanation. The Justice ordered that the girl be committed to Lakelands Industrial School and said that he hoped that he was not making the order too late for the child's sake.[46]

A second case involved a physically disabled child in County Meath:

> "It is an inhuman case," said District Justice Beatty at Delvin Court, when he ordered that a pretty but partially deformed 5-year-old girl be removed to Summerhill Industrial School. The child, Winifred Melia, Mooretown, near Delvin, was in court in the care of Inspector J. Egan, NSPCC, who applied for her removal to Summerhill. The Inspector said that Winifred was never allowed to walk, or to speak and mix with other children. When he went to the house at Mooretown, he found the child in a garret, lying on a bundle of old straw with only an old coat for a covering. The mother had run away from the County Home. The grandmother told him she had no responsibility in the matter. The Justice said both mother and grandmother should be serving a term of six months in jail.[47]

The reason for the child's effective imprisonment is not clear, since the grandmother declined to speak in her own defense. It is likely, in the second case, that the child's physical disability compounded the "shame" of her illegitimate existence. It is impossible to know how common this type of case was – where illegitimate children were removed to industrial schools after being locked away by their families in order to hide their existence. But the fact that details of two such cases were published in newspapers in a three-year span suggests that it was not entirely uncommon.

As was alluded to earlier, it was not unusual for unmarried mothers to hand their children over to the care of local authorities and subsequently begin new lives and new families. This scenario was illustrated again in a case that came before the Tullamore children's court in 1950. In this case, a woman had the care of her two illegitimate grandchildren because her daughter had moved to England, remarried, and refused to support them:

> The pathetic story of how the maternal grandmother of a little girl aged eleven and a little boy aged eight years was unable to maintain them on her income of £2 5s. per week, and of how no contributions towards their care was being made by their mother, was unfolded at Tullamore Children's Court on Friday by Inspector Egan, NSPCC. The Inspector was applying with the grandmother's consent for their committal to approved schools and having heard the application the Justice made an order sending the girl to Clifden and the boy to

Letterfrack…The Inspector said that the grandmother had to pay 4/4 per week rent out of her income, and besides that she was 65 years of age and was now unable to look after them. The mother is married in England but contributes nothing to their support. Her husband, in fact, would not allow her contribute towards their maintenance.[48]

In this case the children's mother chose her new husband over her children, and as a result the children spent the remainder of their childhoods in industrial schools.

For all of the mothers who chose to leave their children in mother and baby homes, or "abandon" them to other family members while they carried on with their own lives, some unwed mothers tried, for months or years, to keep their children but ultimately failed, primarily because of poverty. The Dublin Children's Court was an almost non-stop parade of unmarried mothers seeking the committal of children ranging in age from a few months to ten years.[49] Most of these children were committed on the grounds that they were illegitimate and their mothers were destitute and thus unable to support them. So commonplace was this scenario that district justice Hugh McCarthy expressed "grave concern" about the impact that the Doyle Supreme Court case would have on committals, particularly of illegitimate children who typically were committed solely on the grounds of their mothers' destitution. McCarthy noted "'This is, of course, a very great hardship on the unfortunate mothers who come before me. As a result of the recent decision, we are now back to where we were before the 1941 Act … surely there can be no two views on what should be done in a case of destitution. I am worried about the eventual destiny of these children. If I can do nothing to help them there may be others who will do something.'"[50] Three months later McCarthy was still expressing concern about the fate of illegitimate children whose mothers could find no assistance from the courts in having their children committed to industrial school: "'I'm terribly sorry,' said the Justice to one mother, 'but this does not come within my preserve.'"[51] McCarthy went on to warn unmarried mothers, the ISPCC, and other concerned parties: "'Please don't bring any more cases of this kind before me. I can do nothing about them.'"[52] The Doyle case, combined with the introduction in 1952 of the Adoption Act, had a profound impact on the way illegitimate children were cared for; it perhaps was more likely that they were raised in a home environment, whether their own or a foster or adoptive home, than in an institution.

The handful of autobiographical accounts, combined with ISPCC case files and newspaper accounts of court committals, suggest that the experiences of many illegitimate children were dire no matter what their circumstances. Some children began their institutional lives at birth; by all accounts this existence was austere and loveless at best, and abusive and exploitative at worst. For some of these children, the initial rejection by their families was compounded by the knowledge that their mothers went on to have other families of which they were never allowed to be a part. Many more illegitimate children spent anywhere from a few months to more than ten years with their mothers or extended families before being committed to industrial schools for a variety of reasons. It appears that many mothers wanted desperately to keep their children, and struggled for a number of years to do so before finally giving up in the face of abject poverty, the rejection of family and friends, and the censure of their neighbors. The one thing that children in these cases likely had that other illegitimate children did not, was love and affection. Unfortunately, conditions were such in the first half of the twentieth century that love and affection were not enough to sustain families through hard times, and ultimately it was illegitimate children who paid the highest price.

Conclusion

Twentieth-century Irish social history, if it mentions unmarried mothers and their children at all, assumes that children were ruthlessly ripped from their doting mothers' arms and shunted into institutions. It is true that some government officials and some of the religious orders who ran Ireland's industrial schools and mother and baby homes preferred to institutionalize illegitimate children rather than board them out or allow them to remain in their own homes. But there is no evidence to suggest that the majority of illegitimate children were, in fact, institutionalized. And those that were ended up there for a variety of reasons, and not only or primarily because some people believed this was the best method of dealing with them. The experiences of illegitimate children, as evidenced in first-hand narratives, documentaries, and ISPCC case files, and Department of Health inspection reports, varied widely.

The narrative accounts of institutional life reveal that the lives of illegitimate children could be filled with abuse, neglect, rejection, and instability. However, it is not clear how accurate or representative these accounts are. Undoubtedly children in institutions were subject to some level of neglect and exploitation, and this was in part a function of the system itself, which was poorly funded, administered, and inspected. But the Irish media, and Irish society generally have accepted the autobiographical accounts of institutionalization uncritically, even when there are good reasons to question their validity or accuracy. Illegitimate children who were reared in their own homes or in foster homes did not necessarily fare any better than their institutionalized counterparts. One can only wonder, given the treatment endured by many illegitimate children, how they transitioned to adulthood and self-sufficiency. Many of them, because of lack of training and education or emotional problems wrought by their sense of rejection and trauma, probably faced futures filled with poverty, isolation, and possibly even mental illness and further institutionalization.

Notes

1   "Poor Law" institutions were those, such as county homes, some mother and baby homes, and hospitals, that were funded out of public rates and provided shelter or medical care for those who could not afford to provide it themselves.

2   Adoption was not legalized until the Adoption Act (1952). Prior to this children could not be formally adopted in Ireland; they could be informally "adopted" by foster families, but this practice did not give either party any legal rights. Beginning in the 1930s some religious agencies began sending children to the United States for adoption by American families. There was no legal basis for this practice, and the legal status of the children sent to the US for adoption has never been questioned or explored.

3   In 1929 some 756 women gave birth in county homes and 214 in auxiliary institutions maintained by local authorities. In 1939, the figures were 841 and 315 respectively. It is impossible to know how many more women gave birth at home, in private hospitals and nursing homes, mother and baby homes that were not maintained by the local authorities, or in magdalen asylums. See Department of Local Government and Public Health, *Annual Reports* (Dublin: Government Stationery Office, 1929, 1939).

4   Extern institutions were institutions that operated privately, outside of state administration or control, but that were approved to accept patients/inmates at state expense. Such institutions received capitation grants based on the number of local authority patients/inmates under their care in any given quarter.

5   The religious orders that administered some of these institutions included the Sisters of Charity of St Vincent de Paul, Sisters of Mercy, Sisters of the Sacred Heart of Jesus and Mary, Sisters of St Louis, and Sisters of Charity.

6   NAI, Department of Health P24419/46, opening of home for unmarried mothers in Dublin.

7   NAI, Department of Health KA121179, Ard Mhuire Dunboyne.

8   See, for example, Department of Health, *Annual Report 1935–1936*, p. 390; NAI, Department of Health Augusta McCabe box 1, undated Department of Health report on provisions for illegitimate children (probably from 1943); Cork board of health and public assistance minutes, 4 May 1927; Offaly board of health and public assistance minutes, 23 July 1940.

9   These views were frequently expressed in correspondence between industrial school resident managers and the Department of Health in their requests to have their institutions approved as extern institutions, and in frequent requests that more children be sent to them.

10   Dublin board of health and public assistance minutes, 20 January 1926.

11   Department of Local Government and Public Health *Annual Report*, 1933–34, p. 147.

12 NAI, Department of Health McCabe box 1, undated Department of Health report on provisions for children (probably 1943).

13 NAI, Department of Health A121/74, report on Sean Ross Abbey, 4 October 1944.

14 NAI, Department of Health A121/74, letter from Department of Health to Kildare County Council, 29 April 1945.

15 NAI, Department of Health A121/74, letter from SAO Kildare County Council to Department of Health, 8 May 1945.

16 NAI, Department of Health A121/74, letter from acting SAO Kildare County Council to Department of Health, 21 May 1946.

17 NAI, Department of Health 5/79, Cork South: children boarded out and in institutions.

18 NAI, Department of Health A5/79, inspector's report on children in the county home, Co. Cork, 1 July 1947.

19 References to women escaping from the county home appear frequently in board of public assistance minutes. See, for example, Cork board of health and public assistance minutes, 10 June 1925, 13 December 1937, 23 May 1938, 24 July 1939, 11 September 1939, 26 August 1940.

20 Dublin board of health and public assistance minutes, 1 July 1925.

21 Many regional newspapers carried accounts of hearings at which children were committed to industrial schools. This coverage provides anecdotal evidence of children being committed to industrial schools from mother and baby homes. See, for example, the *Offaly Chronicle* (15 May 1947), p. 3, which tells of three children being committed to industrial schools from Sean Ross Abbey, and the *Evening Mail* (13 January 1949), p. 3, where two children were committed to industrial schools from Castlepollard, Co. Westmeath.

22 When children were committed to industrial schools the cost was split equally between the Department of Health and the local authority in the county of the child's birth. The local authority's contribution came out of local rates (the equivalent of property taxes). However, when children were sent to industrial schools by the local authorities, without benefit of a court committal, the entire cost of the child's maintenance came from local rates.

23 Department of Local Government and Public Health, *Annual Report 1935–36*, p. 390.

24 NAI, Department of Health A8/290 vol. 2, letter from resident manager of St Joseph's School to Dublin board of assistance, 3 August 1956.

25 NAI, Department of Health A30/119, letter from J.J. O'Driscoll, St Joseph's School, Tralee, to Westmeath County Manager, 14 May 1951.

26 NAI, Department of Health A122/61, letter from Sr. M. Colman, St Dominick's School, Waterford to Department of Health, 29 November 1954.

27 The inspection of industrial schools had many layers, and responsibility was shared by both the Departments of Health and Education. The Department of Education employed an inspector who conducted annual inspections of conditions in all industrial schools; separate medical examinations were also carried out annually. Department of Health inspectors were only responsible for inspecting those schools that accommodated local authority children, and they were only responsible for reporting on those children. They did not comment on the schools as a whole, nor were they concerned with children who were committed to industrial schools by the courts.

28 It is possible that the Department of Health inspectors were not as thorough in their inspections because they trusted the inspections conducted annually by Department of Education inspectors.

29 NAI, Department of Education 28740, report of inspection of Newtownforbes industrial school, 1931.

30 The right to apply for certification as a certified institution was first granted under the English poor laws and reaffirmed when the poor law system was overhauled following independence. Local authorities, if they could not provide for individuals seeking relief in their own institutions, could send such people to "certified" institutions. When it came to children, almost all of the country's fifty-two industrial schools were also certified schools, so local authorities did not need to apply for a court committal before sending children to industrial schools. Children maintained in industrial schools by local authorities were called "local authority children."

31 NAI, Department of Health A122/1, report on St Joseph's Industrial School, 9 June 1951.

32 *Suffer the little children*, the book that resulted from the television documentaries, detailed one extreme and unusual case in which a local county councilor became involved in the case of a boy who allegedly suffered extreme physical and sexual abuse while confined to Artane Industrial School, resulting in his official release by the Department of Education. However, although tens of thousands of children lived in industrial schools in the middle decades of the twentieth century this is the only documented case of release for reasons of mistreatment, neglect, or abuse. See Mary Raftery and Eoin O'Sullivan, *Suffer the little children: The inside story of Ireland's industrial schools* (Dublin: New Island Books, 1999), pp. 210–7.

33 *States of fear* narr., Aine Lawlor, writ., prod., dir., Mary Raftery, RTÉ, Ireland, 27 April 1999.

34 Raftery and O'Sullivan, *Suffer the little children*.

35 See Daire Keogh, "There's no such thing as a bad boy: Father Flanagan's visit to Ireland, 1946," *History Ireland*, 23:1 (Spring 2004), pp. 29–32.

36 Raftery and O'Sullivan, *Suffer the little children*, p. 166.

37 Raftery and O'Sullivan, *Suffer the little children*, pp. 243–8.

38 Raftery and O'Sullivan, *Suffer the little children*, p. 319.

39 Raftery and O'Sullivan, *Suffer the little children*, p. 325.

40 Raftery and O'Sullivan, *Suffer the little children*, p. 354.

41 Raftery and O'Sullivan, *Suffer the little children*, p. 354.

42 Mary Phil Drennan, *You may talk now* (Blarney, Co. Cork: On Stream Publications, 1994), p. 7.

43 *Offaly Chronicle* (19 April 1945), p. 1.

44 *Evening Herald* (22 August 1945), p. 1.

45 *Evening Mail* (13 January 1949), p. 6.

46 *Evening Mail* (21 April 1948), p. 5.

47 *Evening Mail* (19 July 1951), p. 5.

48 *Offaly Chronicle* (8 November 1950), p. 4.

49 See, for example, *Evening Mail* (20 February 1952), p. 5; during the sitting of the children's court on that day, applications were made to have nine illegitimate children committed to industrial schools. Although nine was perhaps an unusually large number, almost every sitting of the children's court, which took place

twice per week, heard at least one such application.

50 *Evening Mail* (8 February 1956), p. 5. McCarthy's sinister warning that "there may be others who will do something" is clearly an allusion to the potential for proselytizing.

51 *Evening Mail* (16 May 1956), p. 8.

52 *Evening Mail* (16 May 1956), p. 8.

4

Legislating care and protection: the Carrigan Committee, the age of consent, and adoption

Introduction

The previous chapters have examined the way the state, in the form of the Departments of Health and Education and local authorities, provided for poor, neglected, and illegitimate children through social policy and more informal measures. Two issues in the mid-twentieth century, the age of consent and legal adoption, required more formal action on the part of the state. The debates, both parliamentary and extra-parliamentary, that occurred around these issues provide further insights into how the state conceived of its responsibility to vulnerable children. Even here the best interests of children became secondary to more pressing political issues, such as the official desire to uphold the nationalist image of independent Ireland, to pacify the Catholic hierarchy, and to uphold male sexual privilege. In analyzing the events and debates surrounding passage of the Criminal Law (Amendment) Act (1935) and the Adoption Act (1952) this chapter considers the extent to which vulnerable children were used (or indeed abused), in a variety of ways to prop up the nationalist image of Catholic Ireland that was promoted at home and abroad.

Irish social historians tend to take for granted that for much of the twentieth century the Catholic Church was all-pervasive and all-powerful, particularly in the area of sexual morality, and that the state willingly bowed to pressure to legislate according to Catholic doctrine and principles. Historians point to a number of legislative initiatives, including the mother and child scheme of 1951, the Adoption Act of 1952, and earlier legislation regulating dance halls – as well as to social policy (or lack of it) related to unmarried mothers and their children – as proof of the church's moral authority in virtually all aspects of Irish social and political life.[1] Scholarly examinations of the events surrounding the creation of the Carrigan Committee and its report in the early 1930s tend to reinforce, rather than challenge, these assumptions.[2] James Smith argues that the government suppressed the Carrigan report as part of its policy of "containing" sexual immorality after independence. Mark Finnane acknowledges the role of key Catholic prelates in formulating post-independence social policy, but he also emphasizes the role of other agencies and institutions, including An Garda Síochána and the courts, in shaping the post-independence "moral order." Finola Kennedy wonders whether suppression of the Carrigan report in the early 1930s compounded Irish society's ignorance of the extent of sexual assaults against children. Despite differing approaches and conclusions, all of these articles are rooted in two fundamental assumptions: first that Catholic sensibilities, more than anything else, guided official responses to sexual immorality generally, and to the Carrigan report specifically; and second, that awareness of child sexual abuse did not exist in Ireland in the middle decades of the twentieth century.

Far from being ignorant of the vulnerability of children to sexual abuse in the first half of the twentieth century, lawmakers, jurists, and the public in general were well aware of the problem, even if there was little public commentary. The failure of the government to act on the Carrigan Committee's recommendations stemmed less from ignorance or disbelief of the conditions it revealed than from social and political priorities that were more pressing than their responsibility to protect vulnerable and victimized children. The government's response to information about sexual assaults against children suggests that the poor, disaffected, and marginalized were sacrificed to the "greater good," which in this case meant male sexual license and protecting the newly independent state's legitimacy and reputation in the international arena. Events surrounding the Carrigan Committee and the presentation of its report suggest that the assumptions, beliefs, and behaviors related to sexual morality in post-independence Ireland were far more complex than has yet been acknowledged. The government's decision to suppress the Carrigan report and to suppress subsequent debate on the Criminal Law (Amendment) Act (1935) derived less from ignorance of moral conditions throughout the country, or a desire to "contain" sexual immorality, than from a desire to prevent details of Ireland's "depraved" moral condition from reaching the pages of the foreign, and particularly the British, press.

This fear of international censure or ridicule is, ironically, what finally compelled the government to pass an Adoption Act in 1952. Department of Health inspectors of boarded-out children had been emphasizing the need for legal adoption as early as the 1930s. Their work with boarded-out children convinced them of the need for measures to legally allow children to be subsumed into families other than their own biological families. In the 1940s the Adoption Society and the Joint Committee for Women's Societies and Social Workers joined them in their calls for legal adoption. In spite of mounting public pressure, successive administrations throughout the 1940s and into the early 1950s continued to insist that legal adoption was not necessary. In reality, the Catholic hierarchy opposed adoption on several grounds, and no administration was willing to cross the church on this issue. They were finally forced into adoption by international media attention that chronicled Ireland's informal overseas adoption trade.

The Carrigan Committee

The issue of child sexual abuse has received a great deal of attention in the popular Irish press in recent years, primarily in connection with the alleged physical and sexual abuse of children in industrial schools that were funded by the state and administered by male and female religious orders.[3] However, there have been few quantitative or qualitative analyses of sexual offenses against children in the first two-thirds of the twentieth century, nor of the extent of official awareness or discussion of the issue. Contemporary commentators talk about child sexual abuse as if it has only been "discovered" recently, or as if it either did not exist in earlier times or was so shrouded in mystery and secrecy as to be virtually invisible. Indeed, the phrase "child sexual abuse" gained currency in social and political parlance only in the mid-1980s; prior to this, sexual offences perpetrated against children were not defined or treated any differently from those perpetrated against adults. But the supposed silence or secrecy surrounding child sexual abuse, even if it was not called that at the time, was not as complete as historians tend to assume. And even when relative silence did prevail, this should not be taken as evidence that lawmakers, courts, or even parents were ignorant of the fact that children were vulnerable to sexual assaults.

In the first decade of the Irish Free State's existence, lawmakers amended legislation in a number of areas including the poor law, affiliations orders, and the regulation of dance halls, in an effort to bring Irish statute into line with what they regarded as Ireland's unique social and moral ethos. The law relating to sexual offences, as embodied in the Criminal Law Amendment Acts 1880–85, also came under review at this time. A Criminal Law (Amendment) Bill was introduced in 1929, the primary aim of which was ostensibly to protect girls from sexual assault or exploitation by raising the age of consent to something considered more appropriate to Irish circumstances.[4] However, the Dáil disagreed as to what the age of consent should be; suggestions ranged from sixteen to twenty-one years old. Further, some lawmakers expressed the view that amendments were necessary simply because the existing law was a relic of British administration in Ireland: "The existing law was made by Englishmen, and the general conditions and outlook on such matters here being fundamentally different, it is unsuitable for application to this country."[5] Ironically, the Carrigan Committee's investigation showed that conditions in Ireland were little different from those that prevailed in England.

The 1885 Criminal Law Amendment Act came into existence following a high-profile stunt by W.T. Stead, editor of the sensationalist *Pall Mall Gazette,* that literally shocked respectable English society and shamed the government into legislating a higher age of consent. (The 1861 Offences Against the Person Act raised the age of consent to 13 years). The Stead case occurred against the backdrop of anti-vice and social purity campaigns that had gained steady support and strength in Britain since the 1870s. Stead was joined in his "operation" by Josephine Butler, former crusader for repeal of the Contagious Diseases Acts, and by the Salvation Army. In July 1885 Stead published a series of four articles, "The Maiden Tribute to Modern Babylon," in which he purported to reveal the underbelly of Britain's white sex-slave trade. Stead claimed that he and his reporters spent a month investigating and uncovering London's "trade" in young girls. Stead reported that he purchased a 13-year-old girl, Eliza Armstrong, from her mother for £5. "The 'Maiden Tribute' documented in lurid detail how poor 'daughters of the people' were 'snared, trapped, and outraged, either when under the influence of drugs or after a prolonged struggle in a locked room.'"[6] The series sparked a public outcry the likes of which had never been seen before, and by the time the series had concluded mass demonstrations were being held, demanding that the government enact legislation raising the age of consent; such legislation had stalled in previous parliamentary sessions. It was later revealed that the Eliza Armstrong episode was staged, and that most of the content of Stead's articles was fabricated.[7] In spite of this, however, the series was successful in forcing the government to act on the age of consent, and the result was the Criminal Law (Amendment) Act of 1885. The Act made sexual intercourse with girls under the age of fourteen years a felony, and sexual intercourse with girls under seventeen years of age a misdemeanor.

There was no such public outcry in post-independence Ireland, even as the Carrigan Committee amassed vast evidence of the vulnerability of girls to sexual violence and exploitation. From the beginning, government ministers were reluctant to introduce changes to the Criminal Law (Amendment) Act in spite of the fact that individual TDs had been calling for reforms since 1925. In April of that year, TD Richard Corish raised the issue during oral question time; the Minister for Justice, Kevin O'Higgins, replied that a bill was in the drafting stage.[8] By 1927 there had been no movement on the bill, and again the Minister for Justice was questioned on the matter, this time by TD Seán MacEoin; the Minister replied that other issues had taken priority:

> Materials for Bills dealing with these matters were prepared in my Department a considerable time ago. Owing to the number of other matters of more immediate importance in my Department and other Departments requiring legislation, it has not been found possible to get these materials incorporated in a Bill. It is my intention, however, to have such a Bill prepared at the first available opportunity.[9]

Ten months later, in November 1927, TD William Davin again asked the Minister for Justice (now W.T. Cosgrave) when he planned to introduce the Criminal Law (Amendment) Bill and the Minister again said that other matters were more important.[10] It would be another two years before a bill reached the floor of the Dáil.

The issues raised during Dáil debates on the 1929 Criminal Law (Amendment) Bill may explain the reluctance of successive ministers for justice to introduce it in the first place. The Criminal Law (Amendment) Bill was supposed to protect young girls from sexual assaults, but nearly every TD who spoke during the debates pointed out the Bill's potential to encourage blackmail or false accusations of rape. Lawmakers wanted to ensure that in amending the law they did not inadvertently make it easier for prostitutes or unscrupulous "well grown girls" to entrap "innocent men."[11] Some lawmakers were convinced that, if sexual offenses against young girls were, in fact, on the rise, girls were as much to blame as men for that state of affairs: "Everybody in this House knows, that girls of 16, 17 and 18 years of age are really more responsible for this offence which it is desired to punish under this Bill, than are the persons whom this Bill would punish."[12] In the end lawmakers could not agree on the bill's fundamental principles, nor were they all convinced that changes in the law were even necessary. They agreed to postpone further debate pending the establishment of the Carrigan Committee to inquire into the nature and extent of the country's "morality problem."

Some members of the Dáil doubted that sexual offenses, especially those perpetrated against young girls, represented a significant problem in post-independence Ireland, yet civil servants in the Department of Justice, on the basis of information provided by police commissioner Eoin O'Duffy, could be in no doubt that a problem did exist. A memo prepared by O'Duffy noted that:

> An alarming aspect is the number of cases of interference with girls under 16, and even under 13 and 11, which come before the Courts. These are in most cases heard of accidentally by the Guards, and are very rarely as a result of a direct complaint. It is generally agreed that reported cases do not exceed 15% of those actually happening.[13]

O'Duffy's memo admitted that the roots of this seeming lapse in morality were "indigenous" and thus required a distinctly Irish solution: "The present state of the law is disgraceful in a Christian country, and the whole question of morality crimes should now be dealt with from an Irish point of view."[14] The disparity between the contents of this memo, and the concerns that had dominated the earlier Dáil debates, such as the need to protect men from blackmail, typifies the double standard that was evident throughout much of twentieth-century Ireland whenever moral issues were discussed.

The overwhelmingly male legislature was careful to ensure that new legislative initiatives in areas that governed sexual morality would not either render men vulnerable to blackmail by "conniving" women or force them to be more accountable for their own sexual behavior.[15] The Minister for Justice, James Fitzgerald-Kenney, was the first to raise the specter of blackmail in relation to the age of consent: "This question of the age of consent and whether it should be seventeen or eighteen is a very serious problem. Certainly I myself am of the opinion, to begin with, that it should only be seventeen. Deputies will understand that if a girl of eighteen is a loose woman she may become a most terrible blackmailer. She may look to be very much older, and she may become a most desperate blackmailer."[16]

Gearoid O'Sullivan, while dismissing the Bill's potential for blackmail, noted that:

> What is serious is that two persons commit a crime and that this Bill makes it a crime for one person because of his sex, and makes him liable to be punished and the other person because of her sex and because she happens to be under 18 years of age gets off scot free. That is the principle of the Bill and it is because of that principle that I ask the House to disagree with it and not to give it a Second Reading. There is a good deal to be said about raising the age of consent but not in the fashion in this Bill, namely to the age of 18. There is no sense in that.[17]

Concerns about blackmail, and the conviction that teenage girls were more responsible than men for sexual assaults, surfaced in subsequent debates about the Criminal Law (Amendment) Act.

The Committee on the Criminal Law (Amendment) Act, known as the Carrigan Committee, met for the first time on 20 June 1930. The committee was comprised of six members, four men and two women. Barrister William Carrigan served as chair; other members were Catholic and Church of Ireland clergymen, the matron of a Dublin maternity hospital, a poor law commissioner, and a physician.[18] The committee was only secondarily concerned with juvenile prostitution (although, as will be seen, this issue was foregrounded by many witnesses). Its primary concern was "to examine the proposals which had been repeatedly put forward by various societies and organisations for changes in the law relating to sexual offences, the most important being the raising of the age of consent."[19] One of the committee's first decisions was that its proceedings would be closed to the press and the public, although the press would be "kept informed of the progress of the enquiry."[20] The committee believed that witnesses would be more frank and forthcoming if they knew their evidence would be kept in confidence, rather than featured prominently on the pages of regional and national newspapers.

The concern for the reputation of innocent men expressed in Dáil debates in 1930, as indicated above, was echoed in some of the testimony heard by the Carrigan Committee. One of the most striking examples of this was the heavy emphasis that many witnesses placed on juvenile prostitution, often at the expense of other issues. Almost all of the witnesses commented on juvenile prostitution, and several spoke of little else. One might have expected, given that the committee's task was to investigate the extent of sexual crimes against girls, that those who addressed juvenile prostitution would have done so in the context of the sexual vulnerability or exploitation of girls and young women. In fact, many of the witnesses implied or stated outright that the girls themselves were primarily responsible for their plight and should be dealt with harshly. Most recommended incarcerating suspected juvenile prostitutes in reformatories or similarly penal institutions, and subjecting them to enforced medical inspections.[21]

The strongest condemnation of juvenile prostitution came from District Court justice George Cussen, who rejected the proposal to raise the age of consent "on the ground that young men undoubtedly need some protection from wild girls."[22] Cussen further suggested that "the D.J. should be given power to have the young prostitute medically examined – if she refused she would go to jail – and if diseased she could be committed to serve her sentence in the Lock Hospital."[23] This proposal seems downright draconian, particularly when one considers that women in England had secured repeal of exactly this type of legislation, through the campaign against the Contagious Diseases Acts, in 1886.

Notably, many of the witnesses who gave evidence before a committee ostensibly concerned with the sexual vulnerability of young girls not only concentrated on juvenile prostitution, but also presented their evidence from a perspective that saw juvenile prostitutes more as victimizers than victims. This heavy emphasis on prostitution might have left one with the false impression that juvenile prostitution was a more significant problem than sexual offenses perpetrated against young girls.[24] But much testimony, combined with the debates that occurred in the Dáil in 1929 and 1930, also suggests that, far from assuming that young Irish women were the embodiment of chastity and purity, some segments of "respectable" Irish society regarded them not only as sexually knowledgeable and experienced but, indeed, as sexual predators in their own right.

Several female witnesses suggested that Irish girls were less mature physically, and more innocent of sexual matters, than their English counterparts, and were therefore more easily led astray. Dr Angela Russell testified that "in her experience girls in Ireland were physically more immature than those of equal age abroad and temperamentally they were more trusting and simple."[25] The overall view, however, was that girls were at least as guilty as men of the sexual immorality that was seemingly rampant in the country, and that men needed protection from conniving, blackmailing girls just as much as girls needed protection from predatory men. Undoubtedly the pejorative rhetoric was intended to protect male sexual license, given that in fact the vast majority of victims of sexual crimes that came before the district and circuit courts were under the age of seventeen years and hardly the sexual predators portrayed by lawmakers; however, the conclusions about female sexual promiscuity reached by some observers were not entirely unfounded. Court records of infanticide, and even of sexual assaults, paint a portrait of female sexuality that is often at odds with received wisdom on the subject.[26]

The only witness to address the nature and frequency of sexual assaults against children in any meaningful way was Eoin O'Duffy, commissioner of An Garda Siochána. O'Duffy noted that "the existing statutory provisions in respect of sexual crime were insufficient, also that the position in this matter was alarming and so far from improving was growing worse from year to year."[27] O'Duffy attributed this in part to "wretched housing conditions," which afforded no privacy and, presumably, no protection from sexual assaults. O'Duffy's assumption about the links between housing conditions and the sexual vulnerability of young girls appear somewhat simplistic and naïve because it assumes that sexual crimes were in effect crimes of opportunity. In a memorandum submitted to the committee to expand on his oral testimony, O'Duffy stated that

> [t]here is nothing inherently bad in the majority of our young girls who drift
> into the unfortunate class. In the great majority of cases the cause may be found

in the conditions under which they lived for the first fifteen years of their lives – wretched housing conditions such as where large families sleep in one or two beds in a common room, clothes barely sufficient to cover their nakedness, and no consideration possible as regards dressing, undressing, sleeping and complying with the demands of nature.[28]

In this depiction, male perpetrators of sexual assaults against young girls are portrayed as victims of circumstance, and thus, essentially excused. O'Duffy wrote that "there is nothing inherently bad" in the character of Irish girls but he ignored the character of boys and men entirely. Presumably, given their constant exposure to scantily-clad or even naked young girls in these overcrowded tenements, how could men be expected to keep their sexual urges in check? But O'Duffy's picture also had little bearing on reality. Of the nearly 1,500 sexual assault cases heard in circuit courts throughout the country in the period 1924 to 1960 only a handful occurred under the kind of conditions described by O'Duffy.[29] In fact, many sexual assaults against young girls (and boys) occurred in isolated fields and laneways, in the homes of neighbors, and in their own rural cottages.

But O'Duffy also suggested that there was a "changed rural outlook" that not only tolerated sexual immorality, but almost celebrated as "clever and interesting" those who exhibited signs of "sexual depravity." This changed outlook, in turn, led to increases in sexual crimes and contributed to "the great increase in the number of assaults on very young girls under 11 years old."[30] O'Duffy stated that most cases came to the attention of the gardaí accidentally and that, owing to a reluctance on the part of parents to report assaults against their children, the reported number of assaults was but a fraction of those that actually occurred.[31] If O'Duffy was correct that reported cases represented less than 15 per cent of actual cases, then the number of sexual assaults that occurred throughout the country between 1924 and 1960 can be projected to have exceeded 10,000.[32] O'Duffy was also right to be concerned about the ages of victims in sexual assaults. Of the nearly 1,500 reported sexual assaults against girls detailed in available court records, 81 per cent of the victims were seventeen years of age or younger. Fifty-five per cent were between the ages of fourteen and seventeen, 18 per cent were between the ages of ten and thirteen, and 8 per cent were nine years of age or younger.[33]

O'Duffy assumed that most of these assaults occurred in urban tenements, and that parental neglect was to blame: "Assaults on girls under the age of 10 usually occur in tenement dwellings in the absence of the parents or guardians. In most of the cases it would appear that the parents or guardians did not take proper precautions to guard against such offences … a section providing penalty for neglect by parents or guardians in such cases is recommended."[34] The inaccuracy of this conclusion about the conditions under which sexual assaults occurred was borne out by O'Duffy's own evidence. According to garda statistics for 1929, as presented by O'Duffy to the Carrigan Committee, only six out of thirty-seven prosecutions for assaults of girls between ten and sixteen years occurred in urban areas, and only two in Dublin tenements. The remainder of these assaults occurred in rural or country areas, where one might have expected the less cramped living conditions combined with more traditional ties of family and community to offer a measure of protection to potentially vulnerable children. In portraying sexual crime as a predominantly urban problem, O'Duffy seems to have assumed that sexual immorality generally, and sexual offenses against children specifically, were "crimes of opportunity" rather than the actions of pathological or predatory individuals. Or perhaps he believed, as many people did at the time, in the image of rural chastity and piety that Eamon de Valera and other nationalists were so anxious to promote.

O'Duffy returned to the committee to continue his evidence on 6 November 1930. At that time he commented on thirty-four specific cases that had come to the notice of gardaí around the country in the previous ten months. One case involved a schoolgirl who was sexually assaulted by a man whom she had approached to sell a ticket of some kind. O'Duffy's solution was to "[suggest] to the Department of Education that school children should not be encouraged or permitted to engage in the selling of tickets outside of school hours."[35] Although O'Duffy was one of only a handful of witnesses who spoke openly and frankly about the extent of sexual assaults against young girls, his own assumptions about the roots of the problem implicitly blamed the victim and inhibited his ability to see the problem clearly.

O'Duffy's remedies amounted to saying that the only way to guarantee children's safety was to keep them under lock and key at home. Court records of incest cases show, however, that even this could not ensure children's safety. Given that O'Duffy's solution to the problem of sexual offences against children implied that the victim had put herself in a situation that made her vulnerable, or her parents had failed to protect her, it is no wonder that the courts tended to treat the cases that came before them with relative leniency.[36] Nor is it surprising that the government failed to give the matter the serious attention it deserved. Finola Kennedy has suggested that there was a lack of knowledge that sexual offences against children were commonplace; it might be more accurate to say that the predominantly male establishment was unwilling or unable to understand the roots of the problem or deal with it effectively.

O'Duffy did, however, recommend that sexual offences against children be reclassified and that stiffer sentences be imposed on those convicted of sexual crimes: "The adoption of severe preventive measures is not premature, and in my recommendation I suggest that practically all the misdemeanours [including such offences as indecent assault] should be raised to felonies."[37] The fact that O'Duffy's recommendations were ignored in the final version of the Criminal Law (Amendment) Act suggests that not everyone shared this view. O'Duffy further suggested that "for all offences against girls under 13 years of age, I take the responsibility of very strongly recommending the 'cat' – not a few strokes, but the most severe application the medical advisor will permit, having regard only to the physical condition and health of the offender."[38] Finally, O'Duffy criticized court justices for not availing of the maximum sentences provided under existing law: "Worse still, judges have not been imposing the extreme penalties allowed. To impose a sentence of six months on, or to fine a ruffian who destroys the innocence of a child under 13 is farcical."[39]

In drafting the 1935 Criminal Law (Amendment) Act lawmakers ignored all of O'Duffy's recommendations. The Minister for Justice, P.J. Ruttledge, rejected the recommendation with regard to minimum sentences because he believed that in many cases "the sympathies of the court may be more in favour of the accused than the accusor."[40] Here again, the evidence suggests that, far from doubting the evidence presented in the Carrigan report, government officials were more concerned with protecting men from wayward or, worse, predatory girls than with addressing the problem of sexual assaults against children. He seems to have assumed that in the majority of cases of sexual assaults that came before the courts, an all-male jury would be more inclined to believe the male defendant's rather than the female victim's version of events.

O'Duffy was correct to criticize court justices for their "farcical" sentences, but he overlooked a significant constraint faced by court justices when dealing with young victims: the inadmissibility of the uncorroborated evidence of children, particularly children who were too young to understand the concept of giving evidence under oath. Dermot Gleeson, a district justice from County Clare, addressed this point in his testimony before the Carrigan Committee. Gleeson was less concerned with the fact or extent of sexual assaults against young children than with the admissibility of their evidence in court:

> in the case where the witness is a child not fit to be sworn, the rules of evidence regarding the admission of extraneous evidence might be enlarged. He [Gleeson] considered that the form of caution … given by the Judge (when charging the jury as to the danger or absence of safety in their relying on the uncorroborated evidence of such young person) had a bad effect. In many cases of this kind the jury acquitted the person though his guilt was apparent.[41]

Gleeson recommended that "the attempt to carnally know a girl should be equally punishable without proof of actual penetration at all events in the case of a child under 14."[42]

Hannah Clarke, an ISPCC inspector, echoed Justice Gleeson's concern about the inadmissibility of children's evidence:

> men who had assaulted little girls under 10 years very often escaped conviction owing to the lack of evidence. She [Clarke] suggested that to meet the difficulty the law of evidence might be amended to the effect that when the child assaulted had at once made an outcry or complaint the sworn statement of the person to whom such complaint or outcry had been made should be treated as corroborative evidence; men who assaulted little girls under 10 years appear to be well aware of the loophole of the inadmissibility of the uncorroborated evidence of their victims.[43]

Neither Gleeson's nor Clarke's recommendations with regard to the admissibility of the evidence of very young victims were heeded when the 1935 Criminal Law (Amendment) Act was passed, because the Minister for Justice believed that "on the whole it would be preferable to allow some offenders to escape justice than run the risk of convicting anyone unjustly."[44] Once again, government officials put specifically masculine concerns ahead of the best interests of vulnerable or victimized children.

The Carrigan Committee presented its report to the Minister for Justice, James Fitzgerald-Kenney in August 1931.[45] The committee concluded that "the cogency and unanimity of the evidence laid before us leave no doubt that gross offences are rife throughout the country of a nature from which it [the Irish state] could formerly claim a degree of immunity that may perhaps have lulled it into a false state of security."[46] The report was both scathing in its indictment of the moral conditions that existed throughout the country, and unforgiving in its recommendations for dealing with offenders. It painted a picture of Irish society entirely at odds with the image of Ireland that the government had tried to promote because it undermined the traditional image of piety, purity, and morality.

There is no evidence that Minister for Justice Fitzgerald-Kenney commented on the Carrigan report before he left office in March 1932. His successor, James Geoghegan (who was in office for just 11 months, from March 1932 to February 1933), was reluctant to give the report any credence, although this may have stemmed more from concern that the report would provide fodder for Ireland's "enemies" abroad than from genuine disbelief in the legitimacy or veracity of the committee's conclusions.[47] Geoghegan concluded that "[apart] from the question as to whether the Report should be adopted, is the question whether it should be published. The view of the Department of Justice is that it should not be published.

It contains numerous sweeping charges against the state of morality of the Saorstat and even if these statements were true, there would be little point in giving them currency."[48] Geoghegan went on to say that "[unless] these statements are exaggerated ... the obvious conclusion to be drawn is that the ordinary feelings of decency and the influence of religion have failed in this country and that the only remedy is by way of police action. It is clearly undesirable that such a view of conditions in the Saorstat should be given wide circulation."[49] The conclusion one might reach is that it was not the report's conclusions that concerned Geoghegan, but whether those conclusions should be made public.

Geoghegan circulated the report to members of the Executive Council (made up primarily of ministers from the various government departments) in December 1932. The accompanying memorandum played down the report's conclusions and counseled caution and skepticism in accepting the Carrigan Committee's findings:

> On the whole the Report should be taken with reserve. It leaves the impression that the authors did not face their task in a judicial and impartial frame of mind. Their recommendations are invariably to increase penalties, create offences, and remove existing safeguards for persons charged. Their main concern seems to be to secure convictions: they do not consider the case of a man charged in the wrong.[50]

The minister here echoed concerns first raised by lawmakers in 1930 that changes to the law might leave men vulnerable to blackmail or false rape charges. He rejected the report's findings on two grounds: first, that the committee made sweeping allegations and generalizations about the state of morality in the country without providing substantial supporting evidence; and, second, that the committee had failed to take evidence from a "devil's advocate" who might have provided an opposing viewpoint, or from a circuit or high court justice who had dealt with the issues first-hand.[51] The Executive Council was as alarmed as the Minister for Justice at the state of affairs depicted in the report, so much so that they agreed unanimously not to make the report available to the public or, indeed, to the members of the Dáil who had requested the inquiry in the first place.

While critical of the report's shortcomings, particularly its failure to hear evidence from "devil's advocates" or court justices, the Minister for Justice's memorandum to the Executive Council acknowledged that "unless these statements [made by witnesses before the Committee] are exaggerated, the obvious conclusion to be drawn is that the ordinary feelings of decency and the influence of religion have failed in this country and that the only remedy is by way of police action. *It is clearly undesirable that such a view of conditions in the State should be given wide circulation* [emphasis added]."[52]

The government's primary concern was, thus, not whether the report's allegations were true, or whether young children might be vulnerable to sexual assaults on a wide scale, but whether the attention of the general public (both inside and outside of Ireland) should be drawn to such a state of affairs.

More than three years passed between the presentation of the Carrigan report to the Executive Council in 1932 and the introduction in the Dáil of a second Criminal Law (Amendment) Bill in June 1934. It was agreed that an informal parliamentary committee, made up of seven members including the current Minister for Justice (Ruttledge), the former Minister for Justice (James Geoghegan), the attorney general, and representatives from each of the parliamentary parties, would draft the legislation and then present it to the full Dáil as a *fait accompli*. This informal committee expected the Dáil to rubber-stamp the legislation without discussion or debate. It was further agreed that "any minority on the Committee would be bound by the decision of the majority and would not press their point of view on committee stage or elsewhere."[53] While the government recognized the need to act on the Carrigan Committee's recommendations, it intended to stifle debate and silence opposition. It succeeded: the Criminal Law (Amendment) Act came into force in February 1935 with no debate or dissent.

The Carrigan Committee was important for what it revealed about attitudes toward sexual assaults against children in twentieth-century Ireland. Although the Carrigan Committee's primary objective was to investigate the extent of sexual offenses in the country, and especially those against young girls, many witnesses were more concerned with juvenile prostitution than with sexual assaults, and they often portrayed girls as more victimizers than victims. Witnesses gave evidence about the nature of sexual offenses against young girls that was not borne out by evidence from actual court cases; this misguided view of the problem would have hindered the government's ability to protect victims had they been inclined to do so (although it seems clear, based on the Carrigan report and its aftermath that they were not so inclined).

All segments of Irish society had some knowledge or experience of sexual assaults against children during the first half of the twentieth century. Parents warned their children away from particular individuals, or took steps to protect their children when they suspected assaults had taken place or were about to take place. Similarly, district and circuit court justices acknowledged the extent to which very young children were victimized, and voiced frustration at the constraints imposed by existing law in punishing offenders. But government and religious officials were more concerned with how publicizing the issue would make Ireland appear on the international front or to "our enemies," as the Reverend M.J. Browne put it in his response to a Department of Justice memorandum.[54] And, as has become abundantly clear from the government's obsession with suppressing the Carrigan report in the 1930s, government ministers were well aware of the extent of sexual crimes against children in the first half of the twentieth century. However, political agendas and priorities prevented them from acknowledging the extent of the problem, accepting responsibility for protecting children, or punishing perpetrators as they deserved to be punished.

Exporting the "problem": American adoptions of Irish children

For many illegitimate Irish children, adoption by an American family under American adoption laws provided the only alternative to institutional life or an insecure informal adoption or fostering arrangement in Ireland. The legality of sending Irish children out of the state for adoption under foreign laws was scarcely questioned by those involved in the process; civil servants and Catholic agencies were concerned only that the children in question were sent to "good" Catholic homes. Indeed, the hierarchy and civil servants were so concerned with the Catholic question that they refused to allow children to be removed to Northern Ireland or England for adoption lest they fall into the hands of Protestant families or proselytizers.[55] On the surface, those involved in the unofficial adoption scheme expressed reservations about the wisdom of sending children out of the state for adoption. In fact, however, it was an ideal solution for most of the parties concerned.

Margaret Humphreys and Gillian Wagner have examined the practice, from the 1870s to the 1950s, of sending "unwanted" children from orphanages and industrial schools in Britain to institutions and families in the farthest reaches of the empire, both as a means of disposing of the "problem" at home and perpetuating a white, British population throughout the empire.[56] Orphaned and abandoned children (some of whom were Irish-born) who came into state care became pawns in Britain's late nineteenth-century and early twentieth-century empire-building strategies. Similarly, the institutionalization or overseas adoption of Irish children served as a counterweight to the "paganism" and "liberalism" allegedly inherent in British colonial rule, and protected innocent Irish children from the "evil" clutches of proselytizers even as it denied them constitutional rights and individual identities. The removal of children from their homes and families also helped to protect the veneer of "respectability," piety, and morality that supposedly distinguished the native Irish government's rule from that of the former Protestant colonizer. The ends may have differed, but the politicization of definitions and policies relating to childhood in Ireland mirrored those elsewhere in Europe in spite of early nationalist leaders' insistence on the importance and value of children in the life of the new state.

For religious orders, who operated the mother and baby homes and "adoption" societies from which the majority of children were adopted, overseas adoptions solved an accommodation problem that often reached crisis proportions when babies were born or admitted faster than they could be boarded-out or sent to industrial schools. Sending children to America also relieved local authorities of the financial burden of maintaining them in industrial schools, extern institutions, or foster homes. The only player who did not win, in the official sense, was the Department of Foreign Affairs (DFA). Because of its role in issuing passports to facilitate the removal of children from Ireland, the DFA left itself open to allegations that it encouraged and indeed fostered emigration at a time when the Irish population was in a steady decline due to low birth rates and high emigration. But as long as the Catholic hierarchy in Dublin sanctioned the scheme the Department of Foreign Affairs facilitated it. However, it was not the DFA but the hierarchy, and in particular John Charles McQuaid, Archbishop of Dublin from 1940–1972, who determined the conditions under which passports would be issued to allow children to leave the state for adoption.

It is not possible to ascertain, from available evidence, the number of children sent to America under the informal adoption scheme.[57] The DFA began keeping statistics only in 1950; from the beginning of 1950 through October 1952 the DFA issued 330 passports for children to travel to America for adoption.[58] Anecdotal evidence suggests that children were exported to America from as early as 1940, with one agency alone, St Patrick's Guild of Dublin, arranging sixty-one American adoptions between 1948 and 1950.[59] However, official statistics are not an accurate indication either of the time frame in which the adoptions occurred, or the numerical extent of the practice. Department of Foreign Affairs files reveal that some American couples brought Irish children home without a passport under the United States Displaced Persons Act of 1948.[60] Other couples, mostly US servicemen stationed in England, registered the births of illegitimate Irish children as their own biological children.[61] Given the apparent ease with which some couples secured and removed children without passports, or registered illegitimate Irish children as their own, the practice was clearly more widespread than statistics would suggest and, likely, than government officials or philanthropic agencies would wish to admit.

It is easy to understand why charitable agencies seized on overseas adoptions as a solution to what they regarded as an overwhelming problem. Letters from religious-based philanthropic agencies to Archbishop McQuaid illustrated their dilemma: "Girls are *flocking* here daily, some of them in great distress, and the best I can do for them is to hold out hope that they might be relieved in December or the New Year. Many of them will become disheartened, no doubt, and who can be sure that the children will be safe."[62] There is little doubt that charitable agencies received more requests for assistance than their human or financial resources could grant. Many women turned to these agencies in desperation, often after being rejected by their families or fired from employment when their pregnancies were discovered; many more gave birth in county homes, mother and baby homes, or private nursing homes, and then were encouraged or coerced into giving up their children.

But it also must be remembered that the philosophy that underpinned the majority of charitable Catholic institutions and agencies was the firm conviction that unmarried mothers were fundamentally unfit to have custody of their own children. Pressure was brought to bear on many unmarried mothers, even those who might have been inclined to keep their children, to relinquish custody to agencies that then boarded them out or sent them overseas for adoption. Those involved in the overseas adoption scheme justified the practice on the grounds that it was virtually impossible to convince Irish families to adopt illegitimate children. This claim is somewhat dubious in light of the fact that inspectors' reports on boarded-out children consistently referred to foster families who wished to adopt the children entrusted to their care.[63] Additionally, in the first year of legal adoption the Adoption Board received 2,500 requests for adoption orders, and thereafter received at least twice as many applications as could be processed in a year.[64]

In spite of the legal and ethical dilemmas that the overseas adoption policy presented, healthy children were sent out of the state in their hundreds, if not thousands, from the 1940s into the 1960s.[65] American couples acquired illegitimate Irish children almost for the asking, earning Ireland a reputation, particularly among American servicemen stationed in England, as a "happy hunting ground" for healthy white babies.[66] In some cases American couples called on institutions in person to inquire about adopting a child; other hopeful adoptive parents wrote to convents or adoption societies such as St Patrick's Guild requesting that a child be sent to them.[67] In virtually all cases children were sent with a minimum of paperwork and very little fuss. Preliminary transactions often occurred through the mail, the adopted child was accompanied to America by a paid attendant, and no one in a position of responsibility ever met the adopting family or inspected their home and qualifications, and the adoptive parents did not meet the child until he or she actually arrived in their home. Adoption societies were so eager to secure adoptive families for the children in their charge that, at least until 1950, they required little or no information about an adopting couple's background, home life, or financial position. All they required was an affidavit in which the adopting parents undertook to raise the adopted child as a Catholic (although ironically the couple did not have to prove that *they* were practicing Catholics). These overseas adoptions carried on, in virtual silence and secrecy, from the early 1940s until 1950, when two high-profile incidents shattered official complacency on the matter. These incidents marked a turning point in Ireland's adoption policy: the first set of circumstances prompted Archbishop McQuaid to shut down overseas adoptions temporarily until guidelines could be put into place to regulate them, while the second forced the government's hand in introducing adoption legislation.

In March 1950 the *New York Times* published a story about six Irish children departing from Shannon Airport for adoption by American couples. The story explained that the children had come from St Patrick's Home in Dublin and were accompanied by Miss Nora O'Sullivan, a nurse from the institution.[68] This press attention, coming on the heels of earlier news accounts of wealthy American businessmen flying to Ireland specifically to adopt Irish babies, prompted Archbishop McQuaid to demand that philanthropic agencies suspend overseas adoptions until his staff could fully consider the issue.[69] He also instructed his leading advisor, Cecil Barrett, to initiate a ban on publicity at Shannon Airport.[70] At the same time Department of Health officials, who previously had played only a marginal role in the overseas adoption process, began to raise questions about the "character, suitability and religion" of potential adopters who were able to remove children from the state without undergoing a vetting or screening process, and seemingly without following U.S. immigration laws. Yet, it was not these practices in themselves, but the international press that the adoptions attracted, that caused concern and embarrassment among church and government officials. It is a testament to McQuaid's power and influence that the publicity blackout remained unchallenged domestically for almost two years.

The second incident, which forced the government into action on the adoption issue, involved the Hollywood film star Jane Russell, who traveled to Ireland in late 1951 with the intention of adopting a child:

> I hoped I would be able to find a boy in Europe, but it seems to be impossible ... the British law will not allow me to take a child from England. In Italy I could not get a child because I am under 40; and, anyway, there were difficulties

because Italy is a Catholic country and I am a Protestant. Now I have been advised to try Ireland; but I am worried in case the same difficulties would arise there. My husband is Irish, and he would very much like to adopt an Irish baby. If it is possible, I would like to fly to Dublin this week to pick out a child and make all the arrangements for bringing him to America.[71]

A member of the Church of Ireland Moral Welfare Organisation advised Russell that she would be unable to adopt a child from a Protestant institution or agency without the requisite home studies and background investigations, so Russell set her sights on a young Irish boy who resided with his parents in England. The chain of events that led Russell from Ireland to England is sketchy at best, but somehow Russell convinced an Irish couple, the Kavanaghs, to allow her to adopt their son Tommy, and within hours the Irish legation in London issued a passport in Tommy Kavanagh's name.

The British press gave considerable coverage to the incident, which in turn fueled a flurry of reports in other international newspapers about Ireland's adoption policy.[72] Irish legation staff in London insisted that they had acted correctly as, in spite of the press that had already surrounded the case, Russell swore that she was taking Kavanagh to the United States for "a holiday," and Kavanagh's own father had applied for the passport. The Department of Foreign Affairs responded by issuing the following memo to all Irish legations and consulates abroad:

As from the receipt of this minute, we would be glad if you would refer to the Department any application for a passport made to you by or on behalf of a person of either sex under the age of 18 years … You may have noticed in the Irish papers of the beginning of last week a reference to a case in which the Embassy at London granted a passport to an infant, on the application by the father, and that the child was subsequently brought to the United States by an American film actress. The whole business received a great amount of undesirable publicity in the Press (particularly the English Sunday papers of the 11th inst.) and the reason for this instruction is that we wish to ensure that an Irish passport will not again be issued in such circumstances.[73]

Although Russell's adoption of Tommy Kavanagh violated both British law and Irish regulations, and shortly after returning to the United States Russell admitted that she was considering returning Kavanagh to his parents because she really wanted a girl, it was the ridicule to which Ireland was subjected in the foreign press, and not the violations of law or concern for Tommy Kavanagh's welfare, that precipitated official action on the matter.

When Archbishop McQuaid undertook to regulate the overseas adoption scheme, following the *New York Times* story, religion was the defining issue, as it would be in the debates about the 1952 Adoption Bill. These regulations required that prospective adopters produce a number of documents including a sworn affidavit of their religious devotion and their willingness to raise and educate adopted children in the Catholic faith; a recommendation from the diocesan director of Catholic Charities branches in the United States; financial statements; and "medical certificates for both adopters, stating ages, and that they are not deliberately shirking natural parenthood."[74] Prospective adopters also were supposed to undergo a home study conducted by Catholic Charities, an American Catholic organization with branches throughout the country. However, a leading official of Catholic Charities admitted to DFA officials in 1955 not only that many of the home studies relied more on the word of the prospective adopters themselves, and references from family and friends, than on the assessment of qualified social workers, but also that "the Catholic Charities Organisation was not in fact equipped at all its Branches to deal satisfactorily with adoptions."[75] In other words, while the home study theoretically was the centerpiece of Archbishop McQuaid's regulations, in fact it did little to ensure that adopting couples were suitable in every way to adopt Irish children, and paper religious guarantees remained the sole factor upon which decisions were made regarding the issue of passports for the purpose of adoption.

The state's reluctance to play an active role in the regulation of overseas adoptions persisted following the implementation of McQuaid's regulations. The DFA issued a standard response to all requests for information on overseas adoption: "This department has no function in connection with the adoption, outside the State, of Irish children beyond the issue of a Passport to enable the child to travel."[76] This reluctance stemmed in part from a desire not to infringe on the church's authority in matters of faith and morals, as revealed in this exchange between the Department of Foreign Affairs and the Department of Justice, in which Justice declined to facilitate a background check on a potential adoptive family on the grounds that the hierarchy might object: "A more substantial ground of refusal was, however, that we might lay ourselves open to accusation from high places that we were facilitating the adoption of a child by a person not of the religion in which the child was being reared or not of the religion of one or other of the parents. Very delicate questions might arise and it was felt that Departments of State should keep clear."[77]

DFA officials were well aware that the government had, in the late 1940s, established the Committee on Emigration and Other Population Problems to examine Ireland's population crisis and recommend solutions, and they would have been placed in an awkward position if their activities in the area of adoption had come to light at such a critical time. This was particularly true given that the percentage of the population in the 0–14 years age group fell consistently from 1901, and began to level off only in 1951.[78] The policies set forth by Archbishop McQuaid, and fastidiously upheld by relevant government departments, highlight the extent to which the hierarchy, and especially Archbishop McQuaid, manipulated government agencies in determining the fate of illegitimate children. Some Irish children were placed with American families that, on paper, appeared to be "good Catholics," but were found wanting in other ways. Meanwhile, others remained in institutions because potential adopters who might have made excellent parents could not meet Archbishop McQuaid's religious test.[79]

While it would be easy to fault agencies and individuals of church and state for the callousness with which illegitimate children were treated, one could argue that official attitudes merely reflected a more general hostility within society toward illegitimate children and their mothers. Illegitimate children were institutionalized, or sent overseas for adoption, precisely because their mothers could not or would not keep them, and because their extended families and communities refused to acknowledge or accept them. There was an absence of public opinion in Ireland surrounding the care and protection of children that made it easy for church and state to conspire in sending illegitimate children overseas in virtual secrecy. This secrecy and silence are in part an indication of the success of Archbishop McQuaid's press blackout, but it also epitomized the prevailing attitude toward children, and particularly illegitimate children. It would seem that no one cared enough about the plight of illegitimate children to question or object to the practice of sending children overseas, or to demand that the state accept responsibility for providing for children at home in ways that served children's best interests rather than political or religious agendas.

Church, state, and adoption legislation

By lawmakers' own admission, Ireland lagged woefully behind their western counterparts when they introduced adoption legislation in 1952.[80] And yet, when lawmakers finally did act on the issue they did so not because they acknowledged the utility of legislation but because they were, literally, shamed into it by foreign press coverage of Ireland's informal and unregulated adoption practice. Not only did the Jane Russell incident prompt a flurry of negative reports in the foreign media, it also raised a host of questions in the Dáil, where individual TDs demanded an account from government ministers on the practice and extent of overseas adoption.[81] Once the "secret" was out public opinion began to coalesce around the issue, leaving lawmakers with no choice but to act.

Given the general lack of concern on the part of both church and state for the fate of illegitimate children adopted overseas, perhaps it is not surprising that there was no sense of urgency to initiate legislation that would legalize adoption at home and either regulate or ban the overseas process. Government officials argued, until the Jane Russell incident put the issue on the national agenda, that adoption legislation was unnecessary because there was no public demand, and no apparent need, for it:

> No pressing need for legislation on this subject has been felt in Ireland until relatively recently. In recent years there has been demand for enactment of legislation enabling the adoption of children. This has arisen, partly as a result of the activities of certain aliens who wish to adopt Irish children and held out the inducement of large sums of money to induce Irish parents to allow their children to be taken out of the country. To deal with this situation the government have recently decided to introduce a Bill to legalise adoption in the case of illegitimate and orphan children.[82]

At the same time, lawmakers conceded that by the time the issue was discussed in the Dáil many county councils, trade unions, and other interested parties (including Department of Health inspectors of boarded-out children) had been agitating for adoption legislation for nearly a decade.[83] The Legal Adoption Society of Ireland, founded in 1948, was established for the sole purpose of lobbying for legislation that would allow for the transfer of parental rights from biological to adoptive parents.[84] And as early as 1944 the Joint Committee of Women's Societies and Society Workers had begun exploring the possibilities for legal adoption, and pressuring the government to enact adoption legislation.[85]

As early as 1939 a question was raised in the Dáil about the introduction of adoption legislation primarily, it seems, on the basis of representations from Department of Health inspectors who could attest, from first-hand experience, to the potential benefits of adoption legislation. However, the Catholic Protection and Rescue Society and other Catholic agencies made representations of their own pointing out the "undesirable results" that could stem from adoption legislation.[86] In 1946 civil servants in the Department of Justice engaged in discussions with members of the hierarchy and with leading theologians from St Patrick's College, Maynooth, on the possibility of introducing adoption legislation that was not contrary to Catholic teaching. At this time proposals were put forward that would ensure that adoptive parents shared the religious persuasion of the child they proposed to adopt. In other words, by 1946 not only was the government fully aware of the need for adoption legislation, but Department of Justice officials had already formulated the religious safeguards that were central to the 1952 Adoption Act.[87]

In private, government officials admitted the real reason that adoption legislation was not forthcoming before 1952: an unwillingness to enact legislation that might infringe on the church's authority, and the difficulty of convincing Archbishop McQuaid that the proposals put forward as early as 1939 would effectively protect Catholic children from being adopted by non-Catholic families.[88] In an address to the King's Inn Law Students' Debating Society in 1951, Attorney General C.F. Casey voiced the government's dilemma:

> The subject ... had received much publicity in recent years and efforts had been made to prevail upon the Government to introduce legislation dealing with it, and severe criticism on this has been leveled against the Government for its failure to introduce a Bill. I would ask those who are concerned on this topic to be patient and to avoid emotion ... This country is a predominantly Catholic country. That does not mean that Parliament should penalise any other creed, but it does mean this, that Parliament cannot surely be asked to introduce legislation contrary to the teaching of that great Church.[89]

Casey's statement implicitly acknowledged that there was sufficient public opinion to warrant a fuller discussion of adoption than had yet occurred, but also that, short of an absolute disaster (such as the Jane Russell fiasco), the government would take its cues on the matter from the hierarchy. In delaying the introduction of adoption legislation until they were forced into it, lawmakers placed church–state relations above the well-being and best interests of thousands of illegitimate Irish children who would have benefited enormously from having stable, loving adoptive homes.

Adoption became a hot political issue in 1952 not because of a new-found sense of responsibility on the part of the state for the well-being of unwanted children, or a sudden realization of the need for adoption legislation. Rather, a series of embarrassing and highly critical reports in the foreign press about Ireland's overseas adoption practices, brought to light by the Jane Russell incident, forced church and state to compromise in order to avoid further embarrassment. While McQuaid's blackout on publicity at home proved to be extraordinarily effective, not even McQuaid could control the foreign press's treatment of Ireland's overseas adoption practice. The most damning and worrying article appeared in 1951 in the German *8 Uhr Blatt* newspaper, in response to English press coverage of the Russell case.[90] The article struck a nerve with both the hierarchy and government departments because it raised the specter of a black-market baby ring that allegedly sold "unwanted" Irish children to the highest American bidder, the irony being that while Irish agencies were willing to do almost anything to rid themselves of the moral and financial burden of caring for illegitimate children, American couples were willing to pay dearly for the privilege of adopting healthy, white Irish babies even if they were illegitimate.

According to a Department of Foreign Affairs translation of the *8 Uhr Blatt* article, an Irish welfare worker in England accused the Irish government of turning a blind eye to the export and sale of Irish children: "'Our country has today become a sort of hunting ground for foreign millionaires who believe they can acquire children to suit their whims just in the same way as they would get valuable pedigree animals. In the last few months more than one hundred children have left Ireland, without any official organisation being in a position to make any enquiries as to their future habitat.'"[91] Department of Foreign Affairs officials were hard-pressed to refute the article's allegations and simply wondered at the source of the author's information. Irish legation staff in Bonn wanted to demand a retraction from *8 Uhr Blatt* editors but DFA staff advised against this: "I have to say it is our considered opinion that no such action should be taken – more especially so since, with the exception of the figures given, the article is largely not incorrect."[92] It is indicative of the ambiguous legal and ethical position in which overseas adoptions placed the government, as well as the illegitimate children involved, that government ministers and civil servants were unable to defend themselves against *8 Uhr Blatt's* allegations.

Negative press coverage forced the government to take action on the issue of adoption but, true to form, government officials took their cue from the hierarchy. The first reference in official sources to government ministers actively discussing an adoption bill appeared in Department of Foreign Affairs files in May 1952. However, earlier that year, in January 1952, the hierarchy's Episcopal Committee issued a statement that laid out the position from the Catholic point of view, and this position paper served as the basis for subsequent adoption legislation.[93] The hierarchy acknowledged the state's right to provide for children, and in particular to ensure that "unwanted" children were given good homes, but not at the expense of their Catholic faith and birthright. On the other hand, children's officers and social workers argued that adoption legislation should serve the best interests of vulnerable children and would merely regularize relationships already in existence, albeit without the protection of law. In the end, the state deferred to the hierarchy rather than the "experts" in formulating adoption policy. The fact that lawmakers were willing to defer to the archbishop on such matters, and to place religious obligations above their own civic responsibility to one group of Irish citizens – illegitimate children – lends credence to the view, held among some critics in the 1950s, that Ireland was a confessional state with Archbishop McQuaid the equivalent of an "ecclesiastical Taoiseach."[94]

Lawmakers' singular obsession with religious as opposed to more worldly (and, one could argue, pragmatic) concerns is further underscored by a comparison of the debates on adoption that occurred in the British Parliament in 1925–26, and the Dáil in 1952. The primary distinctions centered on differing perceptions of the state's responsibility for children who lacked the protection and care of "natural" or "normal" families, how far the state could and should go in protecting the rights of the natural mother, and the role of a religious test in assessing the fitness of prospective adopters. Unlike their Irish counterparts, British MPs highlighted the benefits that would accrue to the state as a result of legalized adoption:

> I feel – and I believe my views are shared very largely by all Members of the House – that the English character has been built up on home life. God knows, some of the homes are not worthy of the name; but nevertheless, there is a spirit even in the meanest tenement that has developed the British character, which has made the British nation what it is. I find, too, that institution life tends very largely to a return to institution life, either in the form of prison, workhouse, or homes of that description. It saps the independence of character. It tends to make men, at any rate, with less moral fibre than we associate with the average Britisher. To a person who has been brought up in an institution – even a good institution – prison has not the same horror that it has to the average man or woman, and we complete the vicious circle very often, as magistrates well know, with people who have been brought up to appreciate institution life. Therefore, I welcome the Bill, because I think it will assist us to enable orphan children to be brought back into the normal life of the nation, and to become normal citizens.[95]

The practical benefits that would result from adoption legislation were all but ignored by Irish lawmakers.

Virtually all British MPs who spoke in support of the Adoption Bill insisted that an adoptive family was a far better environment for a needy and vulnerable child than even the best institution, and they acknowledged that wealth and religion alone did not determine a family's ability to love and care for an adopted child. Under British law, a couple wishing to adopt had to file a petition with the courts and submit to a thorough home and background study. Only people resident in England and Wales were eligible to adopt, and only children who were similarly resident could be adopted. As one MP pointed out, the state retained responsibility for adopted children's well-being even after the court issued an adoption order; allowing people to remove children from the state would also remove those children from the protection and jurisdiction of the British court system.[96] This is in stark contrast to the Irish overseas adoption practice, where government departments and charitable agencies disclaimed all responsibility for children once they left the state. In a further effort to protect children from unsuitable foster parents, British law authorized courts to issue interim adoption orders for a two-year period of assessment and supervision.

Although British legislation was concerned primarily with safeguarding the physical and emotional well-being of illegitimate children, British lawmakers also acknowledged the hardships and pressures faced by biological mothers who gave their children up for adoption. The law prohibited the making of an adoption order without the mother's consent, and it required magistrates to "be fully satisfied that the parties understand the nature and effect of the proposed transaction and are acting of their own free will," in other words to ensure that women giving children up for adoption were not pressured into doing so, and understood the irrevocable termination of parental rights that adoption entailed.[97] British legislation implicitly recognized that, just as some women might in desperation seek unsuitable alternatives for dealing with an unwanted child, so too many women were pressured into giving their children up for adoption, either by religious institutions who thought they knew best, or by desperate couples willing to pay hefty fees for the privilege of adopting a healthy white child. The question of maternal rights, as well as the best interests of the child, were consistently ignored in the Irish debates.

The most conspicuous distinction between the British and Irish debates was the role of religion in matching children with adoptive families. British legislation acknowledged the importance of religious faith but also insisted that religion was not the most important criteria for determining the suitability of adoptive parents:

> In these matters we have, first of all, to consider the welfare of the infants. I am not for a moment suggesting that the question of religious belief is not a most important thing, but it is not the only thing, and if we put in the Clause words which make it peremptory that the only person who can adopt a child must be of the same religious faith we may be doing something which in certain cases may be against the interests of the child. Of course, due regard will always be paid to this matter, but I ask the House to leave it to the discretion of the tribunal which will have all the facts before it, and which will see that full consideration is given to the paramount welfare of the infant.[98]

The child-centered tone of the British debates contrasts sharply with the obsessive concern among Irish lawmakers with questions of religion and faith, at the expense of the rights and interests of children and their biological parents.

The differences between British and Irish lawmakers' approach to the adoption issue reflect an investment, on the part of Irish lawmakers, in a particular concept of family life as the foundation of social life and stability. This is not to suggest that British lawmakers discounted the importance of the family, or that vulnerable British children necessarily fared better than their Irish counterparts, but rather that the British conceptualization of "family" was broad enough to include families consisting of two parents and adopted and biological children, and also families comprised of un-married women or men and adopted children. Although Irish lawmakers were willing to solve the problem of illegitimacy by establishing "non-tra-ditional" families, neither lawmakers nor members of the hierarchy antici-pated displacing the traditional, nuclear family as the foundation of Irish social life and in fact were adamant that adoption legislation not "sub-stitute an artificial for a natural family."[99] The language of the Episcopal Committee's statement regarding the place of the family in Irish society was inserted virtually verbatim into Minister for Justice Boland's opening statement on the Adoption Bill:

> The Constitution recognises the family as the natural primary and fundamen-tal unit group of society, and as a moral institution possessing inalienable and imprescriptible rights, antecedent and superior to all positive law. The purpose of this Bill is not to allow the relationship of adoption to be substituted for the family, but to enable children who do not belong to a family, to secure through adoption the benefits of the family.[100]

Because officials were concerned that adoption not supplant or alter "natural" or "appropriate" models of family organization, unmarried people were prohibited from adopting except where an unmarried woman petitioned to adopt a child who was related to her by blood (the same did not apply to unmarried men wishing to adopt blood relatives).

The adoption of legitimate children also presented a challenge in the context of the government's conceptualization of "normal" or appropriate family composition. In his speech presenting the Adoption Bill to the Dáil, Minister for Justice Boland stressed that the government could only legal-ize the adoption of illegitimate children:

> I am advised … that there is a danger that the Bill would be held to be uncon-stitutional if it provided for the adoption of legitimate children whose parents are alive. The Constitution declares the rights and duties of parents towards their children to be inalienable, and any provision for the permanent transfer of those rights and duties, even with the consent of the parents, might be uncon-stitutional. The main need for adoption arises in connection with orphans and illegitimate children.[101]

Here is a clear statement that constitutional rights were not seen to apply to unmarried mothers or their children. Even under the informal, pre–1952 adoptions, DFA officials were quite willing to issue passports to allow il-legitimate children to travel overseas for adoption, so long as Archbishop McQuaid approved, but they consistently refused passports to legitimate, even orphaned, children.

Their refusal was linked to their understanding of parental and family rights enshrined in the 1937 Constitution, as outlined in a 1954 internal DFA memo relating to the adoption of a legitimate child:

> In my view it would not be proper for us to issue such a Passport [to a legitimate child of parents still living] notwithstanding that on the face of it the child's material interests might well be best served by facilitating her adoption. It is relevant to remark in this connection that our own adoption law does not envisage the adoption of legitimate children under any circumstances. This no doubt is based on the principle of the State maintaining so far as is in its power the unity of the family, which is enshrined in the Constitution ... In the light of the above my view is that ... having regard to the terms of Articles 41 and 42 of the Constitution, it would not be open to the parents of this child to execute a valid surrender of the child to a third party, and that consequently the Department could not consider the issue of a Passport in a case such as this.[102]

Yet not all civil servants agreed with this interpretation:

> the Constitution insists upon the natural and imprescriptible rights of the family and refers throughout to the parents, that is to say, both to the mother and the father. It is clear therefore that the Constitution so far from imposing a restriction on the family, recognises that it is entirely free to carry out its own moral obligations which are anterior to positive law. For this reason, if a parent wishes to allow his child to be adopted in America, there is nothing in the Constitution to prohibit it.[103]

The seeming conflict in these two interpretations was one of form more than substance. There was no question that "legitimate" parents possessed fundamental, "inalienable" rights. What was at issue was how best to protect those rights; the question at the center of the debate was whether the state had the right to override a parent's decision to give his or her legitimate children up for adoption. And yet, the fact that illegitimate children were sent out of the state with no official oversight or regulation, and sometimes without the consent of their mothers, suggests that the constitution would be used to protect the rights only of those who conformed to the state's image of a "normal" family. Adoption legislation represented an implicit acknowledgment on the part of lawmakers that those who fell outside the pale were not entitled to full participation, as citizens, in the life of the state, or to full constitutional rights and protections as parents. Indeed, the irony in this debate was that while legitimate children could not be adopted, in Ireland or abroad, even with their parents' consent, an unmarried mother's consent was not required to send an illegitimate child overseas for adoption.

Although the Adoption Act was intended to remedy the defects of the informal overseas adoption, it did not stop the outward flow of children and, in fact, the safeguards established to regulate the adoption of children at home did not apply to overseas adoptions. The debate on this question is revealing and indicative of the fundamental lack of concern on the part of church and state for the fate of illegitimate children. Some TDs insisted that the Act *would* prevent children from being sent to America for adoption:

> We could see these children being taken out, being placed in an aeroplane and going right across to the United States of America to be adopted by parents of whom we had no knowledge except the amount of money they might have for that purpose. There were no precautions in regard to that adoption and nothing could be done about it. The children could be adopted, flown across the Atlantic to America and kept there where they would be under no control of our Minister or of our courts. Under this Bill, they will be under the control of the Minister and of the board set up under this Bill when it becomes an Act, and under the control of this House, if needs be. Deputy Rooney: Does the Deputy mean that the practice will be stopped? Deputy Cowan: Yes, the Bill prohibits it. Deputy Boland: It makes it illegal. Deputy Lynch: It proposes imprisonment if it is contravened.[104]

In fact, the Act did not halt the exodus of children or enact measures to protect the civil and legal rights of children who were removed from the state, and it certainly did not provide for the imprisonment of people who removed children from the state for the purpose of adoption. The only change in the overseas adoption practice was the introduction of a minimum age for removing a child from the state. This measure was aimed not at protecting the child but at preventing proselytism, as it was based on the assumption that desperate mothers would willingly hand newborn infants over to any individual or organization, including Protestant ones, that offered assistance. Imposing an age restriction theoretically reduced the element of desperation that the Catholic hierarchy assumed fueled the proselytizing "menace," and attempted to ensure that children sent out of the state for adoption would not lose their Catholic birthright.

Not only did overseas adoptions not cease, but DFA officials acknowledged that there was no legal basis for them to deny passports for children to travel abroad, so long as the children and adopting parents met Archbishop McQuaid's 1950 regulations:

> I think it essential that I should make it clear that we could see nothing in Section 39 to justify us using the passport machinery to exercise an administrative restraint on the travel abroad, for adoption or other purposes, of children in the exempted categories outlined in subsections (2) and (3) of that Section. Quite the contrary. In fact, we must, it seems to us, regard Section 39 of this bill, even at the present, as a precise statement of Government policy in the matter of what categories of children are to be permitted to go abroad or be restrained from so doing and we must be guided by that in the issue of passports. This being so we have, for instance, decided against the issue of future passports to illegitimate children under one year to travel abroad for adoption purposes.

> Similarly, we must interpret the Government policy reflected in sub-sections (2) and (3) of Section 39 as specifically inhibiting us from exercising an administrative restraint on the travel abroad of the exempted categories of children whose right so to travel the two sub-sections in question so clearly preserve.[105]

Even as DFA officials insisted that they could not impose limits on granting passports to children to be adopted overseas, they continued to insist that they were opposed in principle to such adoptions: "while refusing to give encouragement in a positive way, we did not mean to suggest that you should refuse passports where a child's guardians want to send him out of the country and there is no legal impediment to that."[106] DFA officials were in a difficult position: on the one hand, they had no choice but to adhere to both adoption legislation and constitutional law when determining whether to issue passports; on the other hand, precisely because their role was to issue the required travel documents, they were vulnerable to the charge that they were facilitating emigration. This dilemma plagued the DFA from the time overseas adoptions began in the 1940s, and the adoption bill did nothing to resolve it.

Conclusion

Most of the provisions for children made by the state derived from legislation that was not exclusively directed at children. Two pieces of legislation from the mid-twentieth century, the Criminal Law (Amendment) Act and the Adoption Act, on the other hand, were explicitly intended to protect children in specific circumstances. The debates that occurred around these issues reveal both the ways that church and state conceived of their responsibilities to vulnerable children, and the limits of that responsibility when it interfered with other political expediencies. In the case of the Criminal Law (Amendment) Act, Eoin O'Duffy, then Commissioner of An Garda Siochána, presented evidence that should have caused grave concern throughout Irish society about the vulnerability of young girls to sexual assaults. And, in fact, this evidence and the evidence presented by others to the Carrigan Committee *did* cause grave concern within the inner circles of church and state.

However, it was not concern for the safety and well-being of vulnerable children but, rather, concern for the damage to Ireland's reputation, at home and abroad, that might have derived from publicizing such evidence of Ireland's moral "crisis." An equally worrying issue for male lawmakers was the fear that amending the law in relation to the age of consent might hold men more accountable for their sexual behavior or, worse, leave them open to blackmail or false accusations from predatory teenage girls. Such concerns had no evidentiary foundation, but they do reflect the priorities among the predominantly male political establishment, priorities that often put their own agendas and best interests above those of vulnerable and victimized children.

Similarly, the evolution of Ireland's adoption process up to 1952 reveals the yawning schism between the republican ideal to "cherish all the children of the nation equally," and the way the state dealt with children who for whatever reason could not be cared for and protected by their own biological parents. The practice in the 1940s, 1950s and early 1960s of allowing illegitimate children to be removed from the state for the purposes of adoption, when considered in light of the pressures that finally compelled the state to act on the issue in 1951–52, suggest that lawmakers and the hierarchy were more concerned, at least into the 1960s, with the preservation of Ireland's self-image and reputation abroad, and with the preservation of the faith of illegitimate children, than with the needs and best interests of those children. The overseas adoption practice finally died out in the early 1970s, not because of negative public opinion or a sudden awareness that the practice was wrong or potentially harmful, but rather because there was, by the early 1970s, a growing acceptance (or at least tolerance) of unmarried motherhood; this, coupled with the introduction in 1972 of the Lone Parent's Allowance, effectively dried up the "supply" of healthy children being offered for adoption. In 1970 the governmentally-established Kennedy Commission published a scathing indictment of Ireland's industrial school system, and for the first time in Irish history the plight, needs, and best interests of illegitimate and vulnerable children were considered in their own right and not as part of broader social and political agendas.

Notes

1 The Adoption Act was significant in this regard because lawmakers refused to act on the issue, in spite of the fact that social workers had been highlighting the need for adoption for more than fifteen years, because the Catholic hierarchy was opposed to it.

2 Mark Finnane, "The Carrigan committee of 1930–31 and the 'moral condition of the Saorstát'," *Irish Historical Studies*, 32:128 (November 2001), pp. 519–36; James M. Smith, "The politics of sexual knowledge: The origins of Ireland's containment culture and the Carrigan report (1931)," *Journal of the History of Sexuality*, 13:2 (April 2004), pp. 208–33; Finola Kennedy, "The suppression of the Carrigan report: a historical perspective on child abuse," *Studies*, 89:356 (Winter 2000), pp. 354–62.

3 Law Reform Commission, *Consultation paper on child sexual abuse* (Dublin: Law Reform Commission, 1989); Iseult O'Doherty, *Stolen childhoods: Testimonies of*

the survivors of child sexual abuse (Dublin: Poolbeg Press, 1998); Barry Coldrey, *A Christian apocalypse: The sexual abuse crisis in the Catholic Church 1984–2004* (Melbourne: Tamanaraik, 2004); Chris Moore, *Betrayal of trust: The Father Brendan Smyth affair and the Catholic Church* (Dublin: Marino Books, 1995); *The Ferns report* (Dublin: Government Stationery Office, 2005); Olive Travers and Sylvia Thompson, *Behind the silhouettes: Exploring the myths of child sexual abuse* (Belfast: Blackstaff Press, 1999); Hannah McGee, *The SAVI report: Sexual abuse and violence in Ireland* (Dublin: Liffey Press, 2002); *Report on the inquiry into the operation of Madonna House* (Dublin: Government Stationery Office, 1996). I use the word "alleged" here because although allegations have been made on a number of fronts, they have not been proven in a court of law.

4 The issue of age of consent is not as straightforward as it first appears. The Criminal Law (Amendment) Act of 1885 made it an offense to have sexual relations with a girl under the age of 14 years; sexual relations with a girl between the ages of 15 and 16 became a misdemeanor. Irish lawmakers appear to have interpreted this legislation as setting the age of consent at thirteen. But when the Criminal Law (Amendment) Bill was passed in 1935, it mirrored almost exactly the language of the 1885 Criminal Law (Amendment) Act, except that it raised the upper age limit to 17 years.

5 NAI, Department of Justice H247/41A, Eoin'O'Duffy memorandum on the Criminal Law Amendment Act, 30 October 1930.

6 Judith Walkowitz, *City of dreadful delight: Narratives of sexual danger in late Victorian London* (Chicago: University of Chicago Press, 1992), p. 81.

7 For an excellent and thorough discussion of the Stead case see Walkowitz, *City of dreadful delight.*

8 *Dáil Éireann*, vol. 11 (28 April 1925), col. 369.

9 *Dáil Éireann*, vol. 18 (25 January 1927), col. 9.

10 *Dáil Éireann*, vol. 21 (17 November 1927), col. 1506.

11 *Dáil Éireann*, vol. 34 (27 March 1930), cols 259–63.

12 *Dáil Éireann*, vol. 34 (27 March 1930), col. 265.

13 NAI, Department of Justice 247/41A, O'Duffy Memorandum, 30 October 1930.

14 NAI, Department of Justice 247/41A, O'Duffy Memorandum, 30 October 1930.

15 Similar concerns were expressed during Dáil debates on the Affiliations Orders (Illegitimate Children) Act of 1929. See *Dáil Éireann*, vol. 32 (30 October 1930), cols 521–3.

16 *Dáil Éireann*, vol. 34 (27 March 1930), col. 262.

17 *Dáil Éireann*, vol. 34 (27 March 1930), col. 263.

18 Until 1929 Carrigan was a senior prosecutor in the Central Criminal Court and likely had extensive experience prosecuting sexual assault cases.

19 NAI, Department of Justice 90/4/3, Constitution of the Criminal Law Amendment Committee.

20 NAI, Department of Justice 90/4/3, Criminal Law Amendment Committee (CLAC) Minutes, 20 June 1930.

21 See, for example, NAI, Department of Justice 90/4/3, CLAC Minutes, 26 June 1930; 27 June 1930; 17 October 1930.

22 NAI, Department of Justice 90/4/3, CLAC Minutes, 26 June 1930.

23 NAI, Department of Justice 90/4/3, CLAC Minutes, 26 June 1930. See also 27

June 1930; 18 July 1930; 17 October 1930; 23 October 1930; 20 November 1930.

24 An exhaustive examination of Central Criminal, circuit, and district court records shows that prosecutions for sexual assaults were far more common than prosecutions for prostitution; indeed prostitution cases rarely came before the courts.

25 NAI, Department of Justice 90/4/3, CLAC Minutes, 18 July 1930. See also 1 July 1930; 17 October 1930; 20 November 1930.

26 Many of the prosecutions for sexual assault that involved victims over the age of 15 or 16 years were, in fact, cases of consensual sex where the girl ended up pregnant. In some cases prosecutions were brought against three or more men because the girl did not know who the father of her child was. See, for example, NAI, Clare Circuit Court 1D 14 106, 13 June 1935 in which there were three defendants, all of whom could have been the father of the "victim's" child; Cork Circuit Court 1D 65 40, 14 June 1930, involving five defendants; and Wicklow Circuit Court 1D 19 113, 9 February 1942 involving five defendants. It also was not unusual for women in infanticide cases to name two or more men as the possible fathers of their children.

27 NAI, Department of Justice 90/4/3, CLAC Minutes, 30 October 1930.

28 NAI, Department of Justice 247/41A, O'Duffy Memorandum, 30 October 1930.

29 This is based on an examination of all circuit court records available in the National Archives of Ireland. However, this does not represent *all* of the cases heard in the circuit courts during this period, because the NAI records are not complete for all counties.

30 NAI, Department of Justice 90/4/3, CLAC Minutes, 30 October 1930.

31 NAI, Department of Justice H247/41A, O'Duffy Memorandum, 30 October 1930.

32 This is based on an examination of all *available* circuit court records. The number of cases prosecuted probably was much higher than the 1,500 alluded to here, and therefore the figure of 10,000 is also likely an underestimate rather than an overestimate.

33 This is based on an examination of all circuit court records available in the National Archives of Ireland.

34 NAI, Department of Justice 247/41A, O'Duffy memorandum, 30 October 1930.

35 NAI, Department of Justice 90/4/3, CLAC Minutes, 6 November 1930.

36 O'Duffy's strategy of attempting to eliminate situations in which sexual offences or sexual immorality *might* take place was also evident in official suggestions for dealing with what was regarded as an alarming deterioration of moral standards in the 1930s. Most observers recommended restricting dance halls, giving gardaí greater powers to monitor "courting couples" in motor cars, and patrolling streets and alleys where couples might have an opportunity of an assignation.

37 NAI, Department of Justice H247/41A, O'Duffy memorandum, 30 October 1930.

38 NAI, Department of Justice H247/41A, O'Duffy memorandum, 30 October 1930.

39 NAI, Department of Justice H24741/A, O'Duffy memorandum, 30 October 1930.

40 NAI, Department of Justice 90/4/3, Department of Justice memorandum, 27

October 1932.

41 NAI, Department of Justice 90/4/3, CLAC Minutes, 18 December 1930.

42 NAI, Department of Justice 90/4/3, CLAC Minutes, 18 December 1930.

43 NAI, Department of Justice 90/4/3, CLAC Minutes, 5 February 1931.

44 NAI, Department of Justice 90/4/3, Department of Justice memorandum, 27 October 1932.

45 Several ministers for justice were involved in the events surrounding the Carrigan Committee and passage of the Criminal Law (Amendment) Act. James Fitzgerald-Kenney was Minister for Justice when the Carrigan Committee was established in 1929 and when its report was issued in 1931. James Geoghegan became Minister for Justice in March 1932 and served for just under a year during the time the government was contemplating what to do with the Carrigan report. And P.J. Ruttledge became Minister for Justice in February 1933 and saw the Criminal Law (Amendment) Act through to completion.

46 NAI, Department of Taoiseach S5998, *Report of the committee on the Criminal Law Amendment Acts (1880–1885)* (Dublin: Government Stationery Office, 1931).

47 NAI, Department of Justice 247/41B, letter from M.J. Browne to James Geoghegan, 13 November 1932.

48 NAI, Department of Justice 90/4/3, Department of Justice memorandum, 27 October 1932.

49 NAI, Department of Justice 90/4/3, Department of Justice memorandum, 27 October 1932.

50 NAI, Department of Justice 90/4/3, Department of Justice Memorandum, 27 October 1932.

51 Evidence was taken from at least two district justices, who likely had more experience than any high court justice with cases of sexual assault given that many cases were heard in district courts. Moreover, the chair of the Criminal Law (Amendment) Committee was himself a court justice.

52 NAI, Department of Justice 90/4/3, Department of Justice memorandum, 27 October 1932.

53 NAI, Department of Justice 247/41D, Internal memorandum to the Minister for Justice, 23 February 1933.

54 NAI, Department of Justice 247/41B, letter from M.J. Browne to James Geoghegan, 13 November 1932.

55 NAI, Department of Foreign Affairs 345/164, handwritten note from Mr Fay to Dr Nolan, 4 October 1944.

56 See Margaret Humphreys, *Empty cradles* (London: Corgi, 1997) and Gillian Wagner, *Children of the empire* (London: Weidenfeld and Nicolson, 1992).

57 According to Mike Milotte a total of 2,103 children were sent overseas throughout the duration of the overseas adoption process. See Mike Milotte, *Banished babies: The secret history of Ireland's baby export business* (Dublin: New Island Books, 1997), p. 201. These statistics exclude children sent overseas prior to 1951. They also excluded children whose adoptive parents took them out of the country without securing an Irish passport for them, or who were registered, illegally, as the biological children of the adoptive parents. Milotte culled these figures from various DFA files, which he does not cite, so it is impossible to confirm the accuracy of these figures.

58 NAI, Department of Foreign Affairs 345/164, handwritten note to Mr Commins,

14 October 1952.

59   DDA, American Adoption Policy Files 1950–52. "American adoptions," n.d.

60   Under this act visas could be issued to European orphans who were entering the country for the purpose of legal adoption. NAI, Department of Foreign Affairs 345/164, internal memorandum, 29 December 1950.

61   In 1955 it came to the attention of the Department of Foreign Affairs that at least 8 children were illegally registered as the biological children of American servicemen stationed in England. All of the adopted children were born in the same nursing home, and it seems that the midwife who ran the home arranged the adoptions and facilitated the illegal practice. NAI, Department of Foreign Affairs 345/96/545, Irish children alleged to be illegally registered as American citizens.

62   DDA, American Adoption Policy Files 1950–52, letter from Sister Elizabeth Farrelly, St Patrick's Guild to Father Mangan, Archbishop's Office, 10 May 1950. In expressing concerns for the safety of children whom this agency could not help, this nun was worried not that the children might become victims of infanticide but, rather, that the children would be handed over to Protestant agencies and thus become "victims" of proselytism.

63   See, for example, NAI, Department of Health A124/12, extract from Miss Litster's report on the inspection of boarded-out children, 15 July 1937.

64   *Report of An Bord Uchtala*: (Dublin: Government Stationery Office, 1953).

65   The practice may have begun earlier than the early 1940s; however, no one in authority seems to have been aware of it until the late 1940s, and statistics were only compiled from 1950.

66   NAI, Department of Foreign Affairs 345/96/I, internal memorandum, 29 December 1950.

67   Although adoption was not legalized until 1952, charitable agencies such as St Patrick's Guild and the Catholic Protection and Rescue Society arranged fostering arrangements and informal adoptions and thus they referred to themselves as adoption societies.

68   *New York Times* (18 March 1950), p. 30. It is possible that the St Patrick's Home referred to in the article was the local authority mother and baby home, St Patrick's, at Pelletstown, Co. Dublin. It might also refer to St Patrick's Guild, a Dublin adoption society.

69   NAI, Department of Foreign Affairs 345/164, internal memorandum, 12 July 1950; *New York Times* (29 July 1949), p. 23. The story published on this date told of businessman Rollie McDowell's decision to "surprise the wife" by bringing home two children from Ireland. The legal arrangements were conducted in Ireland without the knowledge or consent of Rollie's wife Thelma.

70   DDA, American Adoption Policy Files 1950–52, letter from Cecil Barrett, Archbishop's House, to Stuart Wilson, sales manager for Pan American Airlines, n.d.

71   *Irish Times* (30 October 1951), p. 5.

72   Department of Foreign Affairs Adoption Policy Files contain clippings of articles that appeared in England, Australia and Germany. See NAI, Department of Foreign Affairs 345/164.

73   NAI, Department of Foreign Affairs 345/96/I, letter to Irish consuls abroad from Horan, 20 November 1951.

74   DDA, American Adoption Policy Files 1950–52, requirements of His Grace, the

Archbishop of Dublin, for American adopters, n.d.

75 NAI, Department of Foreign Affairs 345/96/I, notes of meeting between Monsignor O'Grady, Catholic Charities, and Mr Morrissey, Miss Kenny, and Mr G. Woods, Department of Foreign Affairs, 16 January 1956.

76 NAI, Department of Foreign Affairs 345/164, letter from Department of Foreign Affairs to M.M. Halley, 11 July 1953.

77 NAI, Department of Foreign Affairs 345/96/II, letter from Department of Justice to Department of Foreign Affairs, 2 November 1950.

78 Commission on Emigration and Other Population Problems, *Report 1948–1954* (Dublin: Government Stationery Office, 1954), p. 17.

79 There are references throughout Department of Foreign Affairs files to the fact that Catholic agencies in America revealed the unsuitability of some homes. No one in the DFA appears to have taken the initiative to find out what the problems were, how many children were involved, how those children fared after they were adopted by the "unsuitable" families, or what happened to them when the American courts declined to make adoption orders.

80 *Dáil Debates*, vol. 132 (11 June 1952), col. 1119.

81 NAI, Department of Foreign Affairs 345/96/I, extract from Dáil Éireann report, 21 November 1951.

82 NAI, Department of Foreign Affairs, 345/96/I, letter from Fay, DFA to Irish Embassy in Washington, DC, 3 May 1952.

83 *Dáil Debates*, vol. 132 (11 June 1952), col. 1103.

84 W.A. Newman, "Legal adoption," *The Bell*, 16:4 (January 1951), p. 62.

85 NAI, JCWSSW 98/14/5/2, Joint Committee of Women's Societies and Social Workers (JCWSSW) Minutes, 26 October 1944. The JCWSSW discussed legal adoption with growing frequency at their monthly meetings from 1944 until adoption legislation was finally passed in 1952.

86 NAI, Department of Justice 93/39A, letter from Roche to Archbishop McQuaid, 12 January 1944. Presumably the "undesirable result" was the possibility that non-Catholic couples would adopt Catholic children.

87 NAI, Department of Justice 93/39B, letter from W.J. Conway, St Patrick's, Maynooth to Mr Roche, Department of Justice, 22 November 1946.

88 An internal Department of Justice memo dated 4 April 1933 indicated that although a case could be made for the introduction of adoption legislation, advisors to the Minister for Justice suggested that it would not be politically expedient to act on the issue. See NAI, Department of Justice 93/39A.

89 *Catholic Standard* (16 February 1951), p. 1.

90 NAI, Department of Foreign Affairs 345/164, translation of *8 Uhr Blatt* article.

91 NAI, Department of Foreign Affairs 345/164, translation of *8 Uhr Blatt* article.

92 NAI, Department of Foreign Affairs 345/164, letter from Horan to Irish Legation Bonn, 14 January 1952.

93 The Episcopal Committee, established by the hierarchy in 1951, was comprised of the bishops of Cashel, Derry, and Galway, along with Revd Cornelius Lucey (who in August 1952 became Bishop of Cork). The committee's remit was to advise the hierarchy on whatever matters might be referred to them; in late 1951 the Episcopal Committee was asked to consider the issue of adoption.

94 *John Charles McQuaid: What the papers say,* presented by John Bowman, Radio Telefís Éireann, RTÉ 1 Dublin. 1998. The term Taoiseach refers to the head of the Irish government, the equivalent of the British Prime Minister.

95 *Hansard House of Commons Debates*, 26 February 1926, cols 940–1.
96 *Hansard House of Commons Debates*, 18 June 1926, col. 2661.
97 *Child adoption committee first report*, British Parliamentary Papers vol. 9 (13 March 1925), p. 6.
98 *Hansard House of Commons Debates*, 18 June 1926, p. 2664.
99 NAI, Department of Foreign Affairs 354/164, Episcopal Committee statement on legal adoption, January 1952.
100 *Dáil Debates*, vol. 132 (11 June 1952), col. 1107.
101 *Dáil Debates*, vol. 132 (11 June 1952), col. 1106.
102 NAI, Department of Foreign Affairs 345/96/II, memorandum from Commins to Fay, July 1954.
103 NAI, Department of Foreign Affairs 345/96/II, memorandum from Commins to Fay, July 1954. As it happened the child in question was born in Northern Ireland and not an Irish citizen. The state therefore had no right to issue a passport for the child to travel outside of the country for adoption even with the parents' consent.
104 *Dáil Debates*, vol. 132 (11 June 1952), col. 1125.
105 NAI, Department of Foreign Affairs 345/164, letter from Commins to Berry, Department of Justice, 4 November 1952.
106 NAI, Department of Foreign Affairs 345/164, letter from Berry to Commins, 6 November 1952.

5

The abused child?

Introduction

As previous chapters have suggested, the life of the illegitimate child, or the poor child whose parents for whatever reas on could not or would not care for them according to middle-class standards, could be grim. Many children spent all or parts of their childhood in industrial schools, county homes, or exploitative and abusive foster homes either because their parents violated society's standards of sexual purity and "respectability" or because ISPCC inspectors and district court justices decided their parents were unfit. One can imagine that the system that prevailed to deal with "problem" children in the first half of the twentieth century inflicted a significant degree of psychological violence on them, although the effect on children of social policy was scarcely, if ever, questioned. The plight of children in state care – either in institutions or foster homes – suggests a more general attitude of indifference towards children and childhood that was also reflected in official attitudes toward and treatment of physical and sexual violence against children. ISPCC case files, Department of Education complaint files, court records, newspaper accounts, and autobiographical accounts of Irish childhood, all reveal a sustained pattern of violence that was striking in its regularity and in its acceptance. These sources suggest that children were subjected to a remarkable degree of physical and sexual violence in their homes, schools, and communities. Some of this violence was upheld as legitimate parental authority over children, while other forms of violence, like child sexual abuse, were ignored or minimized because dealing with it would have revealed the shaky foundations upon which Ireland's supposed moral superiority were based.

The "discovery" of child sexual abuse in the 1980s tends to overshadow the fact not only that child sexual abuse has a far longer history than that but, more importantly, that knowledge did exist of the extent and dangers of child sexual abuse in the early part of the twentieth century. But a variety of prejudicial and institutional barriers conspired to prevent the state from protecting children who had no one else to protect them. (Some of these barriers are discussed in Chapter 4.) This chapter, drawing on the wide array of sources mentioned above, examines the physical and sexual violence to which children were subjected in twentieth-century Ireland to again point out the enormous gap between official declarations of concern for "life," and for child life in particular, and the precariousness of life for children, even those who theoretically had two parents to protect them from the vagaries and pitfalls of human existence.

Assault and abuse in the home

One might assume, given the active involvement of the ISPCC in court proceedings that committed children to industrial schools, that ill-treatment or abuse was a significant factor in the committal of children to industrial schools. This was not the case at all; less than 1 per cent of children were committed to industrial schools in any given year as a result of abuse or ill-treatment (including sexual assault).[1] Only 13 of the nearly 400 ISPCC case files examined here dealt with assault or physical abuse, and two of these involved complaints against teachers (the parents in these cases sought the ISPCC's help in bringing their complaints to the attention of the appropriate authority).[2] A small handful of parents were prosecuted for ill-treating their children, but this seems to have been the exception rather than the rule. Only two such cases surfaced in an extensive survey of regional and local newspapers, and fourteen in a survey of circuit court records. John Collins was prosecuted in 1951 for "ill-treating" a 2-year-old child, his wife's illegitimate daughter.[3] According to witnesses and medical testimony, the defendant beat the child repeatedly over a number of months, to the extent that her face was swollen and bruised, and threatened to hang her. Collins was convicted, but his punishment suggests either that the district justice did not view his behavior in all that serious a light, or perhaps he was excused because the child was not his. Collins was fined £5 and ordered to pay court costs. There is no evidence that the child was removed from the home, and therefore no evidence that any action was taken to protect her from future beatings. All of this might suggest that abuse and ill-treatment were not significant issues in twentieth-century Ireland. But when one considers the accounts of twentieth-century Irish childhood that have been published in recent years, it seems that corporal punishment, that by today's standards might be regarded as abuse, was fairly commonplace, so commonplace that many people discuss it in their autobiographical narratives as if it was a normal part of everyday life.

Parents appear to have enjoyed an almost unfettered right to punish their children in whatever way they saw fit, so long as it did not result in serious injury or death (although, as will be seen, even in cases of death exceptions could be made). Public discussion of the right of parents to punish their children was rare in mid-twentieth-century Ireland, and the available evidence indicates that corporal punishment was widely used by parents and generally accepted as necessary to discipline children at home. Children in theory were protected from assault and ill-treatment by the Children Act (1908) (amended by the 1957 Children Act), and the various Offences Against the Person Acts:

> If any person over the age of sixteen years [amended to 17 years in 1957], who has the custody, charge or care of any child or young person, wilfully assaults, ill-treats, neglects, abandons, or exposes such child or young person or causes or procures such child or young person to be assaulted, ill-treated, neglected, abandoned, or exposed in a manner likely to cause such child or young person unnecessary suffering or injury to his health (including injury to or loss of sight or hearing, or limb, or organ of the body, and any mental derangement), that person shall be guilty of a misdemeanour.[4]

The penalties for conviction under this section of the Children Act ranged from a £25 fine or six months' imprisonment for a summary conviction, to a £100 fine or two years' imprisonment on indictment. (These penalties were not increased under the 1957 legislation.) However, the theoretical legal protection afforded to children under the Children Acts was diluted by a provision that specifically upheld a parent's right to punish his or her child: "Nothing in the Part of this Act shall be construed to take away or affect the right of any parent, teacher, or other person having the lawful control or charge of a child or young person to administer punishment to such child or young person."[5] This proviso might explain why there were so few prosecutions for assault or ill-treatment under the Children Act. Parents were more likely to be prosecuted under this Act for failing to support their children than for ill-treating or assaulting them.[6]

ISPCC case files suggest that even the ISPCC, whose founding mission was to protect children from abuse and neglect, turned a blind eye to what they regarded as legitimate or necessary discipline on the part of parents, even if it crossed the line into abuse by twenty-first-century standards. Of the ISPCC case files examined, only 11 dealt explicitly with ill-treatment or assault by parents or other family members.[7] The most extreme cases of what would be regarded as "abuse" seem to have been categorized in ISPCC case files under the heading of "assault" – only 5 files were designated as assault. What is interesting about these cases was the way ISPCC inspectors often dismissed violence against children as a by-product of conflicts between husband and wife. In 1938 Wexford a woman complained that when her husband returned home drunk one night he assaulted one of his sons.

The ISPCC report pointed out, however, that although the father smacked the child with a fist and threw him to the ground, he did not inflict "grievous bodily harm."[8] This was the extent of the report's commentary on the alleged assault against the child, and the father was never held accountable for his actions. The case was officially closed in September 1938, but there is no evidence that the ISPCC inspector conducted supervisory visits in the months between April and September, or took any other action to protect the child. The ISPCC was called to the home again in June 1939 for similar reasons, and this time they noted that the problems in the home were the result of conflicts between husband and wife: "Mother complains that father will not work and is careless of his duties towards his children. Father said he cannot get employment. Both parents are rather difficult, the man is hot-tempered and his wife inclined to nag him which he resents."[9] Reading between the lines, one might conclude that the ISPCC inspector, who was probably male (the ISPCC had a tendency of recruiting inspectors who were male and ex-military) regarded the man's violent behavior as legitimate given that his wife "nagged" him and, presumably, challenged his authority in the home.

The ISPCC's view that a nagged father could not help himself when he accidentally injured his children was also evident in a court case from 1947 Co. Kerry. William Corkery was charged at the Listowel District Court with assaulting his daughter Bridget, aged six: "On April 25 when the defendant arrived home, having drink taken, they had the usual quarrel. He put his wife outside the door and she called out their six year old girl to her. He went out to pull the child in. The mother strove to keep the child outside and the father tried to bring in the child. In the tussle the child's arm was broken."[10] The district justice was extremely cavalier in his attitude towards this case: "If you have a nagging wife, the thing to do is to leave her. Drink won't cure it. So said District Justice Kenny B.L., at Listowel Court when imposing a suspensory sentence of six months not to be enforced if he be of good behaviour for two years, on William Corkery, Muckenagh, Lixnaw, who was charged with wilfully assaulting his six years old daughter, Bridget."[11] The injury Bridget sustained was dismissed as an unfortunate result of the scuffle between her parents: "there was no intent to injure the child. The injury happened in the tussle."[12] The response of court authorities to this case could be considered outrageous by contemporary standards. In suggesting that a man should leave a "nagging wife" Justice Kenny dismissed the effect that the man's drinking had on his family's physical and financial well-being, and he ignored the fact that Irish society in the twentieth century did not provide viable options, whether through counselling, intervention, or divorce, for dysfunctional families. His dismissive attitude towards the child's injury was indicative of the marginalization of children generally in twentieth-century society. The child's injury was secondary to the conflict between husband and wife and was therefore insignificant in the "big picture."

A case from 1953 Wexford reveals the tensions that could exist in a family when its members did not conform to social and moral norms and expectations, tensions that could erupt into violence against children. The complainant in this case was the mother of a 10-year-old girl; she wrote to the ISPCC on at least four occasions between September and November 1953 after returning from England and discovering that her child had allegedly been the victim of repeated assaults at the hands of her father:

> I am sorry to have to make this complaint against my father. But he has been very cruel to my child. I am not living with my husband as he is not the father. I come over here to earn my own living. I shall be most grateful if you will call at [a neighbor's house]. One day he hit her on the head with an ash plant and a big lump rose it, another day he aimed to stick a sprong in her. In any case I am not leaving her there. I must bring her back with me. There are plenty of places here where they don't object to one child. Please inspector don't tell my father I wrote this letter or life won't be worth living. He has a desperate temper.[13]

Although this woman wrote at least four letters calling the ISPCC's attention to her plight, when the ISPCC inspector visited the house the woman and her mother tried to prevent him from confronting the father/husband about the alleged assaults:

> When about three hundred yards from the house I met an aged woman and a child who answered the description of those I wanted. Having told them who I was the grandmother said: "Everything is alright now. Her mother is home and we don't want to have anymore noise about it. Twould only make matters worse and we could not live in the house with him anymore." She then said "Don't go near the house or let him see you." I then sent the child for the mother.[14]

In a postscript to his report the ISPCC inspector indicated his inclination to believe the woman's account of her father's treatment of her child:

> The mother appears honest and truthful. She showed me the marks on the child's legs – already described. She admitted that the child was bold and

difficult to manage and she also stated that the child was not of the marriage and her husband … who is in England knew of the child's existence but was not responsible for her maintenance. Therefore she could not take her to him. The maternal grandfather believed she was of the marriage, if he thought or heard the true story they could not live with him. She asked me not to visit him.[15]

In spite of the mother and grandmother's obvious fear, the ISPCC inspector did confront the man about his treatment of his grandchild:

[the man] appeared and came over the road to us. Told him who I was and the object of my visit. I then gave him the usual caution per Inspector's Page 45. He said "I did beat her with a rod because she broke the locks on my cases. I could not have patience with her. She is too bold and difficult to manage." I then warned him and told him how serious it was for a strong man such as he was to assault a child of tender years. He said "I am sorry but I lost my temper." As already mentioned the mother does not want to hear any more about it. She is taking her to England.[16]

The women in this household clearly lived in fear of their father/grandfather/husband, and the man admitted that he beat the child. And yet the inspector did nothing beyond "warning" the man, and he seems to have accepted the mother's wish "not to hear any more about it."[17] This case had a number of complicating features that likely shaped the ISPCC inspector's response. The child was illegitimate and, although her grandfather did not know this, it likely influenced the ISPCC inspector's view of her "worthiness" when it came to protection. And both the mother and grandfather stated that the child was "bold" and "difficult to manage," which implies that the child brought the assault on herself and that she required correction and discipline. The fact that the ISPCC inspector did nothing more than warn the man suggests that he did not take an overly serious view of the case.

Another case from 1939 further illustrates the ISPCC's cavalier attitude when it came to allegations of assault or abuse of children. A neighbor wrote a letter to the ISPCC in which he alleged that the father of the house was "semi-savage" and beat his children regularly. When the ISPCC inspector visited the home he found that the oldest son, aged 12 years, was in the hospital suffering from a hip injury: "The boy is in the county hospital Wexford for the past month, it is alleged that his hip was injured by a kick inflicted by the father. I interviewed … sister of the boy and she stated that the boy complained to her that his father had kicked him. She took the boy to [doctor] some days later and he ordered him to hospital."[18] The boy's doctor testified that the boy's hip was tubercular and that there was no evidence of violence. On the other hand he acknowledged that if the child had been the victim of blows or kicks to his hip, resulting injuries could render his hip condition "acute." The ISPCC inspector seemed to accept the father's denials and let him off with a warning.[19]

The ISPCC, in spite of its founding mission to protect children from "cruelty," rarely dealt with explicit cases of cruelty, abuse, or assault in the course of their daily rounds. And when they did confront blatant and not so blatant cases of abuse or assault they appear to have looked for reasons to reaffirm a parent's right to discipline his or her children. In some cases the abusive treatment of children was dismissed as an inevitable by-product of conflicts between parents (for example, when a woman "nagged" her husband and drove him to violence). In other cases, the children themselves were implicitly blamed for being "bold," "unmanageable" and, even, illegitimate. There was not a single instance, in the ISPCC case files examined here, in which a parent or grandparent was prosecuted for assaulting his or her child or in any way held accountable.

The right, and indeed the duty, of parents to discipline their children, with corporal punishment if necessary, was often re-affirmed in the courts, where it was not unusual for district justices to exhort parents to "beat" or "thrash" errant children. In a 1930 case before the Roscommon District Court the district justice advised the father of two boys, who were charged with housebreaking, to punish them more severely:

> Justice: "What this boy wants is a good thrashing."
> [Boy's father]: "I gave him the rod severely."[20]

The district justice adjourned the case against the older boy and committed the younger boy to an industrial school where he would receive the punishment he was lacking at home. In another case from 1930 the district justice suggested to a woman that her son might attend school more regularly if she beat him occasionally. The mother replied that she did beat her son, which typically caused him to run away from home for several days at a time.[21]

In the Birr children's court in 1953 a 12-year-old girl was charged with the larceny of a pocket watch. The girl's father told the district justice that when he heard about the theft he gave her "a few right beatings."[22] The district justice was "satisfied the father was the type of man who would look after [the girl]" and he adjourned the case for six months, warning the father that "whether or not the girl would be sent away rested entirely on ... the control he would exercise over [her] during that period."[23] In another case from 1953 a father told the district justice that he had given his sons "a good beating" after they were caught stealing. The justice replied that "he was satisfied that it was not the father's fault that the boys had done what they did. He gave them a good hiding and it was no less than what they deserved."[24] In the Dublin children's court in 1957 District Justice O'Nunain advised a mother that "a few whacks of a stick" would bring her delinquent son "to his senses."[25] In short, some district justices appear to have believed that juvenile delinquency stemmed, in part, from parents' failure to use corporal punishment to keep their children in line, and they encouraged parents to take their responsibilities in this regard more seriously.

Not only did the courts reaffirm a parent's right and responsibility to use corporal punishment, but the *Summary Jurisdiction over Children (Ireland) Act* of 1884 also gave courts the authority to hand down corporal punishment sentences on delinquent children: "When the child is a male the court may, instead of any other punishment, adjudge the child to be, as soon as practicable, privately whipped with not more than six strokes of a birch rod by a constable, in the presence of an inspector or other office of police of higher rank than a constable, and also in the presence, if he desires to be present, of the parent or guardian of the child."[26] In 1949 seven boys were convicted in the Bray children's court of malicious damage; four of the boys' parents were ordered to pay restitution while the remaining three parents were ordered to beat their children in the presence of the police. One parent refused to carry out the sentence, and the district justice insisted that if the boy's parents "were determined to spoil him," he had no choice but to send the boy to Marlborough House for one month.[27] In the aftermath of this ruling a question was raised in the Dáil about the wisdom of allowing district justices to pass corporal punishment sentences, but the Minister for Justice stated that he did not plan to alter the law.[28] The 1997 Criminal Law Act finally abolished the right of courts to impose corporal punishment sentences.

A case that clearly illustrates the judicial affirmation of a parent's right to administer corporal punishment arose in 1967 when a 6-year-old boarded-out child, Mary Josephine Stephenson, died following a severe beating by her foster father, Vincent Dunphy. Dunphy's own testimony suggests that the beating he inflicted on Mary Josephine could not in any way be classified as moderate or acceptable even by the standards of the day, and in fact it appears to have been a brutal, unprovoked assault. Dunphy wakened Mary Josephine at nearly midnight so that he could be punish her:

> He [Dunphy] asked her why she had left her face cloth in the basin and not put it away. She got out of bed to do this. He took a towel off the bed and held it in a ball in his right hand. He struck her on the face. It was more a push than a blow. She staggered back and fell. Then she got up again and came towards him. He asked her why she pretended to be asleep and she said she had been asleep. Then he hit her again with the towel. This went on four or five times. About the fourth or fifth time she looked a bit groggy and she slumped to the ground.[29]

Dunphy justified the assault by claiming that Mary Josephine was "difficult" and told lies. He stated that during the three weeks prior to the assault that led to her death she had become particularly difficult and every day he "had to hit her with the palm of [his] hand across the face."[30] Neighbors testified that they had not seen Mary Josephine in the week or so immediately before her death but that prior to that they often saw her with bruises, scratches, and black eyes, suggesting a sustained pattern of beatings.

The judge's charge to the jury reveals an ambivalent attitude toward Mr Dunphy's actions. He cautioned the jury that they must

> approach this case on the basis that the accused is a man who sincerely believes that physical punishment was the proper way to deal with any offences this child committed. Even if you hold the view that excessive punishment was used that, by itself, does not mean that he intended to do serious injury to the child. *It does not follow from the fact that there was regular punishment that it was necessarily given with the intention of causing serious injury or what was done on this evening was something dangerous.* [emphasis added] It's a matter for you to decide but I think it is probable that when the child fell she struck her head, setting in motion a chain of events that resulted in her death.[31]

In effect the judge seemed willing to absolve Vincent Dunphy of responsibility for Mary Josephine's death, suggesting that Dunphy was justified in inflicting corporal punishment under the circumstances. He could not have foreseen, when he beat her, that she would fall back, bang her head, and die. The jury returned a verdict of manslaughter and Dunphy was sentenced to twelve months' imprisonment. Dunphy's solicitor argued that this sentence was too harsh given a parent's legal right to punish his or her child.[32]

Official data on corporal punishment in the home, while admittedly limited, nonetheless points clearly to the conclusion that parents were free to use corporal punishment without interference from the ISPCC or the courts. Indeed, district justices often expressed the view that parental corporal punishment would compel errant children to attend school regularly or prevent some petty crimes. The law that protected children from assault and ill-treatment also upheld the right of parents to punish their children. It seems that no one, including district justices, wanted to attempt to define the boundaries between legitimate parental punishment, on the one hand, and assault and ill-treatment on the other. The ISPCC, whose founding mission was to protect children from cruelty and abuse, spent more time tracking down parents who failed to maintain their children financially than they did investigating allegations of cruelty and abuse.[33] Even in cases where evidence of "cruelty," ill-treatment, or assault existed, the ISPCC often brushed it off as insignificant or justified given the child's behavior, or as an unfortunate by-product of conflicts between parents.

Corporal punishment in national schools

The Department of Education was responsible for regulating the use of corporal punishment in national schools, and regulations changed very little from the 1930s to the early 1980s when corporal punishment was finally abolished. Official regulations notwithstanding, however, corporal punishment was used widely to maintain discipline in schools, violations of the regulations were commonplace and, for the most part, ignored by the Department of Education. Even as public opinion began to turn against the use of corporal punishment in national schools from the 1950s, successive Ministers for Education consistently refused even to consider abolishing corporal punishment in national schools.[34]

From the 1930s right through to the 1980s the following regulations guided the use of corporal punishment in schools (with some slight modifications):

1) Corporal punishment should be administered only for grave transgression – [never for failure in lessons (this last phrase was deleted in 1931 and added again in 1946)]; 2) The Principal Teacher only should inflict the corporal punishment. An interval of at least ten minutes should elapse between the offence and the punishment; 3) Only a light cane or rod may be used for the purpose of inflicting the corporal punishment. The boxing of children's ears, the pulling of their hair, and similar ill treatment are absolutely forbidden, and will be visited with severe penalties; 4) No teacher should carry about a cane or other instrument of punishment; 5) Frequent recourse to corporal punishment will be considered by the Department as indicating bad tone and ineffective discipline.[35]

The available evidence suggests that corporal punishment was commonplace and that parents themselves generally supported a teacher's right to punish their children.[36] This view is reinforced by the memoirs and autobiographical accounts of Irish childhood in the 1940s, 1950s, and 1960s. In a 1969 newspaper article setting out the argument in favor of abolishing corporal punishment in national schools, Lawrence Murphy recalled his own schooldays and the fear instilled in himself and his classmates by some of the teachers. He recalled that "the slower students – in my class of which I was a member, would be lined up by the teacher's desk each to receive one strap across the hand. This was the corrective measure used to give us more of an incentive to work."[37] Murphy believed that his experiences were not unique:

In some schools we have to admit that the pupils are not instilled with the concepts of human rights and dignity for the individual. Unfortunately, the Irish student in many cases has no individual rights once he enters the classroom. His dignity is stripped away from him like bark from a tree … That is how he learns, not through love of his subjects or his striving for knowledge, but rather through terror of the consequences if he can't come up with the right answer when the questions come around to his side of the room. To say that this is characteristic of all modern Irish schools would be ridiculous, but there are still schools, usually outside the main centres, where the lay of the strap still prevails.[38]

Biographical and autobiographical accounts of Irish childhood contain numerous references to corporal punishment in schools; often such references are made in passing, as if being hit in school was part of the ordinary fabric of childhood. Patrick Boland, who grew up in the Liberties, one of Dublin's poorer neighborhoods, in the 1940s, recalled that: "we children accepted the beatings as being just part of a normal school day."[39] Angeline Kearns Blain remembered, growing up in Dublin's Irishtown in the 1940s and 1950s, that the only adult who ever hit her with a stick or cane was the teacher at the local national school.[40] The writers Frank O'Connor and Patrick Galvin, whose childhoods spanned the 1910s and the 1930s respectively, recalled the canes used by teachers to punish children, and both remembered that it was not unusual for the canes to break in the course of the punishment, suggesting that the punishment was inflicted with a degree of severity.[41]

The anecdotal evidence provided in personal histories, such as those cited above, is supported by evidence from Department of Education files. This evidence suggests that the Department was reluctant to entertain complaints lodged by parents and guardians, and often condoned or ignored even blatant violations of the corporal punishment regulations. As a rule the Department of Education dismissed parents' complaints, even when a teacher admitted inflicting corporal punishment in a manner or for a reason that violated Departmental regulations. When the Department of Education received a complaint from a parent or guardian, the first step was to inform the parent that complaints should be raised with the school manager. This was usually done with a standard letter along the following lines: "With reference to your recent letter regarding the treatment of your son, a pupil of the above-named school, by ... principal teacher of the school, you are informed that complaints of this nature should, in the first instance, be brought before the Manager, who is the person charged with the direct government of the school, and I am to request you to be so good as to state whether this has been done."[42] In many cases parents/guardians bypassed the school manager in favor of direct communications with the Department of Education. It is possible, as some complainants alleged in their letters, that they feared they would not be given a fair hearing from teachers or school managers. There is also evidence that parents/guardians complained directly to the Department of Education in cases where animosity or overt hostility existed between parents and school managers, principals, and teachers.

On receipt of a complaint a Department of Education official wrote to the school manager informing him of the complaint and requesting a statement from himself and the teacher involved, along the following lines:

> I am to enclose for your information a copy of a letter which has been received from [parent] regarding his son, a pupil of the above-named school, and I am to request you to be so good as to obtain a written statement on the matter from the teacher concerned and to forward it to the Department together with your own observations.[43]

If there seemed to be some merit to a complaint, or if it was of a serious nature, the Department also asked a divisional inspector to investigate and report on the matter.

Although the Department went through the motions of investigating complaints, its commitment to enforcing the corporal punishment regulations appears half-hearted at best. One case in particular testifies to the Department's unwillingness or inability to deal with serious and legitimate complaints. In February 1929 a group of parents from Currane in County Mayo wrote to the Department of Education with a litany of complaints against the principal and two assistant teachers (one of whom was the principal's wife) of the local national school, including allegations of frequent violations of corporal punishment regulations. The parents threatened to withdraw their children unless the Department addressed their concerns, and three weeks later 120 of the school's 133 pupils were withdrawn. Gardai initiated proceedings against the parents under the School Attendance Act, but the district justice adjourned the cases and called on the Department of Education to conduct an inquiry. The parents of seventeen children lodged formal complaints that their children had been beaten, while other parents complained in general terms about the way the school was run. After a thorough investigation the Department's divisional inspector found that most of the complaints in relation to the running of the school were unfounded. However, he also concluded: "that the children were punished excessively and irregularly by [the principal, his wife, and another teacher], that the corporal punishment regulations were flagrantly violated, that [the principal] burned the copy book which was stained with blood from the hand of [a pupil] and that [the teacher] did not restrain her tongue."[44]

The divisional inspector recommended the removal of all three teachers; the deputy chief inspector, however, recommended that the teachers be "admonished" and fined amounts ranging from £5 to £25 for "non-observance of the rules regarding the infliction of corporal punishment."[45] The deputy chief inspector also recommended that the school manager "be informed that the inquiry reveals that he has not discharged his duty to the

Department, the teachers and the parents of the pupils."[46] In August 1932, eighteen months after the complaints were first made, the Department of Education followed the recommendations of the deputy chief inspector and fined rather than removed the teachers. In spite of the divisional inspector's findings the Department concluded "the failure of the teachers to observe the corporal punishment regulations in spirit and in fact was probably a temporary lapse on their part."[47]

Three years later additional complaints were lodged against the principal teacher. The case was initially dismissed in the Achill District Court, but upheld on appeal to Castlebar Circuit Court, and the teacher was fined £5 plus costs. Following on from the court case the Department wrote to the principal and his wife advising them to seek an exchange with teachers from another school. The couple ignored this and subsequent directives, and in 1936 it seems that the Department gave up trying to compel the teachers to leave. They issued the following warning, the same warning that was issued in 1932, that

> if it should be proved to the satisfaction of the Department, now or at any time in the future that ... any member of the staff of the school had administered excessive or irregular punishment to children in attendance, the matter would be regarded in a very grave light and the Department, in taking appropriate action, would not refrain from inflicting the maximum penalty of withdrawal of recognition as teacher should such actions be deemed necessary in the circumstances.[48]

In short, after a period of seven years of complaints, inquiries, court cases, and warnings involving the same teachers, the Department was unable to remove the teachers or compel them to abide by corporal punishment regulations, and ultimately they stopped trying. The above case may be unusual in terms of its seriousness and duration, but it is a reflection of the Department's ambivalence and ineffectiveness when it came to addressing complaints about corporal punishment. In at least three cases teachers were fined and warned after serious violations of corporal punishment regulations, but subsequent complaints against the same teachers were ignored.

One teacher was fined twice by the Department, in 1932 and again in 1933, for inappropriately punishing a child. In 1932 he was accused of beating a child severely on the legs for failing in his school lessons. The teacher denied it, but the divisional inspector concluded that although the teacher was "a respectable man and a hardworking teacher," "the boy got two or three slaps on the hands and about six blows of the cane on the legs and that his legs were marked for a few days afterwards."[49] In relation to the 1933 complaint the inspector found that "[the teacher] occasionally beat [the child] and his sister on the back ...; that he used an unsuitable rod when administering corporal punishment; that he is in the habit of punishing pupils for failure at lessons."[50] The teacher admitted punishing the child, although he denied that the punishment was inappropriate, and he suggested that "these children are very pettish in manner, and I have no doubt that they sometimes tell stories at home."[51] The Department fined the teacher £10 and warned him again of the dire consequences of further incidents. Yet another complaint was brought against this teacher in 1935. The teacher admitted slapping the child for poor performance in his Irish lessons, and several other boys gave evidence that they had been punished in similar fashion. However, the teacher denied giving the boy a black eye, as alleged by the mother. In spite of the teacher's own admission, the evidence of three other boys, and the teacher's track record, the inspector recommended that no action be taken in this instance. One gets the sense that, short of removing the teacher (which, for some reason, the Department was not inclined to do), there was little more they were willing or able to do to force the teacher's compliance to Departmental regulations.

Four additional cases illustrate the Department's tendency either to ignore complaints or to do the absolute minimum required to address them. In these cases (from 1930 Kildare, 1931 Donegal, 1935 and 1943 Galway), the parents sought transfers to other schools for their children, and once the Department sanctioned the transfers no further action was taken. The Department appears to have held the view that the transfers essentially solved the problem even when the parents' complaints were upheld.[52] The case from 1935 was particularly interesting because in the course of the investigation both the divisional inspector and the Irish National Teachers Organization (INTO) complained to the Department that they took too much notice of parental complaints, the overwhelming majority of which they believed were frivolous.[53]

It is clear from the way the Department of Education, school managers, and teachers responded to complaints that teachers frequently and knowingly violated Department of Education regulations, and that the Department of Education often overlooked blatant violations rather than take action that might undermine the authority of teachers, principals, or school managers. Only rarely were parents' concerns addressed by the Department of Education; in most cases the Department took months, or even years, to respond to complaints. Even when a teacher was reminded, warned, or reprimanded, the Department rarely informed parents about the outcome of their investigation but simply stated that "appropriate action" had been taken. The overall conclusion to be drawn from the available files is that the Department was, by and large, unresponsive to complaints and reluctant to hold themselves or teachers accountable for breaches of corporal punishment regulations. In effect they tolerated the extensive use of corporal punishment, even very severe corporal punishment, in breach of their own formal regulations, and provided little if any defense of children against abuse by teachers.

Although most teachers, and perhaps even most parents, supported the use of reasonable and limited corporal punishment to maintain order and discipline in schools, a critical voice on the subject began to emerge in the late 1940s. A small but ever-growing and increasingly vocal number of parents began to complain, through the pages of a Dublin evening newspaper, about the extent of violations of corporal punishment regulations in the country's national schools, and the Department of Education's seemingly lackadaisical attitude to the problem. In 1955, following a sustained letter-writing campaign to the *Evening Mail*, a group of concerned parents formed the School Children's Protection Organisation with the exclusive aim of lobbying the Minister for Education to abolish corporal punishment in national schools. The hundreds of letters received by the *Evening Mail* in late 1954 and 1955 gave voice to parents' concerns that violations of corporal punishment regulations were not only commonplace in the country's national schools, but also were largely ignored by the Department of Education:

> Examination of the extracts from the Rules and Regulations for National Schools laid down by the Department of Education might appear to satisfy any reasonable parent that protection of their children is amply provided for. That this view is now open to grave doubt must be obvious to any honest and serious thinking person, in view of the apparently widespread failure to observe the regulations. That such a chaotic condition should exist surely justifies the making of a more conscientious and careful approach to this problem by the authorities concerned, and either the enforcement of the Regulations or the abolition of Compulsory Education.[54]

According to the Organisation, children were punished in national schools for a variety of "offences," contrary to regulations including: failure at lessons; tardiness; not having copy books or other supplies; absences; and neglect of homework. The punishments meted out for these offences, which also were against regulations, included canings on various parts of the body; beatings with straps or pointers; hair pulling; and beatings with hands or fists.[55]

The letters published in the *Evening Mail*, seventy of which were reproduced in a pamphlet called *Punishment in our schools*, highlighted alleged abuses of the corporal punishment regulations and showed that corporal punishment was a regular feature of life in many schools (in spite of the stipulation that "frequent recourse to corporal punishment will be considered by the Department as indicating bad tone and ineffective discipline").

The School Children's Protection Organisation suggested that the protections theoretically afforded to children by the Rules and Regulations were effectively negated by the Department of Education's reluctance to address complaints:

> To administer in this unhappy situation we have thousands of teachers, school managers and attendance inspectors, numerous officials, inspectors and high executives of the Department of Education and a Minister for Education. We soon learned that all these bodies appeared in the most part to have one thing in common and in which they always presented a united front by an antagonistic approach to any voice raised in criticism. This unfortunate attitude practically nullifies the merits of the Rules and Regulations laid down by the Department and from comments in some of the letters published in this booklet, it would appear that in many cases where a conscientious parent attempts to seek an investigation of any incident relating to one of his or her children they are quickly discouraged from pursuing the matter further and very often in a most humiliating manner.[56]

The kind of punishment (and the reasons for the use of corporal punishment) described in these letters was not new: what was noteworthy was the growing depth of public feeling on the matter.

The Minister for Education unequivocally rejected the validity of the allegations made in the *Evening Mail* letters and *Corporal punishment in our schools*: "I want to say that as far as that publication is concerned it shows on its face to be an attack by people reared in an alien and in a completely un-Irish atmosphere and it is carried on here with the help of our Irish newspapers. It is an attack on the whole spirit of our educational system and it is an endeavour to attack our educational roots."[57] The minister also asserted that although the Department received complaints "from time to time," they never received more than one or two such complaints per month, and that complaints were dealt with swiftly and efficiently.[58] An analysis of Department of Education complaint files would suggest otherwise.

The public debate that emerged in the mid-1950s marked the beginning of the campaign to ban corporal punishment in schools, although it would take nearly 30 years to accomplish this goal. Ironically, in 1956, just when opponents of corporal punishment were becoming most vocal, the Minister for Education proposed changes to the corporal punishment regulations, that opponents of corporal punishment viewed rather ominously. The new regulations permitted the use of a strap, in addition to a light cane or rod, on the hand. The move was widely condemned, not least by the School Children's Protection Organisation: "We strongly criticise the action of the Minister for Education in authorising the use of a leather strap in order to facilitate those teachers whose tradition of correction with the leather strap (in defiance of the regulations) is now such an integral part of their nature that they are unable to teach without it."[59] The *Evening Mail* article from which the above is quoted was accompanied by a cartoon depicting two children lying in hospital beds covered in bandages. One child asked the other: "Was it the cane or the strap?"[60] The decision to allow the use of the strap elicited such a storm of protest that the minister was forced to revert to the old regulations, and the Irish Housewives Association joined the Schoolchildren's Protection Organisation in welcoming the minister's decision: "The Association congratulates the Minister on his courage and foresight in withdrawing permission for the use of the strap and hope that this is the first step towards the abolition of corporal punishment in schools."[61]

In June 1957 the Minister for Education again proposed changes to the rules governing the use of corporal punishment. The new regulations omitted all reference to the implements that could be used to punish children, leaving it to teachers' discretion to decide how to inflict corporal punishment. The Minister for Education assured the Dáil, however, that "… any improper or unreasonable punishment will be regarded as conduct unbefitting a teacher and will be visited with very severe sanction."[62] In effect the minister accomplished in 1957 what he was forced to backtrack on in October 1956, which was his Department's tacit sanction of the use of the strap in administering corporal punishment.

Efforts to ban corporal punishment in national schools continued unabated into the 1960s and 1970s. During question time in the Dáil on 4 May 1961 several TDs cited recent court cases in which parents successfully sued teachers who had excessively or inappropriately punished their children, and they asked the Minister for his views on the various cases. The Minister's response was equivocal:

> My responsibility in the matter is twofold. On the one hand it is for me to see to it that the children are not ill treated and on the other that they receive efficient instruction. The teacher holds for the time being the place of the parent and so for the time being carries in this matter the right of the parent. In these circumstances it would be unreasonable for me to forbid the teacher to adopt any deterrent that might be adopted by a just and wise parent, and a just and wise parent might on occasion deem it necessary to inflict an adequate amount of corporal punishment in order to control the child and bring him up in the way he should go.[63]

The Minister re-affirmed the teacher's right to use corporal punishment without addressing the TD's specific concern – that violations of corporal punishment regulations were all too prevalent.

The rules governing the use of corporal punishment in schools were revised again in 1965. It is not clear what prompted these changes, particularly as the Department of Education's fundamental views on the matter had not changed. The gist of the 1965 rules, as outlined in a debate in the Dáil in 1965, is as follows:

> Teachers should have a lively regard for the improvement and general welfare of their pupils, treat them with kindness combined with firmness and should aim at governing them through their affections and reason and not by harshness and severity. Ridicule, sarcasm or remarks likely to undermine a pupil's self-confidence should be avoided.
>
> Corporal punishment should be administered only in cases of misbehaviour and should not be administered for mere failure at lessons.
>
> Any teacher who inflicts improper or excessive punishment will be regarded as guilty of conduct unbefitting a teacher and will be subject to severe disciplinary action.[64]

The new regulations appear to have been more ambiguous, and perhaps more open to abuse, than previous rules, and did little to ease the concerns of opponents of corporal punishment.

The anti-corporal punishment debate was re-ignited in 1967 when a 9-year-old Dublin schoolboy was awarded 1s in damages following what the court deemed to be excessive punishment administered by his teacher.[65] Although the court was convinced that the teacher in question violated Department of Education regulations, the paltry damages awarded perhaps suggest the court did not take the matter all that seriously. Following on from that judgment a group called Reform was founded to lobby against corporal punishment in schools. In 1970 Reform was joined by the Irish Union of School Students (IUSS) in their campaign to end corporal punishment. In 1974 The IUSS published a brochure entitled *Corporal punishment: The brutal facts*, in which they attempted to quantify the use of corporal punishment in the nation's primary, secondary, and vocational schools. According to the IUSS, 84 per cent of the schools surveyed used corporal punishment of some form; the majority of these (92 per cent) were boys' schools, while only 8 per cent of girls' schools used corporal punishment. The survey revealed the variety of implements, including leather straps, t-squares, sticks, hurleys, and tree branches, that were used to administer corporal punishment, all in violation of the spirit, if not the letter, of existing Department of Education regulations. This report concluded that "[w]hile it would seem that many teachers regard corporal punishment as a normal and useful method of class control, it would seem that there are some sadists and other sexual perverts in charge of classes in Irish schools."[66]

Following the publication of this report individual TDs again put pressure on the Minister for Education to re-consider his department's position on the use of corporal punishment. The minister agreed to survey the various teaching organizations for their views on the matter. In May 1978, when the issue was raised again in the Dáil, the minister claimed he was still waiting for responses from some of those groups; in reality it is likely that, true to form, the minister was reluctant to take decisive action on the matter. In December 1978 the minister finally reported to the Dáil on the views of the various teachers' and managers' associations. Of the eight groups surveyed, three opposed all forms of corporal punishment while five expressed the view that the existing rule was adequate (although two of these groups recommended the elimination of the term "corporal").[67]

Those organizations that supported the use of some form of corporal punishment argued that it was necessary both to instill in children a sense of responsibility and accountability for their actions, and to counteract the bad influences and "anti-social behavior" that children acquired in their homes and neighborhoods. At the same time, there was general agreement that parents should have a voice, along with teachers and school managers, in formulating corporal punishment policy and practice. In December 1978 the Minister for Education endorsed this view:

> A high standard of discipline and good behaviour is absolutely necessary in schools if they are to fulfill their educational purpose. How this is to be achieved is a matter for each individual school and each school must develop its own policy, taking into account the general directives of the Department of Education as well as the circumstances obtaining in different areas and even in individual classes. The school policy on discipline should be the result of discussion not only between the teachers and the Board of Management but it should also take into account the attitude of the parents.[68]

The minister also pointed out that, even if corporal punishment in limited form remained part of departmental policy, it was a "non-issue" in practice because it was no longer used in the majority of schools.[69] In short, the minister seemed to be moving away from a rigid or centralized policy of corporal punishment.

But the minister still refused to commit himself to abolishing corporal punishment altogether. After a long and drawn-out statement on the matter in the Dáil the minister ran out of time and the issue was raised again during the adjournment debate, but without the Minister for Education present. During the adjournment debate several deputies voiced their outrage with the way the minister dealt with the question, as illustrated by the following statement from TD Collins:

> I am looking for a clear statement from the Minister in regard to his intentions on corporal punishment and in relation to the rules for national schools, when he will revise those rules and if he will allow corporal punishment to form part of those rules and regulations. The Minister obviously tried to evade the whole question today in the manner in which he treated the House and in the grossly unsatisfactory reply he gave.[70]

The Minister of State at the Department of Education expressed what appears to have been the Department's view on the matter: "a code of regulation is necessary. Such a code must provide for the imposition of sanctions in the event of a deliberate, serious and repeated transgression … Deputies know as well as I do that there are forms of punishment worse than physical punishment which can be imposed on any child. Are we to pursue the elimination of those?"[71] Although the Department of Education was increasingly moving towards a more flexible code of school discipline, they were not yet prepared to eliminate corporal punishment as one tool for maintaining that discipline.

The question of the abolition of corporal punishment surfaced again on several occasions from the time of the 1978 debate until late January 1982, when corporal punishment was finally abolished with effect from 1 February 1982. Department of Education circular 9/82 set out the new regulations relating to corporal punishment:

> The Minister for Education in pursuance of Government commitment to the abolition of corporal punishment in schools, has, following consultations with representatives of Teacher and Managerial Organisations, amended Rule 130 of the Rules for National Schools to read as follows:
>
> 130(1)   Teachers should have a lively regard for the improvement and general welfare of their pupils, treat them with kindness combined with firmness and should aim at governing them through their affections and reason and not by harshness and severity. Ridicule, sarcasm or remarks likely to undermine a pupil's self-confidence should not be used in any circumstances.
>
> 130 (2)   The use of Corporal punishment is forbidden.
>
> 130 (3)   Any teacher who contravenes section (1) or (2) of this rule will be regarded as guilty of conduct unbefitting a teacher and will be subject to severe disciplinary action.[72]

In October 1982 the new Minister for Education, Professor Martin O'Donoghue, appointed a committee to report on how schools were maintaining discipline in the post-corporal punishment era. The committee reported in 1985 that suspension and expulsion had replaced corporal punishment as the preferred methods of dealing with serious transgressions of school rules and that, for the most part, such sanctions were effective. A dissenting memo argued that these sanctions were counter-productive because they denied the children who most needed it of education and special attention.[73] In a footnote to the school punishment debate, the 1997 Non-Fatal Offences Against the Person Act criminalized the use by teachers of corporal punishment, and formally ended the traditional immunity that teachers enjoyed from prosecution under the Offences Against the Person Act.

Child sexual abuse

The issue of child sexual abuse has been in the public spotlight in Ireland in recent years thanks in large measure to reports submitted by the Law Reform Commission and growing allegations of pedophilia against a number of Catholic priests, and of cover-ups by the Catholic hierarchy. The media, elements of which seem to have an anti-clerical bias, has helped to keep the issue of pedophile priests in the public spotlight and would have the public believe that only priests sexually abused children in the past.[74] In fact, children were subject to a significant degree of sexual violence in twentieth-century Ireland, from a variety of sources, and available evidence suggests that parents, jurists, and the police were far from ignorant of children's vulnerability to such assaults. It was not a lack of knowledge that guided official responses to sexual assaults against children but, rather, a lack of political will to do anything about it. Judicial responses to sexual assaults against children are somewhat more difficult to interpret. On the one hand, judges and juries were inhibited from punishing some offenders because of anomalies in the law that were not rectified with the 1935 Criminal Law (Amendment) Act. On the other hand, crimes against young children do not appear to have been treated any more harshly than crimes against older teenagers or adults, and punishments overall tended to be fairly lenient.

Sentencing patterns were roughly similar across age groups: in rare cases defendants were given particularly harsh sentences but the majority of defendants were sentenced to less than twelve months' imprisonment (with or without hard labor), and suspended sentences were not uncommon. This is important in respect of young victims because it suggests that the courts did not view the assault of a 5 or 6-year-old child as any more serious than the assault or statutory rape of a 15 or 16-year-old girl. Sentences in cases of sexual assaults against boys under 15 years of age were, on the whole, harsher than sentences in cases with under-aged female victims. Of the 33 cases examined here, only 9 defendants (or 27 per cent) were acquitted. Of the remaining 24, ten (or 42 per cent) received sentences of between one and two years' hard labor; three (13 per cent) received sentences of 5–7 years of penal servitude. The remaining six, or 25 per cent, received sentences of between three and nine months' hard labor.

An analysis of conviction patterns, in cases where the victims were girls, does not necessarily lend itself to any firm conclusions. The lowest rate of convictions (36 per cent) involved victims of 6–8 years of age, while the highest conviction rates (70 per cent) involved victims of 2–5 years. This is somewhat surprising on the surface given the inadmissibility of the evidence of very young victims; in general, it seems that the older the victim, the more likely the jury was to convict.[75] This discrepancy likely is due to two factors: first, many cases involving victims between the ages of 15 and 17 should be dealt with separately as many of these involved long-term, seemingly consensual relationships that came to court only when the girl involved became pregnant, or when her father or employer became aware of the relationship. Second, and more importantly, the court relied heavily on the testimony of the victim combined with corroborative evidence; in several instances juries were specifically directed to acquit defendants in cases involving very young victims (younger than ten or eleven years of age) either because the victims were unable to state in court precisely what had happened to them, or because although medical evidence confirmed a sexual assault, no corroborative evidence linked the defendant to the crime. In other words, the mere word of a young child, even when combined with medical evidence attesting to an assault having occurred, was not sufficient to secure a conviction.

Sentencing and conviction patterns suggest that sexual crimes against children were not treated as serious, and no one recognized the potentially harmful long-term effects of sexual abuse on children. Even parents seemed to evaluate crimes against their daughters based on the "harm" they caused, although this definition of harm was more physical than psychological.[76] This notion of "harm" was evident in a number of cases, including one from 1929 County Monaghan. In this case a 5-year-old girl was indecently assaulted by a neighbor.[77] The child's mother accosted the neighbor and he confessed, which might account for the fact that he was convicted in spite of the child's young age. The mother herself dismissed the seriousness of the crime because the doctor assured her that "there is no danger ... there was nothing in but the finger."[78] This might have accounted for the sentence handed down: 12 months with hard labor suspended. The age of the child, and the fact that the doctor and mother dismissed the incident as insignificant, may have compelled the justice to "go easy" on the defendant. Another mother concluded that her 11-year-old daughter was "quite well" after a sexual assault, and that it "did her no harm."[79] The defendant in this case was acquitted.

On the other hand, a case from 1942 Donegal poignantly illustrates parental fears and suspicions with regard to sexual assaults against their children, and the lengths they went to to protect their children. MR,[80] aged eleven, was responsible for fetching milk from the neighbor each evening. Her father began to suspect that a neighbor TK was harassing his daughter so he began to follow her, from a distance, each evening. The father followed his daughter on three separate evenings and, on the third evening, caught the neighbour TK in the act of assaulting her. TK was convicted of unlawful carnal knowledge and sentenced to fifteen months' hard labor – a relatively harsh sentence, particularly in a case involving such a young victim.[81] In this case the father was suspicious, either because of rumors he had heard in town or because of the way his daughter was behaving, and he took steps to protect her. His actions likely helped to not only convict TK but also ensure that a harsh sentence was imposed.

Other parents were similarly suspicious and caught defendants in the act of molesting their children. EW, aged nine, took a shortcut home from school one day in September 1931, when she was attacked by a local man, DL. EW's brother saw DL approach his sister and told his father about the encounter between the two. The father immediately became suspicious and ran to the field looking for his daughter. In court, he stated

> My son … came out home at about that time and in consequence of what he told me I went in search of [EW]. After crossing a few fields I saw [DL] rising up out of a dyke. I also saw my daughter [EW]. She got up after [DL] got up. She was crying and sobbing. I shouted to [DL]. I was then about 100 yards from him. I said "stand." He ran away and I followed him until I was stopped. It would be about 150 yards to the point where I saw [DL] get up from where the children came home from school … I took my daughter home and I did not ask her any questions.[82]

DL appears to have had a reputation in the locality, which caused EW's father concern when he heard that DL had accosted his daughter. DL was convicted of unlawful carnal knowledge and sentenced to five years' penal servitude – an extraordinarily harsh sentence that likely would not had been passed without eyewitness testimony.[83]

One of the biggest problems with prosecuting sexual assaults, especially assaults against children younger than ten or eleven years of age, was the inadmissibility of their evidence. Many defendants were acquitted not because the justices who heard the cases believed them to be innocent but because the evidence of the victims was disregarded. This flaw in the system was evident in the case of WN, who was accused of assaulting sisters ER and VR, aged 2 and 4 years respectively.[84] Medical evidence indicated that both children had been assaulted, and VR later was diagnosed with gonorrhea. In spite of this evidence, however, WN was acquitted because the girls' evidence was not deemed to be credible. The case of RJ had a different outcome.[85] RJ was accused of assaulting 4-year-old EM. In her evidence, EM's mother testified that "on account of EM's extreme youth she is unable to come to court to give an account of it."[86] RJ was convicted because he confessed. However, he was sentenced only to keep the peace, suggesting that the justice did not see the crime as all that serious.

A noteworthy characteristic of sexual assaults against children was the tendency of some accused to give money, sweets, or other small gifts to their victims. In some cases these gifts secured the victims' cooperation and/or silence. But some defendants treated the sexual encounters almost as commercial transactions, with the gifts serving as "payments." These small gifts may have ensured the cooperation and perhaps even silence of naïve and innocent young girls, but they also provided vital evidence that in some cases helped secure convictions. Eleven-year-old KC testified that, after MH assaulted her he gave her a penny and told her to "say nothing about it."[87] PJ, also eleven years old, testified that as she walked away from the man accused of assaulting her he threw a penny at her and said "Don't tell anyone or your mother."[88] The case of WM was noteworthy because the two pence he gave his victim led to his downfall.[89] When the victim, 5-year-old MO, returned home she had the two pence in her hand. Her mother asked her where she got the money, and MO confessed that she had been assaulted. In all three of these cases the accused were convicted in spite of the age of the victims, suggesting perhaps that the giving of money or other gifts implied guilt on their part. The sentences in these cases ranged from keeping the peace, in the case of RG (convicted of assaulting PJ), to twelve months with hard labor in the case of MH. WM received a sentence of six months with hard labor.

In his evidence before the Carrigan Committee Eoin O'Duffy stated his belief that the conditions of urban life, specifically overcrowding in tenements that offered no privacy and that presumably exposed young children to the realities of sex and reproduction, rendered young girls particularly vulnerable to sexual assaults. This view would suggest that sexual assaults were crimes of opportunity rather than the actions of predatory men, and that girls were most likely to be assaulted by people in their own homes or tenements – in other words, by people they knew. Court records show just how misguided O'Duffy was. Of the nearly 1,500 cases entered in the various justice minute books, only about 350, or 23 per cent, occurred in urban areas. The remainder occurred throughout the country, in small towns and tiny villages, in the victims' own homes, in isolated fields and secluded laneways. And while many girls were assaulted by friends, neighbors, lodgers, and others who were known to them, a substantial number of victims testified to never having met the accused before the assault occurred. Parents often voiced fears or suspicions about specific men in their locality, and sometimes those fears and suspicions were translated into almost heroic efforts to protect their daughters and bring the perpetrators to justice. Such parents were working, however, against a criminal justice system and a political system that were indifferent to the vulnerability of children to sexual assaults, and that (in the case of parliament anyway) put the protection of male sexual license above the protection of children from sexually predatory men.

An analysis of cases involving male victims under the age of fifteen years raises some interesting questions about how the courts conceived of sexual assaults against children. In their evidence to the Carrigan Committee several witnesses, including Eoin O'Duffy, indicated that sexual assaults against young girls were primarily crimes of opportunities, and not necessarily the actions of "sick" or predatory individuals. This was clearly not the case when courts evaluated the actions of male defendants accused of assaulting young boys. In at least four of the cases, the defendants, although convicted, were recommended for psychological treatment.[90] Additionally, while the term "pedophile" was never used in relation to sexual offenses against girls, the medical report of one of the defendants in a case involving a male victim referred to him as a pedophile.[91]

One aspect of sexual crimes against males that comes to light from an examination of court records is the possibility that it was a "learned" behavior. At least four of the defendants (two of whom were teenagers themselves) admitted that they had been victims of sexual assaults at the hands of older men. The medical officer's evaluation of a 47-year-old defendant is revealing in this regard:

> This man ... gives one a history of indulging in masturbation since his youth. When about 17 years of age he was living in the country and was there initiated into the practice of sexual intercourse with boys. Since that time he appears to have been having regular sexual relations with boys. About 2 years ago he tells me he lost complete control of his sexual impulses and indulged freely in the practice, but during the last year he has been able to curb his desire in this direction. Apart from sexual inversion he has shown no other signs of mental instability.[92]

It was regarded as sexual "inversion" for a grown man to have sexual intercourse with young boys, but it was not considered either "inversion" or "perversion" for grown men to have sexual intercourse with young girls.

The idea that defendants in cases involving male victims might be psychologically disturbed or "sexually inverted" is abundantly clear in a case from 1945. The defendant in this case admitted that he had, on several occasions, put advertisements in local newspapers claiming to have a position available for a messenger. Based on the replies he received, the defendant chose his "prey" based on very specific criteria:

> I placed a number in red pencil on the envelope of those people who appeared to have inferior education judging from the handwriting and style of the reply in each case. My object was that this kind of person would be more suitable for the purpose which I had in mind, namely for committing sodomy. I mean more suitable in the sense that the person would not understand what kind of offence

sodomy was and also that they would be more impressed with the work which I pretended to get for them.[93]

Based on these preliminary evaluations, the defendant visited several possible "candidates," met the parents of the boys and gained their trust, and then asked the parents if he could take the boys with him to meet the potential employer. The mother of one of the victims was actually suspicious enough of the man to follow him as he accompanied her son to "meet" the employer. She essentially caught the defendant in the act and flagged down a passing policeman. Although the defendant appealed for leniency, he was given a very harsh sentence of six years' penal servitude. Not all of the defendants in cases involving male victims were as plotting or predatory as the defendant described here. However, it does appear that male defendants intentionally put themselves into situations, such as advertising a bogus employment opportunity, or frequenting the penny arcade, where they could encounter and gain the trust of unsuspecting boys. This is an element of sexual assaults that was, for the most part, missing from cases involving female victims.

Conclusion

Children in twentieth-century Ireland were subjected to a significant degree of physical and sexual violence at the hands of parents and other family members, teachers, neighbors, friends, and even strangers. Nominal legal measures existed to protect children from such violence, but exceptions and anomalies meant that the real effect of legislation was to uphold parents' right to punish their children, with beatings if necessary, and to protect predatory men from prosecution when they sexually assaulted young children whose evidence was not admissible in court. Regulations also existed to protect children from excessive punishment in school, although the Department of Education was, historically, reluctant to hold teachers to account even when they had clearly and willfully flouted published regulations. In short, Irish society at all levels tolerated a degree of violence against children that was striking in its regularity and routineness. Official responses to physical and sexual violence against children simply serves to reinforce the extent to which children were marginalized and their needs and best interests sacrificed to more pressing social and political agendas.

Notes

1 The term "abuse" did not come into common usage until the 1980s. Ill-treatment and cruelty were commonly used to describe treatment that today would be branded as abuse.

2 This represents nearly 4 per cent of all cases. ISPCC annual reports, that summarize all cases heard by all branches in a given year, indicate that roughly 10 per cent of cases annually comprised some form of ill-treatment or assault. This discrepancy could be a function of the limited sample of the case files examined here, or it could be that ill-treatment as it was categorized in the ISPCC annual reports included cases of extreme neglect as well as assault. See ISPCC *Annual Reports*, 1930–1955.

3 *The Kerryman* (14 July 1951), p. 4.

4 United Kingdom Acts of Parliament, Children Act, 1908.

5 Law Reform Commission, *Report on non-fatal offenses against the person* (Dublin: Law Reform Commission, 1994), p. 21.

6 This conclusion is based on a survey of circuit court and some district court records, which revealed only thirteen prosecutions in the period 1922 to 1960. It is possible that such cases were prosecuted in district courts for which records have not survived. It is also based on a survey of ISPCC records; the ISPCC only rarely sought prosecutions in cases that constituted outright abuse or ill-treatment, but regularly sought the prosecution of parents who failed to provide financially for their children.

7 The term "ill-treatment" seems to have been used by the ISPCC to describe extreme or severe neglect, and not just physical punishments or assaults.

8 ISPCC case files, Wexford, 30 April 1938.

9 ISPCC case files, Wexford, 21 June 1939.

10 *The Kerryman*, First edition, (14 June 1947), p. 5.

11 *The Kerryman*, First edition, (14 June 1947), p. 5.

12 *The Kerryman*, First edition, (14 June 1947), p. 5.

13 ISPCC case files, Wexford, 8 September 1953.

14 ISPCC case files, Wexford, 8 September 1953.

15 ISPCC case files, Wexford, 8 September 1953.

16 ISPCC case files, Wexford, 8 September 1953.

17 It should be noted that the ISPCC definition of "warning" is somewhat sketchy. It did not, for example, imply that the ISPCC inspector believed that the parent had done anything wrong. The warning likely was more of a generic reminder to the parent of his/her responsibilities to his/her child.

18 ISPCC case files, Wexford, 9 May 1939.

19 ISPCC case files, Wexford, 9 May 1939.

20 *Connacht Tribune* (25 January 1930), p. 5.

21 *Connacht Tribune* (1 March 1930), p. 3. See also *Offaly Chronicle* (16 April 1942), p. 1; *Offaly Chronicle* (19 May 1954), p. 1; *Evening Mail* (2 May 1956), p. 5.

22 *Offaly Chronicle* (18 March 1953), p. 1.

23 *Offaly Chronicle* (18 March 1953), p. 1.

24 *Offaly Chronicle* (2 December 1953), p. 4.

25 *Evening Mail* (10 July 1957), p. 5. See also *Evening Mail* (31 December 1947), p. 6.

26 *A report on the law and proceedings regarding the prosecution and disposal of young*

offenders (Dublin: Stationery Office, 1977), pp. 45–6.

27 *Evening Mail* (20 May 1949), p. 5. Marlborough House was a short-term residential center for juvenile offenders administered by the Department of Education.

28 *Evening Mail* (7 June 1949), p. 2.

29 *Irish Times* (2 July 1968), p. 11.

30 *Waterford News and Star* (5 July 1968), p. 5.

31 *Irish Times* (11 July 1968), p. 11.

32 *Waterford News and Star* (5 July 1968), pp. 5, 11.

33 This conclusion is based on a survey of roughly 400 ISPCC case files for the period 1920s to 1960s.

34 National schools are schools that are publicly funded but that were, until the 1960s, conducted almost entirely by male and female religious orders. Children attend national schools until roughly the age of fourteen years, at which point they sit their junior certificate. They then move on to secondary schools to prepare for the leaving certificate.

35 NAI, Department of Education 27678, circular to managers and teachers of national school, 30 September 1930.

36 In at least ten of the Department of Education complaint files parents specifically stated that they supported a teacher's right to use corporal punishment on their child, but objected to either the severity of the punishment or to the reason that it was inflicted.

37 *Irish Independent* (20 March 1969), p. 3.

38 *Irish Independent* (20 March 1969), p. 3.

39 Patrick Boland, *Tales from a city farmyard* (Dublin: Patrick Boland, 1995), p. 63.

40 Angeline Kearns Blain, *Stealing sunlight: Growing up in Irishtown* (Dublin: A. & A. Farmar, 2000), p. 38.

41 Frank O'Connor, *An only child* (Belfast: Blackstaff, 1993), p. 139; Patrick Galvin, *Song for a poor boy: A Cork childhood* (Dublin: Raven Arts Press, 1990), p. 60. See also Christy Kenneally, *Maura's boy: A Cork childhood* (Cork: Mercier Press, 1996), p. 124; Sean Maher, *The road to God knows where: A memoir of travelling boyhood* (Dublin: Veritas, 1998), p 125; Peter Sheridan, *44: A Dublin memoir* (London: Macmillan, 2000), pp. 58–9.

42 NAI, Department of Education 11898, letter from Department of Education to [complainant], 22 February 1957.

43 NAI, Department of Education 16921, letter from Department of Education to Revd J. Masterson, P.P., 3 December 1960.

44 NAI, Department of Education 20412, case of charges by parents and inquiry, 10 July 1929.

45 NAI, Department of Education 20412, case of charges by parents and inquiry, 10 July 1929.

46 NAI, Department of Education 20412, case of charges by parents and inquiry, 10 July 1929.

47 NAI, Department of Education 20412, letter from Department of Education to Revd Gilmartin, Archbishop of Tuam, 5 July 1932.

48 NAI, Department of Education 20412, letter from Department of Education to principal teacher, 25 April 1936.

49 NAI, Department of Education 28229, letter from divisional inspector Thomas O'Connell to Department of Education, 29 February 1932.

50 NAI, Department of Education 28229, report on complaint by [mother] of the ill-treatment of her children, n.d.

51 NAI, Department of Education 28229, letter from teacher to Department of Education, 19 May 1933.

52 See NAI Department of Education 26305, 28565 and 28623.

53 NAI, Department of Education 28623. The Irish National Teachers Organization (INTO) was formed in 1868 and has become the primary trade union for national school teachers.

54 *Punishment in our schools* (Dublin: School Children's Protection Organisation, 1955), p. 3.

55 *Punishment in our schools*, p. 4.

56 *Punishment in our schools*, p. 5.

57 Dáil Éireann, vol. 152 (8 July 1955), col. 470.

58 Dáil Éireann, vol. 152 (8 July 1955), col. 470.

59 *Evening Mail* (1 October 1956), p. 5.

60 *Evening Mail* (1 October 1956), p. 1.

61 *Evening Mail* (11 October 1956), p. 5. The Irish Housewives Association was established in 1942 to enhance the role of Irish housewives in public and community life. For a history of the Irish Housewives Association see Hilda Tweedy, *A link in the chain: The story of the Irish Housewives Association, 1942–1992* (Dublin: Attic Press, 1992).

62 Dáil Éireann, vol. 162 (5 June 1957) col. 308.

63 Dáil Éireann, vol. 188, (4 May 1961), col. 1776.

64 Dáil Éireann, vol. 218 (28 October 1965), col. 761.

65 *Irish Times* (13 July 1968), p. 6.

66 Irish Union of School Students, *Corporal punishment: The brutal facts* (Dublin, 1974), p. 10.

67 The groups surveyed by the Minister for Education included: Irish National Teachers' Organisation; Association of Secondary Teachers; Teachers' Union of Ireland; Association of Principals of Community and Comprehensive Schools; Catholic Primary Managers' Association; Conference of Convent Primary Schools; and National School Boards of Management.

68 Dáil Éireann, vol. 310 (6 December 1978), col. 815.

69 Dáil Éireann, vol. 310 (6 December 1978), col. 815.

70 Dáil Éireann, vol. 310 (6 December 1978), col. 815.

71 Dáil Éireann, vol. 310 (6 December 1978), col. 815. The position of Minister of State is a junior, non-cabinet level position. The Minister of State in the Department of Education would have been "second in command" in the Department of Education, but he would not have had the same authority, or the same status, as the Minister for Education.

72 INTO, *Discipline in national schools* (Dublin: INTO District XI, 1983), pp. 38–9.

73 *Report of the committee on discipline in schools* (Dublin: Stationery Office, 1985).

74 From the time that the *States of fear* documentaries aired in April 1999 newspapers throughout Ireland (both those that would be regarded as "mainstream" such as the *Irish Times* and the *Irish Independent* and the more sensationalist papers such as *Ireland on Sunday*) have regularly published stories about the allegations of abuse in industrial schools and magdalen asylums, and of paedophile priests. Many of these articles were uncritical in their acceptance of church responsibility

for the scandals, and ignore the role of Irish society as a whole.

75 The conviction rate in cases involving children from 2–5 years of age was 70 per cent; from 6–8 years, 36 per cent; 9–10 years, 44 per cent; 11 years, 58 per cent; 12 years, 55 per cent; 13 years, 40 per cent; 14 years, 47 per cent; 15 years, 43 per cent.

76 In this context "harm" probably meant either pregnancy or a ruptured hymen, depending on the age of the victim.

77 NAI, Monaghan Circuit Court 1C 93 23, 24 April 1929.

78 NAI, Monaghan Circuit Court 1C 93 23, 24 April 1929.

79 NAI, Meath Circuit Court 1D 24 77, 21 March 1924.

80 Names in court reports and descriptions have been replaced by initials to preserve the anonymity of victims in these cases.

81 NAI, Donegal Circuit Court 1D 17 42, 30 June 1942.

82 NAI, Cork Circuit Court 1D 65 41, 13 October 1931; see also Cork Circuit Court 1D 65 43, 5 January 1932; Donegal Circuit Court 1D 6 31, 25 February 1930; Donegal Circuit Court 1D 32 107, 16 April 1947; Meath Circuit Court V14 23 38, 29 June 1948; Sligo Circuit Court 1D 14 4, 17 November 1932.

83 NAI, Cork Circuit Court 1D 65 41, 13 October 1931.

84 NAI, Galway Circuit Court 1D 43 111, 28 October 1928.

85 NAI, Cork Circuit Court 1D 14 65, 17 June 1941.

86 NAI, Cork Circuit Court 1D 14 65, 17 June 1941.

87 NAI, Limerick Circuit Court 1D 42 4, 20 October 1927.

88 NAI, Cork Circuit Court 1D 65 39, 11 October 1929.

89 NAI, Cork Circuit Court, 1D 65 40, 3 June 1930.

90 See NAI, Central Criminal Court V15 14 44, 25 October 1954; Central Criminal Court V15 1 1, 29 January 1952; Dublin Circuit Court 1D 24 144, 12 October 1944.

91 NAI, Dublin Circuit Court 1D 28 68, 11 October 1946.

92 NAI, Dublin Circuit Court 1D 28 68, 11 October 1946.

93 Dublin Circuit Court 1D 27 12, 17 April 1945.

6

Sanctity of child life?
Official responses to infanticide

Introduction

Previous chapters have examined policy and practice and, to the extent
possible, the lived experiences of illegitimate children who either remained
with their biological families or came into state care. But a striking feature
of twentieth-century Ireland was the relatively commonplace incidence
of infanticide. This might seem like an extreme method of dealing with
unwanted children, but all of the accumulated evidence suggests that it
was widely tolerated and often excused, if not necessarily condoned. In
February 1929 Helen Dignan stood trial in the Limerick Circuit Court for
the manslaughter of her newborn infant. Although Dignan likely played an
active role in the death of her infant, she was convicted of the lesser charge
of concealment of birth.[1] In imposing what by today's standards would be
seen as a paltry sentence, the judge articulated the ambivalence that characterized official attitudes towards infanticide in twentieth-century Ireland:
"These cases are becoming too common in the country, but I am not going
to inflict any punishment on the accused. I will take her own bail in £1
to keep the peace for two years and pass a suspensory sentence of four
months."[2] Only the barest of details are available in this case, so it is impossible fully to appreciate the judge's decision essentially to free Dignan while
emphasizing the gravity of her crime.

But this judge's decision was far from unique or unusual. Judges typically
paid lip-service to a veneer of moral outrage at the "slaughter of innocents"
while at the same time imposing sentences that must have led some women
to believe that they could neglect their newborn infants, or even murder

them, and essentially "get away" with it. Lawmakers were equally reluctant to hold women accountable for crimes against their newborn children, choosing to be led by prevailing, if misguided, assumptions about the nature not just of unwed motherhood, but of female criminality. When lawmakers finally did act on infanticide, they did so more out of an effort to bring the law into line with what had become standard judicial practice rather than out of any strong sense of social or moral conviction. Although jurists, lawmakers, and religious leaders acknowledged the theoretical respect that Irish society had for the sanctity of child life, their actions conveyed a different reality: that the lives of illegitimate, and thus presumably "unwanted" infants, could be sacrificed in the name of political, social, and economic expediencies.

Part of this ambivalence may have stemmed from the anomalous legal status of child murder. Until the introduction in the Infanticide Act (1949), women suspected of murdering or concealing their newborn infants were charged with murder under the Offences Against the Person Act (1803), although juries often convicted on lesser charges. However, judges had no choice but to impose a death sentence in murder convictions even though they knew full well the sentence would not be carried out.[3] An analysis of court records indicates that only rarely were women convicted on a murder charge, and every death sentence that was imposed on female infanticide defendants after 1922 was commuted to life imprisonment.[4] The Infanticide Act (1949) introduced the crime of infanticide, or the killing of an infant under twelve months old, as distinct from murder, and it was rooted in the belief that women in the final stages of pregnancy, labor, and childbirth were not "in their right mind" and thus could not be held entirely responsible for their actions. (In reality, lawmakers assumed that it was not the pregnancy itself, but the fact that it occurred outside of marriage, that compelled women to resort to infanticide. In his introduction of the bill Minister for Justice MacEoin noted that women who killed their children were not necessarily insane, but that they suffered from a mental "imbalance" at the time of the act. At the same time, he noted that the "usual type of case" was one involving unmarried mothers.[5] Several other TDs referred to the "unfortunate girls" and "unfortunate women" who typically committed infanticide; in twentieth-century Irish code, "unfortunate girl" meant unmarried mother.) At the same time, lawmakers consistently cautioned that infanticide legislation should not be interpreted as a disregard for infant life; rather, it was a pragmatic if implicit acknowledgment of current judicial practice in which death sentences passed on women, as a matter of course, were commuted to lesser penalties.

The Catholic hierarchy was perhaps the least vocal in articulating its views on infanticide, and in fact issued no formal writings or teachings on the subject that were intended for public consumption. The only sustained views that were expressed by the hierarchy came in a memorandum written by Patrick Dargan, a member of the Archbishop of Dublin, John Charles McQuaid's staff, in February 1949. The memorandum suggested that the fundamental principle of the Infanticide Act, the elimination of the death penalty for women convicted of infanticide, was flawed: "I cannot help thinking that it is a pity that the death penalty for this crime has been invariably remitted for so many years past. There must have been during that period cases in which the extreme penalty was fully deserved. The invariable remission of the penalty must have helped to foster the impression that infanticide is not murder, in the proper sense of the term."[6] The memorandum suggested that the law should be changed, not to accommodate the unmarried mother's unbalanced mind during childbirth, but to acknowledge the fact that men often shirked their responsibilities in these cases: "To my mind, the consideration that appears most to the ordinary person is that the man, responsible for her condition, and so often more guilty than she, so often gets away scot free, while she has to bear all the trouble and all the shame."[7] This notion that men were as responsible as women for infanticide appears occasionally in court records as well and is an interesting counterweight to the fears of blackmail and false allegations that surrounded discussions about the age of consent. (Of course, the men referred to in the infanticide debate were working-class, not the respectable middle-class men who presided over the country's judicial and legislative systems.)

Finally, Dargan concluded that even if the death penalty was eliminated in infanticide cases, the legislation should nonetheless make clear that, in the eyes of the law, infanticide was still a form of murder: "I would suggest that the wording of the bill be altered so as to include an explicit branding of the crime of the killing of an infant by its mother as murder … could this implicit feature of the bill not be made explicit, as a means of calling attention to a very important moral truth?"[8] Dargan was clearly in a difficult position: on the one hand, he had to draft a memorandum on the bill, for Archbishop McQuaid's information, that reflected the church's sanctity of life stance. On the other, the views expressed in the memorandum were somewhat hypocritical and unconvincing given the widespread tolerance of infanticide that existed within the criminal justice system and within Irish society generally. The hierarchy's relative silence on the issue of infanticide may not be noteworthy in itself, but is extraordinary when juxtaposed against the hundreds of pages of text, coupled with vociferous debates, that occurred around such issues as adoption and abortion.

The somewhat cavalier attitude on the part of lawmakers, the hierarchy, and jurists to the crime of infanticide became even more noteworthy when viewed against the backdrop of official expressions of concern over alarmingly high rates of infant mortality, especially among illegitimate children. The Commission on Emigration and other Population Problems, established in 1948 to investigate the roots of Ireland's perceived demographic crisis, reported that until the turn of the century Ireland's infant mortality rate compared favorably with rates for Northern Ireland, England and Wales, and Scotland. But while infant mortality continued to decline in Ireland into the twentieth century, it dropped more dramatically elsewhere in the UK, so that by 1952 the Irish rate, at 41 per 1,000, was considerably higher than in England and Wales (28 per 1,000), Scotland (35 per 1,000) or Northern Ireland (39 per 1,000).[9] The report also noted that Irish rates of infant mortality reflected significant differences between legitimate and illegitimate children:

> Important features of infant mortality in the Twenty-Six Counties are the wide difference between the death rates for legitimate children and for illegitimate children – the difference is wider than in other countries – and, in particular, the disparity between the death rates for illegitimate children here and in neighbouring countries. Deaths of illegitimate children are not always recorded as such, so that it would not be correct to attach too much importance to comparisons. Nevertheless, it is significant that, while the general infant mortality rate for the Twenty-Six Counties in 1950 was 46, the legitimate rate was 45 and the illegitimate rate 78. Full registration of deaths of illegitimate children would, no doubt, increase the disparity, a fact which is confirmed by a sample investigation made by us of the infant mortality rate in situations which provide specially for the care of illegitimate infants. While adequate information is lacking as to the extent of infanticide we believe that its incidence is not sufficiently significant to require comment from us. As to the contrast with the neighbouring counties, our illegitimate death rate in 1950 was 78 compared with 65 in the Six Counties, 53 in Scotland and 39 in England and Wales.[10]

While pre-natal and post-natal neglect likely were most responsible for high rates of infant mortality among illegitimate infants, it is telling that the Commission dismissed infanticide as a significant contributing factor. What the Commission failed to recognize was that the general tolerance of infanticide reflected a more general undervaluing of child life that likely contributed to high rates of illegitimate infant mortality.[11]

Contemporary cases of infanticide typically are greeted with revulsion and incredulity within an Irish population firm in the conviction that such things were and are rare and extraordinary, and smug in their supposed compassion for unmarried mothers and their children in the early twenty-first century. This contrasts sharply with the frequent statements by judges from the 1920s to the 1950s that infanticide was an unfortunate and unpalatable, but inevitable, fact of life. This seemingly cavalier attitude in earlier times reflected a tolerance borne of pragmatism: poverty was a fact of life for a significant proportion of the population, and each new mouth to feed stretched a family's already meager resources. The way that the courts dealt with infanticide, as opposed to the enormous political and social hostility that underscored responses to unmarried mothers, suggests that respect for life did not apply equally to all individuals. Child life was valued only insofar as it conformed to the state's expectations of appropriate maternal behavior and family formation, so that illegitimate children have historically been politically and socially marginalized, and infanticide unofficially and implicitly tolerated in spite of judicial outcries against the "slaughter of innocents."

It is virtually impossible to quantify the extent of infanticide in the twentieth century, not only because it was not always detected, but also because there are discrepancies between the number of cases heard in the Central Criminal and circuit courts on an annual basis, and official statistics published annually in Garda reports. Additionally, national and local newspapers regularly reported the finding of infants' bodies in bog holes, rivers, and gardens; many of these deaths were never accounted for, and the mothers of those infants not identified. However, the actual statistical incidence of infanticide is less important than the concern, especially among lawmakers and judges, that it was all too prevalent in the mid-twentieth century, and an all too easy solution to unwed and unwanted pregnancies. The difficulty of quantifying infanticide is not aided by scholarly studies of the subject, given that little has been written about infanticide in twentieth-century Ireland aside from Louise Ryan's examination of media treatment of infanticide cases in the 1920s and Cliona Rattigan's chapter in *Single motherhood in twentieth-century Ireland*, which is based on a very limited reading of Central Criminal Court files.[12]

Infanticide legislation

Prior to the 1949 Infanticide Act the murder of infants was tried under the 1803 British Offences Against the Person Act. The 1803 Act reflected a shift in the judicial treatment of infanticide as it placed the onus on the state to prove the guilt of the accused, where previous legislation compelled accused women to prove their innocence. Under the 1803 Act the death sentence was mandatory in murder convictions. By the early twentieth century, however, all death sentences passed in these cases were commuted to life imprisonment, and one of the most important features of the 1949 Act was the elimination of the death penalty for women accused of killing their newborn infants. Thus the Infanticide Act could be seen as an effort on the part of lawmakers to bring statute into line with what had gradually become standard judicial practice. Many deputies welcomed the act because of its "humanitarian" and "enlightened" treatment of women accused of infanticide. Minister for Justice MacEoin articulated the majority view when he introduced the bill in the Dáil: "Now, it will, I think, be agreed on all sides that it is desirable that the law should be altered so as to eliminate, in appropriate cases, the pronouncement of the death sentence in these cases in which everybody knows that the sentence will not be carried out."[13] At the same time, the minister warned his colleagues that they must not appear to condone the crime: "But, in framing our legislative proposals to deal with the situation, we must, I submit, be careful to avoid any suggestion that the Legislature of this country has become less conscious of, or less concerned about, the sanctity of human life."[14] The challenge that lawmakers faced in drafting legislation that embraced modern criminal justice principles while preserving a distinct moral tone reflected a more general conflict between societal concern for "innocent" illegitimate children, and the economic and social conditions in which the majority of people lived that effectively sacrificed illegitimate children to apparently more pressing social, economic, religious, and political priorities.

Lawmakers navigated the contradiction between the supposed value of child life, on the one hand, and the reduction of the crime of child murder to infanticide, on the other, by including a stipulation that was, in effect, toothless. They argued that women were to be charged with murder initially, and that the charge would be reduced at the discretion of district and circuit court justices:

> The Bill ... clearly implies, though it does not expressly say so, that the charge initially against a woman who willfully causes the death of her infant child will be a charge of murder. It will be for the district court in the first instance, on the preliminary investigation of the charges, after having heard the evidence including the evidence as to the mental state of the woman at the time of the offence, to decide whether or not the accused shall be sent forward for trial on a charge of murder or on a charge of infanticide.[15]

In fact, however, the charge of murder of newborn infants virtually disappeared from the court records following the passage of the Infanticide Act.

Even before 1949 a charge of murder was lodged only rarely in cases of newborn infant death: of the nearly 600 cases of infanticide and related crimes that were heard in the Central Criminal and circuit courts from the 1920s to 1960, only in 62 cases were the defendants charged with murder.[16] The last murder charge was lodged in the Central Criminal Court in November 1949, just six months after the passage of the Infanticide Act. So, in spite of lawmakers' insistence that the Infanticide Act upheld the sanctity of child life by maintaining the murder charge, in fact just the opposite happened. Nonetheless, lawmakers apparently succeeded in convincing themselves and one another that the Infanticide Act would not send the message that the state condoned infanticide, nor would it lead to increases in the murder of newborn infants: "There may be people who will think that this Bill will be a lesser deterrent to those who might be inclined to kill their children, but I do not think so. When such things happen you will find that the woman was in a frenzy or that her mind was disturbed."[17] It would be impossible, given the nature of court records, to conclude that infanticide and similar crimes increased as a result of the Infanticide Act. (On the other hand, in the ten years preceding the 1949 Infanticide Act, 222 cases of murder, manslaughter, and concealment of birth came to the attention of the courts; in the ten-year period after the passage of the Act, a scant 18 cases came to the courts' attention.) But Mr Boland's claim that most women who committed infanticide were in a "frenzy" is patently incorrect. In fact, many women committed infanticide, some of them on numerous occasions, with impunity and without remorse, and it is not unreasonable to suggest that their own cavalier attitude towards the death of their newborn infants resulted in part from the knowledge that the law would treat them leniently.

Not all lawmakers agreed with the "leniency" of the proposed bill, arguing that the state had a duty to uphold, at all costs, Catholic social and moral principles. Some prominent politicians, including Eamon de Valera, insisted that objective codes of right and wrong not only existed, but also could and should underpin legislative and judicial policy and procedure because they were consistent with God's law. De Valera argued that the legislation minimized the seriousness of infanticide and thus provided an inducement to unmarried women to engage in illicit sex and then kill their babies to hide their moral lapses. He also insisted that the Bill conflicted not only with the state's fundamental respect for the sanctity of human life, but more importantly with God's law, in which the state had no right to interfere.[18] De Valera was one of the few lawmakers to articulate a view that most lawmakers were keen to downplay – that many cases of infanticide were not the result of shame, fear, or desperation, but were in fact cases of wilful murder: "The whole category of crime which you have to consider will embrace everything from possible complete lack of responsibility due to complete mental incapacity to cold-blooded, willful and unadulterated murder. In the circumstances I am inclined to ask myself whether fundamentally as a matter of law it is competent to the House to make a distinction in the nature of the crime."[19] De Valera argued that no change to existing law was necessary, and in doing so he was more concerned that women guilty of murdering their newborn infants pay for their crimes, than he was with the life and death of innocent newborn children. Few of de Valera's colleagues agreed with his views, which is not surprising. Admitting that mothers were capable of wilfully and in cold blood murdering their children would have undermined the entire gendered and maternal order on which the Irish Free State was built. In this instance, illegitimate children were sacrificed in the name of the gendered status quo.

The infanticide debate underscored the inevitable tension between the distinctly or inherently Irish values and traditions that defined the independent Irish state, and foreign, "pagan" (in other words, English) values. Lawmakers expressed a particular unease with what they perceived to be a decidedly liberal or English bias in the bill, which was understandable given that the language of the Irish and English bills was similar.[20] These objections were based on little more than the fact that the bill was modeled after, perhaps even inspired by, its English counterpart: "I would not be too happy blindly to subscribe to anything resembling from the traditions of English liberal thought on this matter ... this word 'infanticide' savours a bit too much to my mind of English liberal thought."[21] Even Justice Minister MacEoin, the bill's author, attempted to defend the bill against the charge that it embraced a spirit of English liberalism: "I am not bringing it in because the British have brought in similar legislation, and I do not bring it in in the spirit of liberalism that some may attach to it; I bring it in in a spirit of humanity and charity to people who are among the poorest of our community."[22] The Irish Infanticide Bill resembled its English counterpart in most aspects, particularly in the creation of a new category of crime, but under British law all women accused of killing their infants were automatically charged with infanticide while the Irish law left it to the discretion of district or circuit court judges to reduce a murder charge to infanticide. This difference reflected the desire on the part of lawmakers to project an image of humanitarianism while maintaining the fiction that the state was committed to protecting and cherishing all children, including illegitimate children who likely would ultimately become burdens on public funds.

The Infanticide Bill passed the Dáil with a minimum of fanfare. Official discussions encompassed a mere nine pages of text in the published record, compared with the almost fifty pages that comprised the parliamentary debate on the Adoption Act (an Act that was the subject of significant comment and intervention by the Catholic hierarchy). Similarly, the Infanticide Act elicited only passing notice in the pages of the Catholic or mainstream press. The fact that the proposed legislation prompted no commentary from the editors of either the *Catholic Standard* or the *Irish Catholic* suggests that the hierarchy assented to, or at least did not oppose, either the principle or the form of the proposed legislation. There appears to have been little of the direct communication and negotiation between church and state that occurred in debates around other "moral" issues such as adoption, affiliations orders, dance halls legislation, and the mother and child health scheme. It would seem that church leaders and lawmakers were more concerned with the souls of living children than with the fate of illegitimate newborns who might die at the hands of their own mothers.

Catholic responses to infanticide

Catholic moralist rhetoric consistently emphasized the dangers to Irish social stability, and to the moral fiber of Irish people, of inappropriate expressions of sexuality, and especially of female sexuality. In focusing on female sexuality the church was not simply projecting the Victorian sexual double standard or constructions of femininity and masculinity that demanded chastity of women but excused male sexual transgressions. Catholic moral teaching did not condone or excuse male sexual indiscretions, and Catholic writers often articulated a particular, if veiled, suspicion of working-class male sexuality. In practical terms, however, it was easier to monitor and regulate the sexual and reproductive activities of women, through indirect means such as sermons, pamphlets, and other religious literature extolling the virtues of chastity and emphasizing the sin of lust, or directly through philanthropic organizations whose mission was to eliminate the potentially dangerous effects of unwed motherhood and illegitimacy. Although religious discourse rarely discussed infanticide explicitly, there was an implicit acknowledgment that it was an inevitable by-product of sexual immorality. But not once was the connection made between the church's insistence on the sanctity of child life evident in abortion discourse and rhetoric, and the disregard of child life evident in prevailing attitudes towards infanticide.

The Catholic hierarchy has been consistent, sustained, and unwavering in its condemnation of abortion as the unacceptable destruction of child life, while they have virtually ignored the destruction of *actual* child life resulting from infanticide. Abortion and infanticide may have represented the willful and premeditated destruction of human life, but abortion was far more worrying because it enabled women to control their sexual and reproductive activities privately and secretly, entirely outside of the church's surveilling and carceral authority. Meanwhile infanticide, while perhaps anathema, nonetheless relieved Catholic charitable agencies of the otherwise almost inevitable responsibility for caring for illegitimate children. Sermons and other Catholic writings often portrayed women accused of infanticide as modern-day Mary Magdalens, as sinner-saints who could "return, like the Prodigal, to the feet of the Father" if they acknowledged their sin, sought redemption, and returned to the "correct path" of virtue and purity.[23] Only the church's "supernatural" moralizing influence could repair the rents in their moral fabric and cleanse their souls sufficiently that they could aspire to eternal life in Heaven. The ambiguity evident in infanticide legislation, combined with the tendency of judges to commit female offenders to magdalen asylums rather than prison, facilitated the church's efforts to exert complete and unchallenged authority over a select group of problematic women in ways that otherwise would have been beyond its reach.[24] It would not be unreasonable, then, to suggest that underpinning the Catholic Church's "sanctify of life" rhetoric was less a concern for the fate of children, than a desire to control female sexuality.

The reaction of Catholic writers to infanticide represented a mixture of theology and pragmatism that occasionally conflicted with official Catholic teaching. The theological response is evident in the recognition that illegitimate children were at particular risk of being murdered by their mothers and in the conviction, articulated by Reverend Devane, that judges, in their leniency, tended to minimize the seriousness of the crime of infanticide. Devane insisted that Catholic theology did not distinguish between legitimate and illegitimate children in asserting the sanctity of human life:

> While making all due allowances and extending pity to the unmarried mother at such a time, we must not be sentimentalized into forgetting or whittling down the Law of God, and we cannot help marvelling at the treatment frequently allotted to those cases in our Courts. It would seem as if the Law did not value the life of the illegitimate child, principally because there is no one to make a case or stand up for it: and certainly it is less valued than the life of the ordinary child. This is not law or morality. People must take the consequences of their acts.[25]

But even the hierarchy expressed a certain pragmatism in its response to infanticide that contrasted sharply with the strong condemnation heaped upon unmarried mothers and their children. In the minds of lawmakers and clergy, illegitimate children posed a constant threat to twentieth-century social harmony and stability as well as a drain on public resources, and they devised numerous schemes to neutralize that threat.

Although rarely acknowledged explicitly, the problem of infanticide was a theme that ran throughout religious discussions about the disintegration of moral standards and a decline in traditional concepts of community and mutual responsibility. Infanticide was the inevitable result when Irish Catholics rejected traditional, "acceptable" forms of amusement and socializing in favor of "foreign" amusements such as the dance hall and the cinema, where women and men mingled in "impure" environments that were obvious "occasions of sin." Father Aloysius gave voice to this belief in a fundraising sermon on behalf of the Good Shepherd magdalen asylum: "in many cases their sad lot might be traced to the want of a Christian home, to a cruel liberty to do as they would and go where they liked. They fell prey to the diabolical heartlessness of some foul wretch and too late they learnt how little they were prepared to battle with the foes of their virtue and their happiness."[26] Reverend Devane, in an article on the evils of dance halls, explicitly linked infanticide and illegitimacy with the dance hall: "It is clear that one of the immediate and chief causes of the immorality of recent times, involving particularly the unmarried mother, is the commercialized dance-halls … I think it well to direct attention to the appalling crime of the murder of the illegitimate by its own unnatural mother, about which there may be a danger of a maudlin sentimentality growing."[27] Religious discourse implied that "true" Irish women were inherently chaste and virtuous but were susceptible to outside forces, especially those emanating from Britain, that threatened their virtue, undermined the church's moral authority, and thus led inexorably to infanticide.

The hierarchy's fears of the perceived threat from foreign influences (and especially the dance hall) to Ireland's "traditional" virtue and piety cannot be underestimated. In religious and nationalist rhetoric Ireland was a traditional, pious, and frugal society, insulated and safe from the dangers and pressures of the "outside" world. Infanticide, unmarried motherhood, and illegitimacy were not intrinsically Irish phenomena but, rather, could be traced directly to the influence of "pagan" (in other words, British) ideas about sexuality, marriage, and family life.[28] Religious leaders portrayed the dance hall as the single biggest threat to Irish morality: dance halls replaced traditional Irish music and dance with more modern and pagan forms but, more importantly, dance halls undermined customary practices of rural socializing that monitored and regulated interactions between women and men. If Devane is to be believed, the dance hall was singularly responsible for the majority of infanticide cases in Ireland. Those women who did not commit infanticide, according to Devane, "exported their shame" to England and brought still greater disrepute on Ireland. The *Catholic Standard* and *Irish Catholic* newspapers emphasized the alleged links between immorality and the dance halls to lobby the government for tighter controls on dance halls, resulting in the 1935 Public Dance Hall Act.[29] Even after the passage of the act the hierarchy continued to insist, through the pages of the Catholic press, that dance halls posed a constant danger to Irish girls' maidenhood. In reality, a survey of infanticide and related crimes suggests a negligible link between dance halls, illegitimacy, and infanticide.[30] But the rise in popularity of dance halls reflected the church's worst fears about female sexuality, a decline in respect for traditional Irish values and customs, and the invasion into Irish social and cultural life of foreign values that undermined the church's moral authority. It was not the lives of innocent children that the hierarchy sought to protect, but rather their stranglehold on the moral and sexual behavior of Irish women.

Perhaps it is telling of the overall attitude toward infanticide that the Catholic hierarchy lobbied far more vocally and vehemently for dance halls legislation and against adoption legislation than for or against the Infanticide Bill. At the same time, John Charles McQuaid, Archbishop of Dublin from 1940 to 1972, did not miss an opportunity to place his views before the Dáil. In a strongly worded statement McQuaid rejected the premise of the Infanticide Bill, particularly the idea that infanticide could be distinguished from murder. In fact, McQuaid regarded infanticide as "an aggravated form of murder. It adds to the crime of murder a violation of the virtue of pietas."[31] McQuaid also expressed regret that the courts typically commuted the death penalty and that the proposed legislation eliminated it altogether, believing that the imposition of the penalty, even if not carried out, conveyed the gravity of the crime of child-murder. But another, unattributed, brief on the infanticide bill included in the same diocesan archive file presents an indifferent attitude to the proposed legislation: "the writer is of opinion that the passage into law of the Infanticide Bill, 1949, would not be likely to result in an increase either in sexual immorality or of infant killing, provided that juries conscientiously perform their duties and judges impose sentences consistent with justice and humanity."[32] These two views, incompatible on the surface, suggest that the hierarchy was less concerned with eradicating the crime of infanticide than with preserving the facade of the Catholic "sanctity of life" doctrine while also ensuring that women convicted of the crime be subject to penalties sufficient to punish them for their "sins." These two unpublished briefs appear to be the extent of the hierarchy's involvement in the debate over infanticide legislation.

Infanticide in the courts

The 1949 Infanticide Act, unlike other "moral" issues such as abortion, contraception, adoption, and divorce, owed less to the influence of the Catholic Church than to a combination of British criminal justice principles, current judicial practice, and basic pragmatism. But to fully appreciate official responses to infanticide and official concern for the fate of illegitimate children, one must look at the way judges and juries understood and interpreted the actions of the women who appeared before them for crimes against their newborn infants. The most compelling insight into the adjudication of infanticide emerges from court records and newspaper accounts of Central Criminal and circuit court trials, and Court of Criminal Appeal records, which include accused and witness testimonies, judges' instructions to juries and, occasionally, insight into sentencing decisions. The majority of court records consist of written depositions, recorded by gardaí in the course of their investigations; full trial transcripts are available only when a defendant appealed her or his conviction or sentence. However, regional Irish newspapers often published extensive and sometimes verbatim accounts of infanticide trials, which offer extraordinary insights into the attitudes of judges, solicitors, and juries.

What becomes clear from an analysis of trial proceedings is that judges paid lip-service to the view that infanticide was a crime perpetrated against "innocent" and "defenseless" illegitimate children. In reality, the death of an illegitimate child often was at the bottom of the list of priorities when juries evaluated guilt or innocence, or when judges passed sentence on women convicted of infanticide and related crimes. Juries looked for a reason to acquit, or to convict on lesser charges even when the available evidence strongly indicated that a child had been murdered in a violent and brutal fashion. Judges tended to be sympathetic to women who appeared before them in court, but they also sought opportunities to make examples of particular defendants for reasons of their own. This was the case, for example, on the rare occasions when male defendants appeared before the courts, but it was also common when numerous cases of infanticide came before a single court sitting. When this happened judges were reminded just how frequently infanticide and related crimes occurred, and they sought to reaffirm the official respect for the sanctity of child life.

There is no doubt that some of the women who appeared before the courts fit the image of the seduced, abandoned, and desperate young woman who killed her baby in a fit of panic, fear, or intense shame. The case of Mary Harris was fairly typical of this scenario. Harris was acquitted of the murder of her newborn infant in 1931 despite the fact that she admitted tying a belt tightly around the child's neck. In acquitting her the jury likely took her circumstances into consideration. Hogan admitted that she was a willing partner in the sexual encounter that resulted in her pregnancy: "I was keeping the company of a boy ... of Drogheda. He took advantage of me on one occasion. I was a consenting party as he had already promised to marry me. I knew I had become pregnant at the end of last November 1930. I did not tell [the boy] of this fact, nor did I tell anyone else."[33] It is entirely possible that Harris did not tell her partner of her pregnancy because she feared he would leave her.

Harris's sense of desperation was compounded by her tenuous employment situation; Harris worked as a live-in domestic servant, and her employer had given her a month's notice, in early September 1931, that she would have to leave. Harris's employer admitted that Harris was a good worker, and she knew Harris had nowhere else to go, but she fired her because she suspected the pregnancy. The fact that Harris gave birth just two weeks after being fired probably contributed to her sense of fear and desperation. At her trial the county medical officer who conducted the post mortem on the infant acknowledged that: "It was quite possible that a girl in the circumstances of the accused might lead to an act of which she would not be responsible."[34] The fact that the jury acquitted Harris, rather than convicting her on a lesser charge, suggests that Harris conformed perfectly to the jury's assumption about the "typical" infanticide defendant, who in their eyes was as much a victim as a victimizer. The death of an innocent child in this case stemmed, not from malice or a disregard for child life, but from a desperate and unfortunate, but all too common, set of circumstances.

A case from 1946 similarly conformed to jurists' expectations of the "typical" infanticide defendant, perhaps even more so than Mary Harris. In this case the defendant, Ellen Davis, was only eighteen years of age. Davis admitted that she knew she was pregnant, but that she did not know who fathered her child: "I never knew the names of the men who used to accompany me home from dances, and none of them ever told me their names. During the times I was accompanied from those dances three or four different men had connection with me on two or three different occasions each, and I would say as far as I can remember that my periods stopped some time in July 1945."[35] Davis's age and situation likely contributed to the less than ideal circumstances in which she gave birth: "I was feeling bad with a pain in my stomach, and I knew then that my baby was about to be born. About two or three minutes after arriving at the potato pit, and while I was standing, my baby was born. I heard the baby dropping to the ground from me, immediately the baby dropped to the ground I looked at it and saw it was a baby."[36] According to the medical evidence, the fact that the umbilical cord had been torn rather than cut indicated "inattention at birth," and the cause of death was asphyxia resulting from pressure on the windpipe. Davis was convicted of concealment of birth and sentenced to eighteen months in a Dublin magdalen asylum. It is interesting that the jury in this instance convicted Davis, albeit on a significantly reduced charge, while the jury in the Harris case acquitted her in spite of her admission of guilt.

It is possible that the jury convicted her so the judge would be in a position to send her to a magdalen asylum, where she would receive the protection he thought she needed.

But for every case that was fuelled by fear, desperation, or shame, there was another that did not fit the "mold" at all, although this did not stop judges and juries from looking for an excuse to be lenient. One case that is particularly intriguing, and indicative of the judicial ambivalence referred to earlier, involved Molly Larkin and her granddaughter Helen. Molly and Helen were charged with the murder of Helen's newborn illegitimate infant. Medical evidence showed that the child died of a fractured skull that was inflicted intentionally rather than accidentally. More extraordinarily, however, some of the child's vital organs had been removed, and the doctors who conducted the post-mortem concluded that this was done deliberately to prevent them from determining that the child had been born alive. The medical evidence clearly pointed to a deliberate and particularly brutal murder. The only witnesses, however, were Molly and Helen themselves, and each implicated the other. The jury concluded that Molly Larkin was entirely responsible for the child's death, and she was convicted of murder and sentenced to death while Helen was acquitted. On appeal, however, Molly's conviction was quashed and on re-trial she was acquitted. In his summation, Molly Larkin's solicitor stressed that Larkin had absolutely nothing to gain from murdering the child. In this instance, neither Helen nor Molly paid for the crime committed against the newborn child, and the fact that the child was murdered and mutilated did not matter in the final analysis.[37]

A second case that illustrates the leniency of juries, and their tendency to overlook the violence perpetrated against illegitimate children, is noteworthy because the woman involved was Protestant, she was married to the putative father of the child (although the husband denied that he was the father), and the child was nine months old when she died. Fanny Ryan gave birth to a child in November 1948. At that time she was unmarried, and the rector of the local Church of Ireland parish, W.M. Giff, helped Ryan place the child in a children's home in Dublin, at a cost to Ryan of 10s per week. In January 1949 Ryan married Joe Bolger, who she claimed was the father of the child. Fanny Bolger (née Ryan) ceased paying to maintain her child in the Dublin children's home in July 1949, at which point Reverend Giff brought the child to the Bolger home, believing that the marriage of the child's parents legitimized her. Fanny Bolger was angry with Giff for returning the child: "Her attitude seemed to be that she had disposed of it and it should not have been brought back to her."[38] The baby died some time in late August 1949, and the circumstances surrounding her death were somewhat cloudy and suspicious. According to Fanny Bolger, she accidentally dropped the child, and the child died several hours later. After the child's death, according to Bolger, she asked her husband Joe to bury her; Joe refused and told her to do it herself. She subsequently buried the child. Interestingly, it was Joe Bolger himself who notified the police of the child's death and illicit burial, and Fanny Bolger's solicitor made much of the fact that Bolger's husband was unsupportive and unsympathetic.

Medical evidence indicated that the child died of shock and hemorrhage due to bruises and skull fractures that could not have been caused by a fall, as Fanny Bolger claimed. Bolger testified that her husband was not present when the child died and refused to participate in its burial. In spite of all of this evidence, the judge cautioned the jury that "the husband had equal if not a stronger motive and that weakened the case as regards motive against the accused."[39] It took the jury just five minutes to acquit Fanny Bolger, and Joe Bolger was never charged with the crime. Here again, the violence perpetrated against an illegitimate child was all but ignored in the jury's eagerness to acquit female defendants whenever possible, even when those defendants clearly did not conform to the image of the "typical" infanticide defendant.

Judges were similarly eager to be lenient whenever possible, but they also took the opportunity, when it presented itself, to make an example of particular kinds of defendants. They often found themselves swamped with infanticide and related cases, and they sometimes felt compelled to pass unusually harsh sentences to perpetuate the façade that crimes against newborn infants would not be tolerated, and to pay lip-service to the assertion that the lives of illegitimate children were valued as highly as the lives of any other individuals. Ultimately a small handful of defendants paid the price, in the form of extraordinarily harsh sentences, for the large number of defendants who were not punished at all. The higher price, of course, was paid by the children who were murdered by occasionally desperate but more often selfish and callous parents.

One case that epitomized the occasional desire among judges to punish excessively certain categories of defendants involved an unmarried couple, James Lynch and Mary Sullivan. Sullivan was homeless and gave birth in a field in Co. Tipperary in June of 1929. Lynch was present when Sullivan gave birth, and in the days before and after the birth he did his best to make Sullivan comfortable by bringing her food, milk, and sacks to sleep on. Both Sullivan and Lynch testified that the baby lived only a short time, and the postmortem indicated that the baby died as a result of "inattention at birth." Lynch's defense counsel suggested that Lynch was "of [a] primitive type. In his own clumsy way he had done his best for the woman."[40]

The judge denigrated Lynch's efforts and told him that "[it] is in savage south Africa you should be."[41] The prosecutor pointed out that "although the crime of infanticide was unhappily, but far too frequently, the source of investigation in the court, the circumstances here were of an exceptional character, inasmuch as here it was the man, the origin of the wrong doing, who was in the dock."[42] The prosecutor also noted that "[it] was a disgustingly barbarous murder."[43] The medical evidence clearly indicated that this was a case of concealment of birth or, at most, neglect rather than a "disgustingly barbarous murder." There certainly were any number of cases of deliberate, violent murder that were far more "barbarous" than anything Lynch had done. The judge and prosecutor acknowledged that they had the rare opportunity to hold a man accountable for the unwanted pregnancy that led to infanticide in the first place. Lynch was sentenced to three years of penal servitude, which was an extraordinarily harsh sentence under the circumstances. But in this instance the judge was less concerned with how or why the baby died than with making an example and scapegoat of Lynch.[44]

It was not only men who became the targets of frustrated judges' wrath. It was not unusual for judges in some circuit courts around the country, and in the Central Criminal Court, to hear three, four, or even five separate cases of infanticide and related crimes in a single court sitting. And when this happened it was not unusual for judges to express frustration at the frequency of such cases and to voice the belief that they should be treated much more seriously. (It should be noted that some judges acted on this impulse and found scapegoats for their frustration, while others paid lip-service to the view while continuing to pass what often ended up being paltry sentences.) The judge in the case of Betty Murphy chose to hold Murphy up as an example, and it is clear that the sentence passed on Murphy had less to do with either concern for her dead baby or with the severity of her actions, but with the judge's utter frustration: "Mr. Justice Meredith said that the case was so serious that he could not impose a less sentence than three years' penal servitude. That would be easier for the prisoner than two years' hard labour. There were four of those cases for trial at the present court, and the situation was such in respect of the class of crime that it would have to be faced. If there were to be any remission of sentence, it would have to be obtained through the usual state channels."[45] Interestingly, a week later, while presiding over another infanticide trial, the judge expressed regret with the harsh sentence he passed on Murphy.[46]

A case from 1940 Longford illustrated the mixed messages that judges often sent in their effort to present a façade of concern for the fate of illegitimate children while acknowledging the realities of Irish life that, in fact, placed very little value on such lives. Margaret Gallagher was charged with murder but convicted of concealment of birth even though medical evidence indicated that the child died from shock and hemorrhage as a result of having its throat cut. On the one hand, the judge adopted a hard-line stance in the case: "It is a most difficult case but the fact remains that a life has been taken and I cannot allow it to go forth from this court that the crime went unpunished."[47] On the other hand, the judge passed a suspensory sentence provided Gallagher voluntarily entered a magdalen asylum.

In recent years there has been a great deal of press coverage of Ireland's magdalen asylums, prompted in part by the allegations that first surfaced in the mid-1990s about the treatment of children in a host of religious-run institutions. The literature about magdalen asylums reinforces the view that women, particularly unmarried mothers, were locked away forever for their "sins."[48] James Smith highlights the use made by the courts of magdalen asylums in lieu of prison for some of the women who were convicted of infanticide and related crimes. Smith concludes: "Government archives suggest that these asylums were always considered available to the state as sites of confinement. Moreover, there was a general awareness of the institutions' punitive regime, in particular, the fact that many women remained confined for life."[49] Smith provides no evidence from the "government archives" to which he refers to support this conclusion. Smith further asserts that the magdalen asylum was the preferred method of dealing with women convicted of infanticide and related courses. Again, Smith's conclusion is based on a limited examination of available sources. Smith used only those cases that were heard in the Central Criminal Court. But of the nearly 600 crimes of infanticide and related crimes that came before the courts in the period 1923 to 1960, only about 200, or one-third, were heard in the Central Criminal Court; the remainder were heard in circuit courts around the country. And the story that is told by an analysis of *all* court records is one of tolerance and lenience. Of the 506 sentences in the Central Criminal and circuit courts, 87 (17 per cent) involved imprisonment for periods of one day to five years; 109 (or 21 per cent) involved confinement in magdalen asylums for periods ranging from six months to three years; and 285, or a staggering 56 per cent of defendants, received sentences that essentially freed them. (These sentences included probation, fines, and orders to keep the peace.)[50]

Conclusion

Official attitudes towards infanticide paid lip-service to the conviction that the lives of all Irish children were sacred and valued. In reality, however, the lives of illegitimate children were low on the list of priorities when it came to official responses and attitudes. The Catholic hierarchy had little to say on the subject of infanticide, even when the Dáil debated infanticide legislation in 1949. This silence is somewhat surprising given the church's sustained and often vehement anti-abortion stance, and its extensive intervention in other "moral" issues like adoption and contraception. In fact the hierarchy appears to have been more concerned with controlling female sexuality than they were with saving the lives (and souls) of the child victims of infanticide. And lawmakers appear to have been more concerned with the semantics of the 1949 Infanticide Act than they were with protecting newborn illegitimate children or of punishing those guilty of child murder.

The official ambivalence towards infanticide, in policy and practice, was seen most clearly in the way judges and juries dealt with infanticide cases in the courtroom. Judges and juries usually approached infanticide cases from the assumption that the "typical" infanticide defendant was a poor, seduced, desperate woman who committed infanticide on the spur of the moment, out of a sense of panic and shame. Such defendants were often perceived as "more sinned against than sinning." This depiction was accurate in some cases, but a significant proportion of the infanticide cases did not conform to this image. Even in cases where women committed brutal acts of violence against their newborn infants, and showed no remorse after the fact, judges and juries sought every opportunity to convict on lesser charges and pass reduced sentences. Illegitimate children were effectively sacrificed in the name of upholding traditional maternal and gender roles, but more importantly in the name of protecting the façade of Catholic morality and purity upon which the independent Irish state was built.

Notes

1   Prior to the 1949 Infanticide Act, many women accused of infanticide were initially charged with murder. However, all but a handful were convicted of either manslaughter, if there was significant evidence linking them to the death of a child, or concealment of birth, if medical evidence was inconclusive as to the cause of a child's death. After 1949 women suspected of killing their newborn infants were rarely charged with murder, instead being charged with infanticide. But most defendants continued to be convicted of the lesser charges of manslaughter and concealment of birth.

2   *Limerick Weekly Echo* (18 February 1929), p. 4.

3   Until 1949 infanticide was not an official category of crime although the term was used commonly before 1949 in legal and legislative parlance. Prior to 1949 the majority of defendants charged with murder were convicted of manslaughter or concealment of birth. Murder implied a wilful act, manslaughter suggested

negligence or ignorance rather than malice, and concealment of birth indicated insufficient evidence to link the defendant with the infant's death, and thus the defendant could only be charged with failing to report the child's birth and death.

4 Central Criminal Court records relating to infanticide consist of trial record books that summarize the charges, convictions, and sentences of all trials heard before the court, as well as depositions and statements in individual cases. All of the records in which the death sentence was imposed, except one, are appended with a handwritten note in the trial record book indicating the commutation of the death sentence to life imprisonment. In the exceptional case, newspaper coverage of the trial indicated that the sentence had been commuted. Annie Walsh was the last woman to be executed in Ireland. She was hanged in August 1925 for murdering her husband.

5 *Dáil Debates*, vol. 115 (28 April 1949), col. 265.

6 DDA, McQuaid Papers government box 1, Patrick Dargan, "The proposed infanticide bill 1949."

7 Dargan, "The Proposed Infanticide Bill."

8 Dargan, "The Proposed Infanticide Bill."

9 Commission on Emigration and Other Population Problems, *Reports 1948–54* (Dublin: Government Stationery Office, 1955), p. 111.

10 Commission on Emigration, *Reports*, p. 112.

11 See Brian Crichton, "Infant mortality in Dublin," *Irish Journal of Medical Science*, 4th series, 42 (July 1925), pp. 302–5; H.M., "Illegitimate," *The Bell*, 2:3 (June 1941), pp. 78–87; NAI, Department of Health M18/1; Department of Health *Annual Reports* (Dublin: Government Stationery Office, 1946–52); and National Society for the Prevention of Cruelty to Children, *Annual Reports of the Dublin Branch* (Dublin: NSPCC, 1930), pp. 7–8.

12 Louise Ryan, "The massacre of innocence: Infanticide in the Irish Free State," *Irish Studies Review*, 14 (Spring 1996), pp. 17–21; see also Louise Ryan, "Press, police, and prosecution: Perspectives on infanticide in the 1920s," in *Irish women's history*, ed. Alan Hayes and Diane Urquehart (Dublin: Irish Academic Press, 2004), pp. 137–51; Cliona Rattigan, "'Dark spots' in Irish society: Unmarried mothers and infanticide in Ireland from 1926 to 1938," in *Single motherhood in twentieth-century Ireland: Cultural, historical and social essays*, ed. Maria Cinta Ramblado-Minero and Auxiliadora Perez/Vides (Lewiston, NY: Edwin Mellen Press, 2006): pp. 83–102.

13 *Dáil Debates*, vol. 115 (28 April 1949), col. 265.

14 *Dáil Debates*, vol. 115 (28 April 1949), col. 265.

15 *Dáil Debates*, vol. 115 (28 April 1949), col. 266.

16 This is based on the author's examination of all of the available trial record books for the Central Criminal and circuit courts. The National Archives of Ireland has a complete set of trial record books for the Central Criminal Court, however, there are some small gaps in the circuit court records. So while the information here is based on all of the *available* evidence, and it likely represents the vast majority of cases that were heard, it is not entirely complete. "Related crimes" include manslaughter and concealment of birth.

17 *Dáil Debates*, vol. 115 (28 April 1949), col. 268.

18 *Dáil Debates*, vol. 115 (28 April 1949), cols 279–80.

19 *Dáil Debates*, vol. 115 (28 April 1949), col. 276.

20 *Public general acts of 1922, Public general acts of 1937–38* (British Infanticide Act); *Infanticide Act, 1949* (Act 16 of 1949). Republic of Ireland, *Irish statute book: Acts of the Oireachtas 1922–1997* (Oxfordshire, UK: Jutastat UK, 1999), CD-Rom.

21 *Dáil Debates*, vol. 115 (28 April 1949), cols 276–8.

22 *Dáil Debates*, vol. 115 (28 April 1949), col. 283.

23 *Catholic Standard* (17 January 1931), p. 2. This image of the fallen woman as sinner-saint appeared frequently in the *Catholic Standard*, especially in annual fundraising sermons on behalf of convents and magdalen asylums.

24 Much of twentieth-century history tends to assume that the church's efforts at total control were entirely successful. This was not the case. The vast majority of unwed mothers lived their lives, with or without their children, in obscurity in their own homes and communities. Only a small percentage ended up in mother and baby homes or magdalen asylums, and it was decisions made by themselves and their families that consigned them to this fate.

25 Revd Richard Devane, "The dance hall," *Irish Ecclesiastical Record,* 37 (January–June 1931), p. 180.

26 *Catholic Standard* (24 September 1932), p. 2.

27 Devane, "The dance hall," p. 178.

28 The term "pagan" was used frequently in religious and legislative rhetoric, and typically was applied to any idea or trend that was seen as distinctly "British," and thus inherently contrary to Irish values.

29 The 1935 Public Dance Halls Act required individuals wishing to hold a dance for commercial purposes to apply to the district court justice for a license. Upon granting of a license the person responsible for the dance hall had to abide by a series of regulations as to the serving of alcohol, start and end times, and car parking facilities. See *Public Dance Halls Act* (Act 2 of 1935), *Irish Statute Book*, CD-Rom.

30 In only 4 of the 209 cases heard before the Central Criminal Court did the defendant indicate that she had met her sexual partner at a dance hall, or that the sexual encounter that led to pregnancy occurred at or on the way home from a dance hall.

31 DDA, McQuaid Papers government box 3, untitled, unsigned handwritten statement.

32 DDA, McQuaid Papers government box 3, untitled, unsigned handwritten statement.

33 NAI, Central Criminal Court 1C 94 66, 17 November 1931.

34 *Cork Examiner* (20 November 1931), p. 4.

35 NAI, Central Criminal Court 1D 29 11, 24 April 1946.

36 NAI, Central Criminal Court 1D 29 11, 24 April 1946.

37 *Cork Examiner* (6 June 1929), p. 13; *Cork Evening Echo* (7 June 1929), p. 3; NAI, Central Criminal Court 1C 94 55, 4 June 1929; Court of Criminal Appeals 1928/29.

38 *Sligo Champion* (25 November 1949), p. 1.

39 *Sligo Champion* (25 November 1949), p. 1.

40 *Limerick Weekly Echo* (21 July 1928), p. 3.

41 *Limerick Weekly Echo* (21 July 1928), p. 3.

42 *Tipperary Star* (21 July 1928), p. 3.

43 *Tipperary Star* (21 July 1928), p. 3.

44   See *Tipperary Star* (23 June 1928), p. 5; *Tipperary Star* (21 July 1928), p. 3; *Limerick Weekly Echo* (21 July 1928), p. 3; NAI, Central Criminal Court 1C 90 24, 19 June 1928.

45   *Offaly Independent* (25 November 1933), p. 5. Medical evidence indicated that the child died of asphyxiation as a result of a band being tied around its neck; in his charge to the jury the judge reminded them that they could find Murphy guilty of the lesser charge of manslaughter if they believed Murphy was not cognizant of the seriousness of her actions. It took the jury just ten minutes to reach their conclusion, and they issued a "recommendation to mercy."

46   "Mr Justice Meredith said that the jury had made a recommendation to mercy, and since he had dealt with the case a large number of similar cases had come before him. He had reconsidered the present case, and was satisfied that the sentence was out of line with other sentences. He, therefore, reduced the sentence." *Tipperary Star* (2 December 1933), p. 12.

47   *Longford News* (8 June 1940), p. 1.

48   Two scholarly examinations of magdalen asylums that reinforce this view are Frances Finnegan, *Do penance or perish: Magdalen asylums in Ireland* (Oxford and New York: Oxford University Press, 2004) and James Smith, *Ireland's magdalen laundries and the nation's architecture of containment* (Notre Dame, IN: University of Notre Dame Press, 2007).

49   Smith, *Ireland's magdalen asylums*, p. 47.

50   This conclusion is based on an exhaustive analysis of the roughly 600 cases entered in all of the available Central Criminal and circuit court trial record books.

7

Desperate act or wilful choice? Infanticide and unwanted children

Introduction

Perhaps one of the most interesting aspects of infanticide in twentieth-century Ireland is that, while lawmakers, the judiciary, and the clergy responded to it as if it were an inevitable but unpalatable fact of life, in fact infanticide was the exception rather than the rule when it came to dealing with an unexpected or unwanted pregnancy. The question then becomes: why, when the majority of unwed mothers found less drastic solutions to their dilemmas, did a small but not insignificant percentage of women resort to infanticide? It is clear that there was a certain element of desperation inherent in some of the cases that came before the courts. But it is also clear that many of the parties involved, including accused women and their families, regarded the life of an illegitimate child as expendable in the context of their priorities and values. Although they were not treated as such in the courts, many defendants were, in fact, criminally or maliciously motivated. An important aspect of infanticide, that rarely is considered in historical research, is the fact that while thousands of women coped with unwanted pregnancies in legal and "moral" ways, a small subset of women adopted extreme and criminal methods. While lawmakers and jurists acknowledged the official respect for child life at the same time that they absolved women for even the most violent of actions, defendants themselves had to negotiate possible legal sanctions, the disapproval of family and friends, and their own human desires and weaknesses. Women who committed infanticide generally put the fate of their newborn children low down on their list of priorities.

Infanticide should not be viewed only as the act of desperate women confronted with an unwed pregnancy in a society that placed a high premium on premarital celibacy and stigmatized unmarried mothers and their children. Infanticide also must be examined within the context of a general societal disregard for the life and well-being of illegitimate, poor, and vulnerable children, and of the values and priorities that dominated family and community life. The image, perpetrated in popular literature as well as scholarly writing, of a mid-twentieth-century society dominated solely by the Catholic Church and characterized by repressive and oppressive attitudes and practices relating to sexuality is not entirely accurate. Admittedly Catholic moral codes influenced legislative and social policy, and church and state certainly attempted to exact conformity to narrowly defined codes of sexuality, maternity, and family life. And without doubt the refusal on the part of lawmakers, into the 1970s, to lift prohibitions on the importation and availability of contraception, coupled with the near impossibility of securing abortion, and the widespread disapproval of unmarried motherhood, meant that sexual activity among unmarried couples was a risky proposition.[1] But unmarried women and men tempted fate and engaged in unmarried sex more frequently than historians have thus far acknowledged, and women were not always passive in these encounters. Nor were they always the victims of male seduction or sexual aggression portrayed in official rhetoric. In this kind of climate, infanticide can be seen as little more than a form of birth control for women who wanted to engage in sexual activities without having to care for the offspring that might result.

Transcripts and newspaper accounts of infanticide cases suggest that the sexually ignorant, innocent, and demure woman, so common in late nineteenth-century and early twentieth-century prescriptive literature, does not necessarily reflect the experiences and motivations of ordinary Irish women. In official rhetoric women who experienced sex outside of marriage were either prostitutes or victims of male sexual aggression, which coincided with a mid-twentieth-century social policy that effectively gave women two options: celibacy or married motherhood. Catholic teaching insisted on premarital chastity for unmarried women, and on the mutually exclusive demands of purity and abundant fertility for married women, whose sexuality was framed by the Marian ideal that defined sex as a perfunctory act of procreation rather than an expression of sexual desire or physical and emotional intimacy. Lawmakers, jurists, and the clergy assumed that the "typical" infanticide perpetrator was a young, unmarried, sexually innocent and ignorant woman who was seduced and then abandoned to cope alone with the consequences.

While this depiction is evident in some infanticide cases heard before Central Criminal and circuit courts it is by no means accurate for all, or even a majority. Trial records reveal that many women were active agents in the sexual liaisons that led to unwed pregnancy, that they had numerous sexual partners before they became pregnant, and that for some of them sex was an accepted part of courting relationships and infanticide an effective, if primitive, method of birth control. Historians must be careful not to accept uncritically the assumption that infanticide was only or inherently a desperate act committed by frightened or victimized women who believed they had no other option. The level of violence perpetrated on some newborn infants, the complicity of family and friends, the number of women who committed infanticide repeatedly over a number of years, suggest a less benign interpretation of the crime, even if judges and juries often gave women the benefit of the doubt. Some women expressed regret in their statements to police over the deaths of their infants but most did not, and it is not unreasonable to suggest that of all the things that went through a woman's mind when she made the decision to commit infanticide, the fate of the child itself was probably the least important.

Infanticide and female sexuality

The alarmist rhetoric of contemporary social observers concerned with the growing rate of unwed pregnancy, especially among teenagers, may leave one with the impression that sexual immorality or promiscuity are distinctly modern social phenomena that can be linked to the emergence of popular culture and the "disintegration of the family." Statistical evidence would indicate that the number of births outside marriage has risen sharply since the 1980s even as contraceptive methods have become more readily available. But recent trends should not obscure the fact that sex, and births outside of marriage, were more common than scholars thus far have acknowledged. Women interviewed by gardaí in the course of infanticide investigations demonstrated a degree of sexual knowledge, agency, and experience that is entirely at odds with the chaste, demure, innocent Irish woman portrayed in moralist and prescriptive literature.[2] It would be foolhardy, based solely on the small sample of evidence analyzed here, to generalize about sexuality in mid-twentieth-century Ireland, but it is not unreasonable to raise questions about the accuracy of prevailing assumptions about extramarital sex and female sexuality in post-independence Ireland.

Maureen Green's testimony echoed that of many women accused of infanticide for whom sex was a normal feature of romantic attachments and unwed pregnancy an unfortunate, but not necessarily disastrous or unexpected, side effect.[3] Green pleaded guilty to manslaughter in November 1943 in the death of her newborn infant. In statements to gardaí she admitted that she "kept company" with several different men from the time she was 18 years of age (she was 22 at the time of the crime), and that "four or five different boys had connection with me during the past four years."[4] It would not be far-fetched, given Green's sexual history and the lack of effective contraceptive methods at the time, to wonder if Green had been pregnant more than once. She likely realized that her sexual activity could lead to pregnancy, and her crime could be interpreted as an extension of her sexuality – a way to engage in sexual relationships without the inevitable related burden of motherhood.

Green and many other women accused of infanticide would have been regarded as "promiscuous" by contemporary standards, engaging in many short-term relationships before becoming pregnant and committing infanticide. Phyllis O'Neil was 19 years old when she was charged in March 1935 with the murder of her child. In her deposition O'Neil stated that: "In April or May 1934 I was working for a man named Mr. Leahy, near Annekisha Mallow, Co. Cork. I was working in this place for a month, during that time I went with a good many boys, and I got in the family way."[5] O'Neil appears not to have been concerned either with preserving her reputation or with becoming pregnant, two of the strongest motivations for remaining celibate. Tess Clark, aged 17 years, was charged in 1934 with the murder of her newborn infant; she testified that she had "kept company" for the previous two years, but that she could not be sure that man was the father of her child.[6]

The behavior of women like Green, O'Neil, and Clark prompted enormous concern among Catholic prelates about the dangers of "foreign" cultural influences: they interacted with many men in unsupervised environments (sometimes in unregulated dance halls) and engaged in sexual activity as part of that routine. They represented the church's worst fears regarding the moral and sexual behavior of young unmarried women.[7] Contemporaries would have described many of these women as "giddy," and it is difficult to equate their actions with the fear, shame, and desperation that motivated some women to commit infanticide. And the widespread tolerance of infanticide on the part of the state and the courts may have led women like Green and O'Neil to believe that they could engage in illicit sexual activities, and "get rid" of the resulting babies, without real fear of repercussions.

Green, O'Neil, and Clark's sexual histories challenge the traditional assumptions about unmarried women's celibacy, and portrayals of unmarried mothers as the unfortunate or unlucky victims of a "fall" or lapse in morality. This is not to suggest that all women, or even a majority, were as sexually experienced as these women. But the records of infanticide trials suggest that women did not always avoid opportunities for sexual experimentation, nor were they always shy and embarrassed about discussing sexual matters with gardaí and court officials. References in the Irish Folklore Commission archives to folk contraceptive and abortion methods, assessed in light of strenuous efforts on the part of the state to prevent books on family planning and English newspapers containing advertisements for contraceptives from falling into the hands of working-class women and men, suggest that women actively sought out methods to prevent or abort unwanted pregnancies. [8] Clearly at least some of them were not averse to simply killing their newborn infants, or allowing them to die, when all else failed. Admittedly those methods were untrustworthy, but the fact that women used them indicates a desire to control their fertility. Some women may have turned to these folk methods hoping to avoid pregnancy while fulfilling their husbands' sexual demands; however, there is no reason to assume that married women wishing to avoid another pregnancy were the only consumers of folk contraceptive methods. [9] This possibility is bolstered by the surprisingly numerous instances in which women arrested on a single count of infanticide subsequently were found to have committed the crime more than once as part of either a long-term union or numerous short-term relationships.

Family and community responses to infanticide

In many cases the lack of concern for illegitimate children in infanticide cases reflected as much on families and communities as on female defendants. The testimony of witnesses and co-conspirators – family members, partners/mates, and friends – demonstrate the subtle and overt ways that families and communities guided the decisions women made in coping with their pregnancies, as well as the stake that families and communities had in determining the fate of illegitimate children. While some women committed infanticide because they were convinced that family and friends would reject them, others hoped that killing their babies would spare their families disgrace and shame. How families responded to unwanted pregnancy and infanticide was rooted not only in legal, religious, or moral considerations but also in "what the neighbors would think." The last thing that anyone seems to have thought about was the child. Some family members conspired in the crime, believing it less unpalatable than having other family members or neighbors discover the pregnancy of an unwed sister or daughter. Others claimed ignorance of the pregnancy and infanticide, and sacrificed their daughters to the mercy of the courts or the magdalen asylum regime in order to preserve their own standing in the community. Some of the most revealing testimonies are those that suggest that family members, and mothers in particular, not only knew of their daughters' pregnancies but also were present at the birth and assisted in ending the child's life or concealing its birth. The involvement of family members in individual cases of infanticide offers insight into the role families and communities played in defining and regulating the moral and sexual behavior of their members. It also reveals the value, or lack of value, that families placed on child life when their status, reputation, or livelihood were at stake.

The reaction of Tara Murphy's father to her suspected pregnancy was an extreme but not necessarily unusual example of the way that fathers responded to their unmarried daughters' pregnancies, and perhaps accounts for Tara's sense of desperation. Murphy testified that two months before she was due to give birth her father demanded to know if the rumors he had been hearing – that his daughter was expecting a child – were true. Murphy denied it at that time, and her father threatened to "cut her throat" if the rumors proved to be true.[10] After she gave birth Murphy tied twine around the infant's neck to stop it crying, and when asked why she killed the child she said: "I was afraid of [my mother] and father, because if my mother knew it she would tell my father."[11] Murphy's mother also suspected Murphy's pregnancy, although she seems to have been more fearful of her husband's reaction than she was angry with or ashamed of her daughter. During the trial the judge castigated Mr Murphy's behavior as "unchristian" and suggested that while he understood the shame and anger that parents naturally felt when their daughters disappointed them, nonetheless as parents they had a responsibility to support their children unconditionally.[12] In this case, the judge's expectations of parental support and mutual responsibility clashed with the priorities that framed family and community relationships and informed responses to unwed pregnancy, illegitimacy, and infanticide. Mr Murphy's status in the community outweighed his parental obligations, his affection for his daughter, or the fate of her newborn infant.

Tara Murphy's mother suspected that her daughter was pregnant but took no active role in concealing the child's birth and death. Other women whose unmarried daughters were pregnant were not so reticent in conspiring to kill or conceal the birth of illegitimate children. A case from 1934 Wexford illustrates the lengths that some women were willing to go to protect their family's "good name." In this case Kathleen Kelly was charged, along with her mother Margaret, of concealing the birth of her newborn infant. Kathleen Kelly testified that she gave birth to a "dead born" baby in August 1933, and that shortly after its birth she buried the child in a neighbor's field. She also insisted that neither her mother nor her sister, Jane, was aware of the birth, death, or burial of the child. But another part of her testimony suggests that she may not have been entirely truthful in her account of the baby's birth:

> I was home with my parents about the year of 1921 and I gave birth to a baby boy in the house. It lived only a few minutes and my mother buried it in the garden immediately. About the year 1927 I was working at Mr. Edmond Johnson's at Glandoran, Gorey, and I gave birth to a baby girl in Johnson's house about November ... it was born alive and I secretly brought it downstairs and buried it in Johnson's garden ... About last May twelve months I was working at home at Tomaboley. I gave birth to a baby boy. It was born alive and my mother buried it in the garden about a day after it being born. It was partly crying all the time since I gave birth until it was buried by my mother.[13]

Not only did Margaret Kelly admit her role in the burial of some of Kathleen's children, she also admitted that her other daughter, Julia, had also had four children between 1923 and 1933, and that these children were also buried. Margaret Kelly apparently thought it was perfectly reasonable to kill or conceal the births of eight newborn children, and the courts must have agreed since not one of these three women was ever convicted of a crime.

The kinds of cases mentioned above were fairly typical not necessarily in the number of children who were killed or neglected at birth to the point that they died, but in the sense that an illegitimate newborn child's life appears to have been a small price for some families to pay to preserve a façade of respectability and piety. It might be useful, for the sake of illustration, to cite one of the extremely rare occasions when parents endeavored to support their unwed pregnant daughter and voiced at least a small measure of respect for the life of an illegitimate child. Eileen Keane was charged, along with her daughter Cate, with the murder of Cate's illegitimate child. Cate Keane already had two illegitimate children whom her parents helped to support, and she had informed her parents about the third pregnancy. Cate falsely accused her mother of killing the child, and initially her mother was charged with murder. In spite of the false accusation, Eileen Keane continued to stand by her daughter: "My daughter ... is there present and she knows I was not present when the child was born. I did what I could when I returned. She knows the child was dead when I came in. God forgive her for drawing that on me. That is all have to say. I would be very sorry to have a hand in any of her children if she had twenty-five of them."[14] While it is clear that in some cases parents responded to unwed pregnancy and infanticide based on their own concerns and priorities rather than their children's or grandchildren's well-being, the Keane case is a rare illustration of the bonds of support, loyalty, and affection that sustained families in hard times, even when that meant accepting an illegitimate child in the face of possible public censure. The Keane family was atypical, at least in the context of infanticide cases, both in their vocal and vehement defense of their daughter, and in their willingness to place the well-being of their daughter and illegitimate grandchildren above the possible censure and disapproval of family, friends, and community.

Religion and class in infanticide cases

The vast majority of women accused of infanticide were Catholic, which is not surprising in a country where roughly 95 per cent of the population professed Catholicism.[15] Although their actions violated central strictures of their faith system, Catholic women accused of infanticide did not necessarily reject their faith and, indeed, often drew on it for guidance, comfort, and forgiveness. Many women's testimonies reveal that they attended church and the sacraments regularly, in some cases confessed their "sins" to the parish priest, and made genuine, if clumsy, efforts to ensure that their dead infants would not spend an eternity in limbo.[16] The words and experiences of women who appear in infanticide records illustrate the ways that ordinary women and men integrated Catholicism into their daily lives, but also suggest that their understanding of the expectations of their faith was a more complex affair than simply going to church on Sunday, saying the rosary, and abiding by the priest's dictates. Sex outside of marriage and the deliberate murder of newborn infants may have been "wrong" according to Catholic teaching, but the women and men involved appear to have had no difficulty in reconciling their actions with their personal sense of sin, contrition, and forgiveness. If ordinary women and men had clearly defined notions of sin, they also seem to have been confident of forgiveness.

Mary Williams confessed her crime to her parish priest, which led ultimately to a full confession to gardaí.[17] What is particularly striking about Williams's confession, however, is that she had killed two children previously, apparently without a guilty conscience. Had she not confessed to the priest in the third instance she might well have got away with all three crimes. The fact that she sought the priest perhaps suggests that her guilty conscience caught up with her, and perhaps that she believed only the direct intercession of the priest could put her right with God. Like Williams, Molly McCormack made a confession to her parish priest, after which she also confessed to gardaí.[18] McCormack admitted giving birth to a child on the beach, claiming that as the child was being born she pulled it and flung it into the sea.[19] Medical evidence contradicted McCormack's account of the birth and death of her baby but, in her eyes, confession to the parish priest meant forgiveness, even if her confession was tainted by lies or half-truths. For both Williams and McCormack it was not only the strength of their faith that mattered, but also the appearance of piety that they projected in the community and in the courts.

Although the evidence provided in infanticide cases is not sufficient to explore the issue to a significant degree, the behavior of McCormack, Williams, and other women accused of infanticide raises compelling questions about religious practices and beliefs in post-independence Ireland, and the links between "immorality," outward shows of piety, and a genuine belief in Catholicism as both a faith system and a way of life. There was evidence of a deep and abiding faith among Irish women and men, even among those who repeatedly and wilfully killed illegitimate newborn children. But one wonders whether this appearance of piety reflected firmly-held beliefs and deep convictions, or whether some segments of the population embraced Catholicism superficially as a matter of convenience in a society that expected no less than full acceptance of and adherence to Catholic principles. On the other hand, given the ambivalence of both the political and religious establishments on the question of the "sanctity" of the life of newborn infants, it is perhaps not surprising that some segments of Irish society showed a similar ambivalence and, indeed, disregard, that did not diminish the strength of their Catholic convictions and beliefs.

Only rarely did non-Catholic women appear in infanticide cases, so it is impossible to draw conclusions about how religious persuasion might have influenced women's actions, the responses of families and communities, or their own perceptions of their behavior in relation to unwed pregnancy. What is striking, however, is the role played by the local Protestant clergyman in the two cases involving Protestant defendants that appeared in surviving court records. The nature of this involvement raises the possibility of differences in how the churches as institutions, and individual clergymen of the two faiths, perceived their responsibility to vulnerable members of the community, particularly unmarried mothers and their children. Chapter 6 chronicled the case of Fanny Bolger, who gave birth in 1948 to an illegitimate child; Bolger's pastor, Reverend Giff, sent the child to the Protestant Children's Fold Home. Bolger subsequently married the father of the child, prompting Giff to return the child to her in August 1949. Bolger pleaded with Reverend Giff to keep the child but he refused based on his firm conviction that the best and most appropriate place for the child was with her natural parents.[20] Giff reported the child's return to the local gardaí, perhaps indicating his concern that Bolger would harm the child. Gardaí visited the Bolger home regularly to check on the child and on one such visit was informed by Bolger's husband that the child was dead.

Reverend Giff returned the child to Bolger following her marriage because, according to law and Protestant theology, marriage legitimized the child so that it could be raised "in all respects as a legitimate child, and so save her from the stigma of illegitimacy."[21] This belief was common to Protestant and Catholic teaching but it was more theoretical than real in the Catholic context. In Catholic thinking a child born outside of wedlock was inherently tainted and flawed, and even the marriage of its parents could not eradicate the stain of its moral weakness. Catholic social observers believed that the best place for illegitimate children was a religious institution that would provide the moral guidance necessary to help the child overcome, to the extent possible, the social and moral disadvantages associated with illegitimacy. Bolger's case alone is not a firm enough foundation upon which to base comparisons between Catholic and Protestant attitudes toward and treatment of unmarried motherhood and illegitimacy. But it does suggest possibilities for further scholarship, particularly in the ways that the two communities in Ireland conceived of motherhood and morality, and of sin and forgiveness, loyalty and mutual responsibility, and concern for marginalized children.

Official discourses assumed that the "typical" infanticide defendant was a poor woman, and the judicial treatment of infanticide sometimes represented a clash between middle-class values and notions of respectability, and the priorities and realities that guided decision-making among ordinary women and men. Only rarely did middle-class women appear before the courts on infanticide charges, and the judicial handling of these cases elucidated the class assumptions that underscored official and popular treatments of infanticide. Ethel Allen was an atypical infanticide defendant because she was a Protestant whose family was affluent and highly respected in the community. The lengths to which Allen's parents went to protect her, and their efforts in court to prove their respectability, illustrate the stake that middle-class families had in dealing privately and discreetly with unwanted pregnancies. Allen was charged in 1937 with the murder of her newborn infant. In their testimony Allen's parents, neighbors, and friends insisted that she was "not right in the head" and unable to care for herself, and thus not responsible for her actions. According to her stepmother, Vanessa Allen, Ethel: "was very excited in the yard when we met her. We had to force her into the house. I don't think she was accountable for what she was doing. She is not normal."[22] The prison medical officer, who examined Allen prior to trial, testified as to her mental state: "She apparently understands the seriousness of the charge against her, but it does not seem to worry her. I doubt if she would be able to instruct Counsel for her defense. Although I cannot find any delusions or hallucinations present, I don't think she is mentally stable. She is not, in my opinion, certifiable as Lunatic, but she is mentally defective."[23]

Allen was convicted of concealment of birth and sentenced to two years' confinement in the Bethany Home, the Protestant equivalent of a magdalen asylum. With the support of family, friends, and their local rector, the Allen family actively lobbied for her release. While these efforts acknowledged Ethel Allen's crime, they also insisted on the family's respectability and status in the community, implicitly pressing the point that a "respectable" middle-class woman like Ethel Allen could only commit a crime like infanticide if she was mentally unbalanced.[24] It is not clear if the Allens knew that Ethel was pregnant and about to give birth, but their efforts to exonerate her suggest that, had they known, they would have ensured that the matter was handled appropriately, but also privately and discreetly.

While it would be unwise to generalize based on Ethel Allen's case, it is safe to suggest that middle-class women did experience unexpected and unwanted pregnancies, although their families and communities had a greater stake in dealing privately and quietly with such "indiscretions" than did their working-class counterparts. They also had the financial resources to send their daughters abroad for the duration of their pregnancies or hide them away in private nursing homes in Ireland. The majority of unmarried middle-class pregnancies went unnoticed, at least by lawmakers, judges, and juries, projecting the false impression that immorality and illicit sexual activity occurred only in working-class relationships, and thus that immorality was a distinctly working-class problem. That falsehood is compounded by the fact that official conventions of morality and sexuality specifically targeted the sexual and reproductive activities of the working class, and working-class women especially. Infanticide was seen as a distinctively working-class crime not only because lawmakers and judges assumed that poverty and desperation were primary motivating factors, but also because working-class women and men were thought to be inherently morally weaker than their better-off counterparts, and thus more susceptible to the temptations of illicit sex and the "easy" solution of infanticide to hide their immorality.

What about the children?

As indicated in Chapter 6, the men who dealt with infanticide in an official capacity believed that women accused of infanticide took the drastic step of murdering their newborn infants because they had been seduced by unscrupulous men uttering promises of marriage, but who were then abandoned to deal alone with the consequences of their seduction. While arguing against traditional conceptualizations of both infanticide and female sexual agency, it is important to acknowledge that for some women infanticide was, in fact, a desperate act committed "in the heat of the moment," or was the least unpalatable of a range of unattractive options. But the ways that different women "did away" with their children suggests a clear distinction between women who truly were desperate, and women who did not regard their illegitimate children as "real" human beings with needs and feelings. One common scenario was the woman who gave birth to an illegitimate child either at her place of employment or in her home, without assistance, and was desperately anxious to hide the birth from employers, co-workers, and family members. In almost all of these cases the women simply did nothing once the child was born: they did not try to clean, cover, or clothe the child, nor did they attempt to feed it. After the child died, typically by what medical professionals deemed "inattention at birth" or "lack of skilled assistance," the women continued to try to hide the pregnancy by disposing of the baby's body. Most, if not all, of these women were convicted not of infanticide but of the less serious charge of concealment of birth. Rarely was a convicted woman sentenced to a prison term or magdalen asylum in these cases. Those women who allowed their children to die out of fear or desperation voiced a striking sense of defeatism that only served to underscore their desperation and helplessness. While they articulated a desire to keep their children, their own survival often rested on getting rid of them. It was a difficult dilemma, and one that women faced largely with resignation, as reflected by Kate Doyle's lament upon arrest: "I was worrying about it all the time since it was a nice baby but I couldn't manage to keep it."[25]

The quiet desperation of the women who fell into this category contrasts sharply with the women, sometimes in complicity with family members, who showed not only callousness but also, often, a remarkable degree of violence, that suggests less a sense of desperation than a patent disregard for the lives of illegitimate newborns. What becomes clear is that the illegitimate children were expendable in the desire of women and their families to "save face" at whatever cost. This is particularly evident in the cases where violence was used or when women committed infanticide repeatedly over a number of years in order to hide adulterous or illicit affairs.

In the Central Criminal Court case against Nelly O'Brien in June 1927, medical evidence indicated that the child had been "practically choked and drowned."[26] O'Brien testified that she had gone to a cousin's house because she knew she was about to give birth. She remained with the cousin for a week after the child was born, at which point she returned home accompanied by her mother Margaret and cousin Desmond Lynch. According to O'Brien: "My mother was carrying the child. I went down to the river-bank and threw the child into the river. The child was alive when I threw it into the river. Neither my mother or Desmond Lynch made any attempt to take out the child after I threw it into the river. We all went home after throwing the child into the river."[27] Margaret O'Brien alleged that Nelly was intent on throwing herself and the child into the river, and that she, Margaret, tried to stop it. Margaret testified that she chased Nelly to the river and pulled her back just as she was about to throw herself in. However, by this time "the child was gone from her into the river and was swept away by the flood."[28] The main intent in this case was to get rid of the child before Margaret and Nelly arrived home. This does not fit within the classic "desperation" mold because some family members were aware of the pregnancy and made arrangements for Nelly's confinement. And a full week passed between the birth and death of the child, a week during which the family had ample time to make arrangements to board the child out, to hand the child over to an "adoption society," or to apply for home assistance for Nelly and the child, if poverty was a barrier against it.

Another case from 1935 Limerick illustrates the callousness displayed by many of the women accused of infanticide. Kathleen Keating, 35-year-old mother of three illegitimate children, gave birth to a fourth child in March 1935. She testified, "I gave birth to a child in the garden. I then threw it into the Morning Star River."[29] Keating alleged that she threw the child into the river, even though she could hear it screaming, because she did not want her mother to know about it. And yet, Keating herself was illegitimate and she already had three children, each with a different father. "Morality" and "shame" clearly were not issues in this family, so Keating's plea of desperation rings somewhat hollow. Keating was charged with murder but pleaded guilty to manslaughter and was given a sentence of six months imprisonment with hard labor.

Perhaps the most extraordinary example of utter disregard not only for the life of a newborn infant, but also for the law and for other family members, was the case of 66-year-old Ruth Maguire and her 27-year-old daughter Christine. Both were charged, in the Central Criminal Court in October 1937, with the murder of Christine's newborn son. Medical evidence showed that a handkerchief had been tied tightly around the child's neck, but also that the child had several deep, lacerated wounds, which suggested that excessive violence was perpetrated on it. Not only was the level of violence significant in this case, but the defendant Ruth Maguire tried to implicate other family members in order to hide her own and her daughter's guilt. Maguire testified that Christine gave birth at the Coombe

Hospital in Dublin and that, four days later, Christine left the hospital and the two of them traveled to the city center. There, they claimed, they handed the child over to Ruth's sister Eileen Broderick, who had allegedly agreed to care for the child. (In other words, Ruth Maguire claimed that she had not seen the child since handing him over to her sister, and that Broderick must have been responsible for whatever fate befell the child.) Broderick denied that she had even seen the child, much less agreed to care for him. The case was noteworthy because of the level of violence used against the child (for which both Ruth and her daughter received relatively harsh sentences) and because of both complicity between mother and daughter, and the mother's efforts to hide her own guilt by implicating other family members.[30]

While all of the women discussed above likely experienced some degree of fear, shame, or desperation in killing their newborn children, it becomes clear that newborn children were easily expendable in their efforts to protect their own and their families' reputations. And if some women expressed regret that they felt compelled to resort to such drastic measures to cover up an unexpected or unwanted pregnancy, many others expressed not regret but resentment at being saddled with a burden (i.e. an illegitimate newborn infant) that they were not prepared to face and that might have threatened their status in the family or community or their employment prospects. These women were no victims: they treated their newborn children with a level of callousness, violence, and antipathy that was completely at odds with prevailing assumptions about natural maternal instincts. But the courts generally did not hold them as accountable for the crimes they committed against their newborn children.

The sense of callousness towards the lives of illegitimate children is conveyed even more strongly in the case of women who committed multiple infanticides over a number of years, or who came before the courts on numerous occasions. The most extreme example of this involved Mary Alice Smyth, who was convicted in February 1954 of five infanticides over a span of years. Smyth was charged in June 1953 with murdering her newborn infant after telling a public health nurse that she had borne and murdered many children over the years. When they dug up the floor of Smyth's home gardaí uncovered the bones of several children, although the precise number that Smyth killed over the years was never determined. Smyth was married during the entire time that the murders were committed; while her husband worked in England she carried on a longstanding affair with Peter Clark, the father of all of the murdered children. After her arrest Smyth was taken to the Carlow Mental Hospital for evaluation, and although the doctor concluded that she was mentally unbalanced he believed the veracity of her statements about the children:

> She told me she had killed six or seven of her babies, that she wasn't sure of the number. She didn't say when she had killed them, that is she did not give the dates, but she said she had killed them shortly after their birth. She said she wanted to inform the Guards, so that she might be punished for what she had done. I believed that it was not a delusion, that what she was saying was true.[31]

The fact that Smyth became pregnant on almost a yearly basis and systematically murdered the resulting children suggests the possibility that her extramarital affair, and the death of her children, were not moral issues for her. Infanticide perhaps became a means through which Smyth carried on a sexual relationship outside of marriage while avoiding the burden of motherhood (not to mention the scandal associated with bearing a child in an adulterous relationship). Smyth was married, sexually active outside of marriage, and unwilling to accept the reproductive ramifications of her sexual activity. While Smyth's case was extreme relative to other infanticide cases, there are examples of other young women, married and unmarried, who sought similar means of exercising some control over their sexuality and fertility, and who did not accept as inevitable the maternal responsibilities that resulted from their sexual liaisons. In all of these cases there is no evidence whatever that the fate of the murdered children caused any undue concern, shame, or guilt.

Mary Williams, mentioned earlier, was convicted in 1933 of concealment of birth after her newborn infant was discovered wrapped in a blanket in her bedroom. Williams insisted that she had not murdered the child, although she admitted wrapping it in a blanket while it was alive, knowing and intending that it would die. When asked who the father was she replied: "The same fellow as before, [Michael Treacy] it is three times – he is the father of my third baby and the third time I have been arrested."[32] There was a certain matter-of-factness in Williams's attitude: her previous arrests indicate that she knew what she was doing, and the possibility of legal action and even imprisonment apparently served as no deterrent to extramarital sexual activity or infanticide. Williams had already been convicted, in 1929, of concealing the birth of a child that was found buried in her garden. In this instance she claimed the child was born dead. The judge appears not to have believed her, however, because although she was only convicted of concealment of birth, a relatively minor offense in the eyes of the court, Williams was given a sentence of eighteen months' confinement in a magdalen asylum.

In the 1933 case Williams was given a eighteen months' term of imprisonment, a relatively harsh term compared to other concealment cases, but fairly lenient in light of her previous history.[33] Williams's history of infanticide underscores the leniency that typically was extended to female defendants, even when they appeared before the courts on more than one occasion over the years. The judicial system was so attached to its tradition-al image of the female "victim" of seduction and abandonment by "rogues" that they failed to consider the implicit message that they were sending: that the death of illegitimate children was not taken all that seriously by the judicial system. Seeing women as criminals rather than victims would have forced them to admit that their preconceived assumptions about female sexuality and "natural" maternal instincts were not entirely accurate. More importantly, looking more objectively at the defendants who came through Irish courtrooms on a fairly regular basis would have revealed the lie in the "sanctity of life" rhetoric and façade of sexual purity that were so central to Irish Catholic morality and, indeed, to the very definition of "Irishness."

While "promiscuous" women, and women who committed infanticide on more than one occasion, violated Irish society's most fundamental tenets of appropriate maternal, moral, and sexual behavior, courts did not always use a woman's previous sexual history as an excuse for excessive harshness. Mary Alice Smyth pleaded guilty to infanticide and was sentenced to three years' penal servitude, a harsh sentence relative to other women, but mild considering that she admitted to killing seven children. Had Smyth been convicted prior to the 1949 Infanticide Act likely she would have been convicted of murder and sentenced to death, commuted to life in prison. Williams came before the courts on at least two occasions in a four-year period, charged each time with the exact same crime. Although she was given a moderately harsh sentence the second time around, when com-pared with other women convicted of the same crime, it was still lenient when one considers that she likely murdered three newborn infants. The fact that courts were willing to take a more lenient view of women com-mitting infanticide essentially meant that women who used infanticide as a regular form of "birth control" were treated no more harshly than those who resorted to it out of fear, shame, or desperation. The fact that children had to die to achieve this objective was apparently irrelevant.

The case of Mary Alice Smyth was extraordinary primarily because of the number of children she was convicted of killing. But Smyth was also married, and married women's desperation to hide illegitimate pregnancies cannot be underestimated, even in cases where the women were estranged from their husbands.[34] Married women pregnant as the result of an adul-terous affair had an even greater stake than their unwed counterparts in getting rid of the evidence of their liaison. Not only could married women not expect to be treated with sympathy by an all-male jury, they also ran the risk of being ostracized from their biological families and communities and being rejected by their husbands who, in most cases, were their only sources of financial support.[35] Christine Farrell was married with two children and became pregnant while her husband worked abroad. Farrell claimed that she was raped, although she refused, under interrogation, to identify the rapist, nor did she report the assault at the time. Although the fact that Farrell sought medical advice during her pregnancy indicated an absence of premeditation Farrell's physician testified that he advised Farrell to enter the county home as she neared her due date, so that she could give birth discreetly and arrange for the child to be boarded out. Farrell refused, fearing that as a married woman she would be forced to keep the child, or that she would not be able to hide it from her husband: "If I don't do away with this child I will have no life with him."[36] Her doctor warned her that: "it would be murder to take the child's life and that she would regret the consequences. She asked me to baptize the child and I refused to do so and told her that it was unnecessary because the child was not in danger of death and that it could be brought down to the Church and be baptized."[37] Farrell's request that the doctor baptize the child could be seen as an indication of intent, as "lay" or "private" baptism was a common feature in infanticide cases where the mother wanted to ensure the eternal life of her illegitimate newborn child even as she denied it an earthly existence. But what is particularly striking was her fear that she would have "no life" with her husband if she did not do away with the child, perhaps suggesting that her claim of rape was fabricated.

Conclusion

Infanticide was the most extreme method of dealing with an unwed or unwanted pregnancy, but it must be understood as just that: one option on a spectrum of options available to unmarried women facing an unexpected and unwanted pregnancy. In the minds of both lawmakers and the courts, the "typical" infanticide defendant was a young, unmarried girl, seduced and abandoned, driven to infanticide by shame and desperation. And while a small percentage of women did, in fact, fit this stereotype, the majority did not. For many women, infanticide was simply an extreme form of birth control in a society that restricted access to more traditional forms of contraception and censured unwed motherhood. The lives of illegitimate newborns were at the bottom of the list of priorities as women, and sometimes their families, sought to conceal the pregnancies, save their jobs, and preserve their reputations and respectability.

Fear and desperation may have been significant factors in many cases, but for some women infanticide also was a logical means of balancing their ambivalence about motherhood with sexual temptation and desire. Religious moralist discourse extolling the virtues of celibacy for unmarried mothers, and fertility and a natural "maternal instinct" for married women, had little resonance in the lives of ordinary women for whom sex may have been customary in their relationships with men, and for whom children represented a drain on financial resources or simply an impediment to their way of life. It is clear from these accounts of infanticide that not all women wanted to be celibate, nor did they want to be mothers. The evidence presented in infanticide cases begs a re-evaluation of constructions of sexuality, maternity, family life, and childhood that were disseminated through moralist literature and have been accepted almost uncritically by feminist and social historians. Such a re-evaluation would facilitate a greater understanding of the interplay of official values and assumptions and popular realities, priorities, and beliefs, in shaping ordinary women's and men's perceptions and experiences of Catholicism, maternity and paternity, morality, and sexuality.

Family responses to infanticide reflected a complex evaluation of practical and moral considerations in which affection between parent and child did not always play a central role. Most families responded to the pregnancy of a daughter or sibling first and foremost based on a consideration of how it would affect their standing in the community. Some family members actively participated in the death or concealment of the child, placing the risk of being caught lower in their scale of priorities than bringing an illegitimate child into the family. But court records also reveal family relationships based on genuine affection and mutual responsibility that withstood the external pressures of social censure or disapproval or even legal action. As with most other aspects of social history, the intimate interactions between families and communities, the values and attitudes that tied them together as well as the disappointments and dashed hopes that could tear them apart, thus far have been neglected by Irish historians. The records of infanticide cases offer one window into these relationships and interactions, facilitating a greater understanding of the intricate ways that intimate family relationships shaped and were shaped by community values and priorities, and indeed the way the lives of innocent children factored into these relationships.

Notes

1   Women availed of abortions in Britain, although the cost of transportation put it out of reach for the poorest of women. It should also be noted that some pregnant women traveled to England to have their babies, so as to hide it from

families, friends, and communities. Catholic relief agencies worked in tandem with the Catholic Protection and Rescue Society and local authorities to repatriate pregnant Irish women, or Irish women who had recently given birth in English institutions.

2 Many of the women accused of killing or concealing the birth of their infants acknowledged that they had numerous sexual partners; many others had other illegitimate children or admitted to committing infanticide on more than one occasion.

3 NAI, Central Criminal Court 1D 22 84, 15 November 1943.

4 NAI, Central Criminal Court 1D 22 84, 15 November 1943.

5 NAI, Central Criminal Court 1D 56 24, 19 March 1935.

6 NAI, Central Criminal Court 1D 44 42, 19 November 1934.

7 In fact only four of the women accused of infanticide admitted that the sexual liaisons that led to their pregnancy occurred as part of an evening out at a dance hall.

8 All of the best-selling family planning guides appeared on the Register of Banned Books from the late 1930s to the 1960s, as were newspapers that consistently carried "lewd" advertisements for contraceptive devices. See *Register of banned books* (Dublin: Government Stationery Office, 1930–1960).

9 Michael Solomons, former obstetrician with the Rotunda Hospital, recalled that as a young trainee doctor he and a colleague delivered a child with a Guinness bottle-cap embedded in its forehead, a misguided effort on the part of the mother to prevent conception. See Michael Solomons, *Pro-life? The Irish question* (Dublin: The Lilliput Press, 1992), p. 6.

10 NAI, Central Criminal Court 1D 44 47, 11 June 1934.

11 NAI, Central Criminal Court 1D 44 47, 11 June 1934.

12 *Offaly Independent* (23 June 1934), p. 7.

13 NAI, Wexford Circuit Court 1D 21 87, 27 February 1934.

14 NAI, Central Criminal Court 1C 94 57, 19 November 1929.

15 In some cases the religion of the defendant was obvious in their statements or those of witnesses. When the religious persuasion was not explicitly stated the most obvious way of discerning the religion of the accused was in her sentence, as magdalen asylums did not accept non-Catholic defendants. In some cases, particularly where the defendant was Protestant, religious persuasion was noted in the Central Criminal Court's trial record books.

16 These measures included giving the child a "lay" or private baptism, saying prayers over the body of the infant, or burying the infant in consecrated ground.

17 NAI, Central Criminal Court 1D 33 64, 14 November 1933.

18 NAI, Central Criminal Court 1D 11 94, 16 October 1939.

19 NAI, Central Criminal Court 1D 11 94, 16 October 1939.

20 NAI, Central Criminal Court 1D 22 96, 15 November 1949.

21 NAI, Central Criminal Court 1D 22 96, 15 November 1949. See also *Legitimacy Act, 1931* (Act 13 of 1931) Republic of Ireland, *Irish statute book: Acts of the Oireachtas 1922–1997* (Oxfordshire, UK: Jutastat UK, 1999), CD-Rom.

22 NAI, Central Criminal Court 1D 60 58, 19 October 1937.

23 NAI, Central Criminal Court 1D 60 58, 19 October 1937.

24 NAI, Central Criminal Court 1D 60 58, 19 October 1937.

25 NAI, Central Criminal Court 1D 56 31, 3 November 1936.

26 NAI, Central Criminal Court 1C 90 9, 21 June 1927.

27 NAI, Central Criminal Court 1C 90 9, 21 June 1927.

28 NAI, Central Criminal Court 1C 90 9, 21 June 1927.

29 NAI, Central Criminal Court 1D 56 22, 24 June 1935.

30 NAI, Central Criminal Court 1D 60 61, 19 October 1937.

31 NAI, Central Criminal Court V15 14 47, 1 February 1954.

32 NAI, Central Criminal Court 1D 33 64, 14 November 1933.

33 Williams was not convicted of these earlier crimes in the Central Criminal Court. She may have been accused but released without charge, or she may have been tried in a district or circuit court. Without knowing when the earlier crimes were committed it would be difficult to trace circuit court records or newspaper accounts, and impossible to trace the crimes if she was tried in the district court.

34 Of the 23 married women accused of infanticide 6 were pregnant prior to marriage; 7 were married to husbands who were away for long periods of time (in some cases 3 or more years); 5 were separated from their husbands; 2 were widows; 2 were found insane, and one had a husband who was infirm.

35 Irish women were given the right to sit on juries in 1919, under British administration. The 1924 Juries Act allowed Irish women to opt out of jury duty if they chose, and in a 1927 debate on another Juries Bill, evidence was presented that the vast majority of eligible women opted out of jury service. The 1927 Juries Act aimed at taking the right to sit on juries away from women altogether, on the grounds that as many of the cases involved sexual and "moral" crimes women would not choose to attend court. The 1927 Juries Act did not take the right to sit on juries away from women, but it did exempt them as a whole, and women who *chose* to sit on juries had to opt in (whereas the 1924 legislation gave them the right automatically, and women could opt out). As a result, the juries in infanticide trials were entirely male. For a discussion of women and Irish juries see Maryann Gialanella Valiulis, "Power, gender and identity in the Irish Free State," *Journal of Women's History*, 6/7:4/1 (Winter/Spring 1995), pp. 120–2. Tony Ward points out that although English women were eligible for jury service from 1919, defense attorneys often sought to dismiss female jurors on the basis that male jurors would be more sympathetic to their clients. See Tony Ward, "Legislating for human nature: legal responses to infanticide, 1860–1938," in *Infanticide: Historical perspectives on child murder and concealment, 1550–2000*, ed. Mark Jackson (Burlington, VT: Ashgate, 2002), pp. 249–69.

36 NAI, Central Criminal Court 1D 33 65, 14 March 1933.

37 NAI, Central Criminal Court 1D 33 65, 14 March, 1933.

Bibliography

Primary sources

Archival material

National Archives of Ireland (NAI)
Department of Education files
Department of Foreign Affairs, Adoption Policy Files
Department of Health files
Department of the Taoiseach files
Joint Committee of Women's Societies and Social Workers Meeting Minutes

Dublin Diocesan Archives (DDA)
Archbishop McQuaid papers
American Adoption Policy Files

University College Dublin (UCD)
Irish Folklore Commission Manuscript Collection

ISPCC
Irish Society for the Prevention of Cruelty to Children case files

Books and pamphlets

Barrett, Cecil. *Adoption: The parent, the child, the home.* Dublin: Clonmore & Reynolds Ltd., 1952.
Barrett, Rosa. *Guide to Dublin charities.* Dublin: Hodges & Figgis, 1884.
Cahill, Edward. *Framework of a Christian state: An introduction to social science.* Dublin: Gill, 1932.
Cherish. *Conference on the unmarried parent and child in Irish society.* Dublin: Cherish,

1974.

Cherish. *Singled out: Single mothers in Ireland*. Dublin: Women's Community Press, 1983.

Concannon, Helen. *The queen of Ireland: An historical account of Ireland's devotion to the blessed virgin*. Dublin: Gill and Son, 1938.

Directory of services in Ireland for the unmarried mother and her child. Dublin: Working Party for the Further Development of Services for the Unmarried Mother and her Child, 1973.

Duff, Frank. *True devotion to the nation*. Dundalk: Dundalgon Press, 1966.

Griffith, Patrick. *Christian mothers: Saviours of society*. Dublin: Browne and Nolan, 1926.

Medical Missionary of Mary, A. *The Irish mother*. Dublin: Irish Messenger, 1945.

National Society for the Prevention of Cruelty to Children, *Annual Reports of the Dublin Branch*. Dublin: NSPCC, 1930.

O'Doherty, Thomas. *Catholics and citizenship*. Dublin: Catholic Truth Society, 1921.

Schmitz, Reverend Peter. *The dignity of motherhood*. Dublin: Irish Messenger, 1947.

Sheehy, Reverend J.S. *The influence of women in Catholic Ireland*. Dublin: Catholic Truth Society, 1921.

Sisters of Charity. *Manual for children of Mary*. Dublin: Browne and Nolan, 1928.

Sommer, Reverend Father. *Mother and child: an exhortation to parents and teachers*. Authorized translation from the German by Isabel Garahan. Dublin: Irish Messenger, 1933.

Sutherland, Halliday. *Irish journey*. New York: Devin-Adair, 1958.

Journal/magazine articles

Anonymous. "I live in a slum," *The Bell*, 1:2 (November 1940), pp. 46–8.

Barrett, Cecil J. "The dependent children," *Studies*, 44 (1955), pp. 419–28.

Brooke, William. "Report on the differences in law of England and Ireland as regards the protection of women," *Statistical and Social Inquiry Society of Ireland Journal*, 6 (April 1973), pp. 202–29.

Brophy, Liam. "The homeless child and the childless home," *Irish Monthly*, 80:855 (July 1952), pp. 263–7.

Browne, Most Reverend Michael J. "Why Catholic priests should concern themselves with social and economic questions," *Christus Rex*, 1:1 (1947–48), pp. 3–9.

Byrne, Reverend George. "The problem child: A solution," *Irish Ecclesiastical Record* 5th series, 69 (July 1947), pp. 588–601.

Cahill, Edward, S.J. "Notes on Christian sociology: The family, general principles," *Irish Monthly*, 52:614 (August 1924), pp. 408–20.

Cahill, Edward, S.J. "Notes on Christian sociology V. the family (b) husband and wife," *Irish Monthly*, 52:615 (September 1924), pp. 473–83.

Cahill, Edward, S.J. "Notes on Christian sociology: Social status of women – Christian woman," *Irish Monthly*, 52:616 (October 1924), pp. 537–40.

Cahill, Edward, S.J. "Notes on Christian sociology VI. the status of women," *Irish Monthly*, 52:618 (December 1924), pp. 646–54.

Cleary, Reverend M.P. "The Church of Ireland and birth-control," *Irish Ecclesiastical Record* 5th series, 38 (1931), pp. 622–9.

Coyne, Edward J., S.J. "Mother and child service," *Studies*, 40 (1951), pp. 129–49.

Crichton, Brian. "Infant mortality in Dublin," *Irish Journal of Medical Science* 4th series, 42 (July 1925), pp. 302–5.

Dallat, Michael. "The Christian citizen," *Christus Rex,* 11:4 (1957–58), pp. 684–91.

Daly, Reverend C.B. "Family life: The principles," *Christus Rex,* 5:1 (1951–52), pp. 1–19.

de Cleir, Sean. "Marriage and the family in Irish Life," *Christus Rex,* 6:4 (1951–52), pp. 303–13.

Devane, Richard, S.J. "The unmarried mother: Some legal aspects of the problem. I. The age of consent," *Irish Ecclesiastical Record,* 23 (January–June 1924), pp. 55–68.

Devane, Richard, S.J. "The unmarried mother: Some legal aspects of the problem. II. The legal position of the unmarried mother in the Irish Free State," *Irish Ecclesiastical Record,* 23 (January–June 1924), pp. 172–88.

Devane, Richard, S.J. "The dance hall," *Irish Ecclesiastical Record,* 37 (January–June 1931), pp. 170–94.

Devlin, Kevin. "Single and selfish," *Christus Rex,* 6:3 (1951–52), pp. 223–31.

Dillon, T.W.T. "Slum clearance past and future," *Studies,* 34 (March 1945), pp. 13–20.

Dillon, T.W.T. "The social services in Eire," *Studies,* 34 (September 1945), pp. 325–336.

Dunne, John P., "Poverty problems for a patriot parliament," *Journal of the Statistical and Social Enquiry Society of Ireland,* 14 (1921–22), pp. 189–98.

Eithne. "Unwanted ones," *Irish Monthly* 55:644 (February 1927), pp. 102–9.

Epstein, M.B., *et al.* "The incidence of rickets in Dublin," *Journal of the Medical Association of Eire* (1950), pp. 19–24.

Exile. "Women in public life," *The Bell,* 5:4 (January 1943), pp. 266–71.

Fahy, Edward. "The boy criminal," *The Bell,* 1:3 (December 1940), pp. 41–50.

Fahy, Edward. "Reformatory schools in Ireland," *Hermathena,* 60 (November 1942), pp. 54–73.

Fahy, Edward. "Probation of offenders," *Hermathena,* 62 (November 1943), pp. 61–82.

Gordon, M., "The impact of television on family life," *Irish Monthly,* 82:877 (May 1954), pp. 180–4.

Gore, Charles Clancy. "Nutritional standards of some working class families in Dublin, 1943" *Journal of the Statistical and Social Inquiry Society of Ireland,* vol. 17 (1943–44), pp. 241–53.

Harty, J.M. "The sacredness of fetal life," *Irish Theological Quarterly,* I (1907), pp. 35–46.

Hegarty, Edward J. "The principles against state welfare schemes," *Christus Rex,* 4:4 (October 1950), pp. 315–33.

H.M. "Illegitimate," *The Bell,* 2:3 (June 1941), pp. 78–87.

Hogan, J.F. "Catholic marriage and the decree 'Ne Temere'," *Irish Ecclesiastical Record* 4th series, vol. 29 (1911), pp. 196–203.

James, Stanley B. "Virgin and mother," *Irish Monthly,* 62:738 (December 1934), pp. 747–53.

Joyce, J. Cyril. "The school medical service in a rural county," *Journal of the Irish Medical Association* (1956), pp. 135–41.

Kenny, Ann. "The deprived child," *Christus Rex,* 10:2 (1955–56), pp. 99–114.

Kent, M.P. and J.J. Sexton. "The influence of certain social factors on the physical growth and development of a group of Dublin city children," *Journal of the Statistical and Social Inquiry Society of Ireland*, 22:5 (1972–73), pp. 188–206.

King, Patrick. "Family allowances," *Catholic Bulletin* 28 (January–June 1938), pp. 310–12.

Lucey, Cornelius. "Family allowances," *Irish Ecclesiastical Record* 5th series, 54 (1930), pp. 470–81.

Lucey, Cornelius. "The problem of the woman worker," *Irish Ecclesiastical Record* 5th series, 48 (July–December 1936), pp. 449–67.

Lucey, Cornelius. "Rerum Novarum and the Family," *Christus Rex*, 5:4 (1951–52), pp. 325–35.

Lydon, Mary. "The need for a child guidance service," *Irish Journal of Medical Science* (February 1946), pp. 56–63.

Macauley, Mrs. M. "Our children," *Christus Rex*, 9:2 (1955–56), pp. 126–33.

May, Sheila. "Two Dublin slums," *The Bell*, 7:4 (1944), pp. 351–6.

McCabe, Anna M. "Institutional care of children," *The Irish Journal of Medical Science* 6th series, 291 (February 1950), pp. 49–58.

McCabe, E.W. "The need for a law of adoption," *Statistical and Social Inquiry Society of Ireland Journal* 102nd Session (1948–49).

McCarthy, Justice H.A. "The children's court," *Christus Rex*, 2:4 (1947–48), pp. 3–12.

McCarthy, Reverend John. "A report on abortion," *Irish Ecclesiastical Record* 5th series, 55 (1940), pp. 337–53.

McGrath, Fergal. "Homes for the people," *Studies*, 21 (1932), pp. 269–81.

McKenna, Lambert. "The housing problem in Dublin," *Studies*, 8 (1919), pp. 279–95.

McKenna, P. "A primal duty of motherhood," *Irish Theological Quarterly*, 2 (1908), pp. 16–34.

Meehan, Ita. "Woman's place in the community," *Christus Rex*, 13:1 (1959–60), pp. 90–102.

Millen, S. Shannon, Esq. "Slums: A sociological retrospect of the city of Dublin," *Journal of the Statistical and Social Inquiry Society of Ireland*, 13 (December 1914), pp. 130–59.

Millen, S. Shannon, Esq. "Child life as a national asset," *Journal of the Statistical and Social Inquiry Society of Ireland*, 13 (September 1917), pp. 301–16.

Murphy, C.B. "Sex, censorship, and the church," *The Bell*, 2:6 (September 1941), pp. 65–75.

Murray, Donal. "The ideology of the family," *Social Studies*, 2:6 (December 1973), pp. 537–47.

Newman, W.A. "Legal adoption," *The Bell*, 16:4 (January 1951), pp. 59–66.

N.G. "Wanted: Homemakers," *Irish Monthly*, 56:656 (February 1928), pp. 70–4.

O'Brien, Catherine M. "The city child," *The Irish Journal of Medical Science* sixth series, 233 (May 1945), pp. 133–45.

O'Brien, Flann. "The dance halls," *The Bell*, 1:5 (February 1941), 44–52.

O'Callaghan, Reverend Denis F. "Dilemma in birth control," *Irish Ecclesiastical Record* 5th series 105 (1966), pp. 232–45.

O'Callaghan, Reverend Denis F. "The unborn child and the law," *Irish Ecclesiastical Record* 5th series, 105 (1966), pp. 358–70.

Philbin, William J. "The individual and the state," *Irish Ecclesiastical Record* 5th series, 79 (January–June 1953), pp. 3–19.

Prendergast, Mary Claire. "The family that isn't," *Christus Rex,* 14:2 (1959–60), pp. 92–104.

Reilly, James, "Family law in Ireland," *Social Studies (Irish Journal of Sociology),* 2:6 (December 1973), pp. 599–604.

Senex, "The new girl," *Irish Monthly,* 55:632 (February 1926), pp. 738–44.

Shannon, Reverend G.J. "Woman: Wife and mother," *Christus Rex,* 5:2 (1951–52), pp. 155–74.

Spain, Alex W. "Maternity services in Eire," *The Irish Journal of Medical Science* 6th series, 229 (January 1945), p. 11.

Stanislaus, Sister. "The plight of the one-parent family," *The Cross,* 64:2 (June 1973), pp. 24–6.

Newspapers/magazines

Bean na hEireann
Bell, The
Catholic Bulletin
Catholic Standard (The Standard)
Clare Champion
Connacht Tribune
Cork Evening Echo
Cork Examiner
Donegal Democrat
Donegal Vindicator
Eire: The Irish Nation
Evening Herald
Evening Mail [Dublin]
Galway Observer
Ireland on Sunday
Ireland's Eye
Irish Catholic
Irish Catholic Directory
Irish Housewife
Irish Independent
Irish Law Times
Irish Press
Irish Statesman
Irish Times
Irish Weekly Independent
Irish Workers' Voice
Kerryman, The
Kilkenny Journal
Limerick Chronicle
Limerick Leader
Limerick Weekly Echo
Longford Leader
Longford News
Mayo News

Meath Chronicle
New York Times
Offaly Chronicle
Offaly Independent
Roscommon Herald
Roscommon Messenger
Sligo Champion
Sligo Independent
Sunday Tribune
Thom's Directory
Tipperary Star
Waterford News and Star
Waterford Standard
Westmeath Examiner
Wicklow People

Government reports/White papers

The child health services: Report of a study group appointed by the minister for health to inquire into the child welfare clinic service and the school health examination. Dublin: Stationery Office, 1967.

Corporal punishment: The brutal facts. Dublin: Irish Union of School Students, 1974.

Department of Health. *National nutrition survey.* Dublin: Government Stationery Office, 1948.

Discipline in national schools. Dublin: INTO District XI, 1983.

The Ferns report. Dublin: Stationery Office, 2005.

Household budget inquiry. Dublin: Stationery Office, 1969.

Law Reform Commission. *Consultation paper on child sexual abuse.* Dublin: Law Reform Commission, 1989.

Law Reform Commission. *Report on non-fatal offences against the person.* Dublin: Law Reform Commission, 1994.

National nutrition survey. Dublin: Stationery Office, 1948.

Punishment in our schools. Dublin: School Children's Protection Organisation, 1955.

Report of inquiry into the housing of the working classes in the city of Dublin. Dublin: Stationery Office, 1943.

Report of the commission on emigration and other population problems. Dublin: Stationery Office, 1955.

Report of the commission of inquiry into the reformatory and industrial school system. Dublin: Stationery Office, 1936.

Report of the commission on the relief of the sick and destitute poor, including the insane poor. Dublin: Stationery Office, 1927.

Report of the commission on youth unemployment. Dublin: Stationery Office, 1951.

Report of the committee of inquiry into widows' and orphans' pensions. Dublin: Stationery Office, 1933.

Report of the committee on discipline in schools. Dublin: Stationery Office, 1985.

Report of the tribunal of inquiry into fire in St. Joseph's Orphanage, Cavan. Dublin: Stationery Office, 1943.

Report of the tribunal of inquiry into the "Kerry babies case". Dublin: Stationery Office,

1985.

Report on the inquiry into the operation of Madonna House. Dublin: Stationery Office, 1996.

Report on the law and procedures regarding the prosecution and disposal of young offenders. Dublin: Stationery Office, 1977.

Some of our children: A report of the residential care of the deprived child in Ireland. London: Tuarim, 1966.

White paper: Housing – progress and prospects. Dublin: Stationery Office, 1964.

White paper: Reconstruction and improvement of county homes. Dublin: Stationery Office, 1948.

White paper: The status of children. Dublin: Stationery Office, 1985.

Annual reports

An Garda Siochana. *Report of the commissioner of the Garda Siochana on crime for the years 1947–1970.*

Department of Education. *Annual reports, 1927–1961.*

Department of Health,
. *Annual reports, 1946–1960.*

Department of Health. *Quarterly report on births, deaths, and marriages, 1932, 1945.*

Department of Local Government and Public Health. *Annual reports, 1922–1946.*

Department of Social Welfare. *First report, 1947–1949.*

Department of Social Welfare. *Annual reports, 1947–1970.*

Irish Society for the Prevention of Cruelty to Children (ISPCC). *Annual reports, 1930–1955.*

Register of banned books, 1930–1960.

Report of An Bord Uchtala, 1953–1970.

Report of the Offaly county medical officer, 1945.

Returns of the registrar general, 1901–1981.

Parliamentary debates and legislation

Bunreacht na Éireann Constitution of Ireland. Dublin: Stationery Office, n.d.

Child adoption committee first report, British Parliamentary Papers vol. 9 (13 March 1925): 6.

Debates of Dáil Éireann, 1923–1985.

Hansard House of Commons Debates.

Minutes of proceedings of the first parliament of the Republic of Ireland 1919–1921. (Dublin: Stationery Office, 1921.

Public general acts of 1937–38 (British Infanticide Act)

Republic of Ireland. *Irish statute book: acts of the Oireachtas 1922–1997* (Kidlington: Jutastat UK, 1999), CD-Rom.

Court records

Adrahan/Kinvara District Court

Athenry District Court
Central Criminal Court Trial Record Books
Cork Circuit Court
Court of Criminal Appeals
Donegal Circuit Court
Galway Circuit Court
Galway District Court
Gort District Court
Limerick Circuit Court
Meath Circuit Court
Monaghan Circuit Court
Sligo Circuit Court
Wexford Circuit Court

County Council archives

Balrothery board of health and public assistance minutes (1943–44)
Cork board of health and public assistance minutes (1924–1948)
Dublin board of health and public assistance minutes (1924–43)
Offaly board of health and public assistance minutes (1925–43)
Wicklow board of health and public assistance minutes (1923–43)

Autobiographies

Argabright, Sheila. *Wild was the way: An Irish orphan memoir*. Philadelphia: Xlibris, 2001.
Boland, Patrick. *Tales from a city farmyard*. Dublin: Patrick Boland, 1995.
Bracken, Pauline. *Light of other days: A Dublin childhood*. Cork: Mercier Press, 1993.
Devlin, Edith Newman. *Speaking volumes: A Dublin childhood*. Belfast: 2000.
Doyle, Evelyn. *Evelyn: A true story*. London: Orion, 2002.
Doyle, Evelyn. *Tea and green ribbons*. New York: Free Press, 2002.
Doyle, Paddy. *The God squad*. London: Corgi Books, 1989.
Drennan, Mary Phil. *You may talk now*. Blarney, Co. Cork: On Stream Publications, 1994.
Durkan, Teresita. *Goldenbridge: A view from Valparaiso*. Dublin: Veritas, 1997.
Fahy, Bernadette. *Freedom of angels: Surviving Goldenbridge orphanage*. Dublin: O'Brien Press, 1999.
Flynn, Mannix. *Nothing to say: A novel*. Swords, Co. Dublin: Ward River Press, 1983.
Galvin, Patrick. *Song for a poor boy: A Cork childhood*. Dublin: Raven Arts Press, 1990.
Goulding, June. *The light in the window*. Dublin: Poolbeg, 1998.
Kearns, Angeline Blain. *Stealing sunlight: Growing up in Irishtown*. Dublin: A. & A. Farmar, 2000.
Kenneally, Christy. *Maura's boy: A Cork childhood*. Cork: Mercier Press 1996.
Kerrigan, Gene. *Another country: Growing up in '50s Ireland*. Dublin: Gill and Macmillan, 1998.
Maher, Sean. *The road to God knows where: A memoir of traveling boyhood*. Dublin:

Veritas, 1998.

Matley, Mary. *Always in the convent shadow.* West Sussex: Poppy Publications, 1991.

McCourt, Frank. *Angela's ashes: A memoir of childhood.* London: HarperCollins, 1996.

McGrath, Paul (with Cathal Dervan). *Ooh aah Paul McGrath: The black pearl of Inchicore.* Edinburgh: Mainstream Publishing Co., 1994.

Noble, Christina (with Robert Coram). *Bridge across my sorrows: The Christina Noble story.* London: J. Murray, 1994.

O'Connor, Frank. *An only child.* Belfast: Blackstaff, 1993.

O'Malley, Kathleen. *Childhood interrupted: Growing up under the cruel regime of the Sisters of Mercy.* London: Virago, 2005.

Sheridan, Peter. *44: a Dublin memoir.* London: Macmillan, 2000.

Taylor, Alice. *To school through the fields: An Irish country childhood.* New York: St. Martin's Press, 1990.

Touher, Patrick. *Fear of the collar: Artane industrial school.* Dublin: O'Brien, 1991.

Warrin, Kate. *Childhood interrupted: A true story of growing up in an industrial school.* London: Virago, 2005.

Secondary sources

Books

Ardagh, John. *Ireland and the Irish: Portrait of a changing society.* New York: Penguin, 1994.

Arnold, Mavis and Heather Laskey. *Children of the Poor Clares: The story of an Irish orphanage.* Belfast: Appletree Press, 1985.

Augusteijn, Joost (ed.) *Ireland in the 1930s: New perspectives.* Dublin: 1999.

Barnes, Jane. *Irish industrial schools, 1868–1908: Origins and development.* Dublin: Irish Academic Press, 1989.

Barrington, Ruth. *Health, medicine, and politics in Ireland 1900–1970.* Dublin: Institute of Public Administration, 1987.

Bock, Gisela and Pat Thane. *Maternity and gender politics: Women and the rise of the welfare state, 1880–1950s.* London: Routledge, 1991.

Bolger, Pat (ed.) *And see her beauty shining there: The story of the Irish Countrywomen.* Dublin: Irish Academic Press, 1986.

Bourke, Joanna. *Husbandry to housewifery.* Oxford: Oxford University Press, 1993.

Bradley, Anthony and Marianne Gialanella Valiulis (eds). *Gender and sexuality in modern Ireland.* Amherst, MA: University of Massachusetts Press, 1997.

Brown, Terence. *Ireland: A social and cultural history, 1922 to the Present.* Ithaca, NY: Cornell University Press, 1985.

Browne, Noel. *Against the tide.* Dublin: Gill and Macmillan, 1986.

Burke-Brogan, Patricia. *Eclipsed.* Galway: Salmon Publishing, 1994.

Burrows, Edna and Patricia Mayes. *Specially concerned: The Mothers' Union in Ireland, 1887–1987.* Dublin: Mothers' Union, 1986.

Caherty, Thérèse, Rita Corley and Patricia Dixon. *More missing pieces: Women in Irish history.* Dublin: Attic Press, 1985.

Carlson, Julia. *Banned in Ireland.* London: Routledge, 1990.

Chubb, Basil. *The government and politics of Ireland.* Stanford, CA: Stanford University

Press, 1971.

Chubb, Basil. *The constitution and constitutional change in Ireland*. Dublin: Institute of Public Administration, 1978.

Clarke, Desmond (ed.) *Morality and the law*. Cork: Mercier Press, 1982.

Clear, Catríona. *Women of the house: Women's household work in Ireland, 1926–1961: Discourses, experiences, memories*. Dublin and Portland, OR: Irish Academic Press, 2000.

Cohen, Sherrill. *The evolution of women's asylums since 1500: From refuges for ex-prostitutes to shelters for battered women*. Oxford and New York: Oxford University Press, 1992.

Coldrey, Barry. *A Christian apocalypse: The sexual abuse crisis in the Catholic Church 1984–2004*. Melbourne: Tamanaraik, 2004.

Coldrey, Barry. *The devoted, the dull, the desperate, and the deviant: The staff problem in traditional residential care*. Melbourne: Tamanaraik, 2003.

Conlon-McKenna, Marita. *The Magdalen*. London: Bantam Books, 1999.

Connelly, Alpha. *Gender and the law in Ireland*. Dublin: Oak Tree Press, 1993.

Cook, Hera. *The long sexual revolution: English women, sex, and contraception 1800–1975*. Oxford: Oxford University Press, 2004.

Corish, Patrick. *The Irish catholic experience: A historical survey*. Dublin: Gill and Macmillan, 1985.

Coulter, Carol. *Ireland: Between the first and the third worlds*. Dublin: Attic Press, 1990.

Daly, Mary. *The church and the second sex*. New York: Harper & Row, 1968.

Daly, Mary E. *Women and poverty*. Dublin: Attic Press, 1989.

Daly, Mary E. *Women and work in Ireland*. Dublin: Economic and Social History Society of Ireland, 1997.

Daly, Mary E. *Population decline and independent Ireland, 1922–1973*. Madison, WI: University of Wisconsin Press, 2006.

Earner-Byrne, Lindsey. *Mother and child: Maternity and child welfare in Dublin, 1922–1960*. Manchester: Manchester University Press, 2007.

Fallon, Brian. *An age of innocence: Irish culture 1930–1960*. Dublin: 1998.

Farrell, Brian (ed.) *De Valera's constitution and ours*. Dublin: Gill and Macmillan, 1988.

Fennell, Desmond. *State of the nation: Ireland since the sixties*. Dublin: Ward River Press, 1983.

Ferriter, Diarmaid. *Mothers, maidens, and myths: A history of the Irish Countrywomen's Association*. Dublin: FAS, 1995.

Ferriter, Diarmaid. *The transformation of Ireland*. Woodstock, NY: Overlook Press, 2005.

Finnegan, Frances. *Do penance or perish: A study of magdalen asylums in Ireland*. Piltown, Co. Kilkenny: Congrave Press, 2001.

Finnegan, Richard B. and James L. Wiles (eds). *Women and public policy in Ireland: A documentary history*. Dublin and Portland, OR: Irish Academic Press, 2005.

Fogarty, Michael, Liam Ryan and Joseph Lee. *Irish values and attitudes: The Irish report of the European value systems study*. Dublin: Dominican Publications, 1984.

Foster, R.F. *Modern Ireland 1600–1972*. London: Allen Lane, the Penguin Press, 1988.

Fuller, Louise. *Irish Catholicism since 1950: The undoing of a culture*. Dublin: Gill and Macmillan, 2003.

Gordon, Linda. *Pitied but not entitled: Single mothers and the history of welfare 1890–1935*. New York: Free Press, 1994.

Hannon, Patrick. *Church, State, Morality and Law*. Dublin: Gill and Macmillan, 1992.

Harkness, D.W. *Ireland in the twentieth century: Divided island*. New York: St. Martin's Press, 1996.

Hayes, Alan and Diane Urquhart (eds). *The Irish women's history reader*. London and New York: Routledge, 2001.

Hayes, Alan and Diane Urquhart (eds). *Irish women's history*. Dublin and Portland, OR: Irish Academic Press, 2004.

Hayes, Joanne. *My story*. Dingle, Co. Kerry: Brandon Books, 1985.

Hesketh, Tom. *The second partitioning of Ireland? The abortion referendum*. Dublin: Brandsma Books, 1990.

Hill, Myrtle. *Women in Ireland: A century of change*. Belfast: Blackstaff, 2003.

Hill, Myrtle. *Women in Ireland 1900–2000*. Belfast: Blackstaff, 2003.

Holden, Wendy. *Unlawful carnal knowledge: The true story of the X Case*. London: Harper Collins, 1994.

Horgan, John. *Noel Browne: Passionate outsider*. Dublin: Gill and Macmillan, 2004.

Howe, Stephen. *Ireland and empire: Colonial legacies in Irish history and culture*. Oxford and New York: Oxford University Press, 2000.

Hug, Chrystel. *The politics of sexual morality in Ireland*. London: Macmillan Press, 1999.

Humphreys, Margaret. *Empty cradles*. London: Corgi, 1997.

Inglis, Tom. *Moral monopoly: The Catholic Church in modern Irish Society*. Dublin: Gill and Macmillan, 1987.

Inglis, Tom. *Moral monopoly: The rise and fall of the Catholic Church in modern Ireland*. Dublin: Gill and Macmillan, 1998.

Inglis, Tom. *Lessons in Irish sexuality*. Dublin: University College Dublin Press, 1999.

Inglis, Tom. *Truth, power, and lies: Irish society and the case of the Kerry babies*. Dublin: University College Dublin Press, 2004.

Innes, Catherine. *Woman and nation in Irish literature and society, 1880–1935*. Athens, GA: University of Georgia Press, 1993.

Jackson, Alvin. *Ireland 1798–1998: Politics and war*. Oxford, UK and Malden, MA: Blackwell Publishers, 1999.

Jackson, Mark (ed.) *Infanticide: Historical perspectives on child murder and concealment, 1550–2000*. Burlington, VT: Ashgate, 2002.

Kearns, Kevin Corrigan. *Dublin's lost heroines: Mammies and grannies in a vanished city*. Dublin: Gill and Macmillan, 2004.

Kennedy, Finola. *Cottage to crèche: Family change in Ireland*. Dublin: Institute of Public Administration, 2001.

Kennedy, Patricia. *Motherhood in Ireland: Creation and context*. Cork: Mercier Press, 2004.

Kenny, Mary. *Goodbye to Catholic Ireland: A social, personal, and cultural history from the fall of Parnell to the realm of Mary Robinson*. London: Sinclair-Stevenson, 1997.

Keogh, Dermot. *The Vatican, the bishops, and Irish politics, 1919–1939*. Cambridge and New York: Cambridge University Press, 1986.

Keogh, Dermot. *Twentieth-century Ireland: Nation and state*. Dublin: Gill and Macmillan, 1994.

Kilfeather, Siobhan. *Dublin: A cultural history*. New York: Oxford University Press, 2005.

Kirby, Peadar. *Is Irish Catholicism dying? Liberating an imprisoned church*. Westminster, MD: Christian Classics, 1984.

Kirby, Peadar and Mavis Arnold (eds). *The abortion referendum: The case against*. Dublin: Anti-Amendment Campaign, 1983.

Koven, Seth and Sonya Michel (eds). *Mothers of a new world: Maternalist politics and the origins of the welfare state*. New York and London: Routledge, 1993.

Kunzel, Regina. *Fallen Women, problem girls: Unmarried mothers and the professionalization of social work, 1890–1945*. New Haven and London: Yale University Press, 1993.

Lane, Fintan and Donal Ó Drisceoil. *Politics and the Irish working class, 1830–1945*. New York: Palgrave Macmillan, 2005.

Larkin, Emmet. *The historical dimensions of Irish Catholicism*. Dublin: Four Courts Press, 1976.

Larkin, Emmet. *The making of the Roman Catholic Church in Ireland*. Chapel Hill, NC: University of North Carolina Press, 1980.

Lee, J.J. *Ireland 1912–1985: Politics and society*. Cambridge: Cambridge University Press, 1989.

Luddy, Maria. *Prostitution and Irish society, 1800–1940*. Cambridge: Cambridge University Press, 2007.

Luddy, Maria and Cliona Murphy. *Women surviving*. Swords, Co. Dublin: Poolbeg, 1989.

MacCurtain, Margaret and Donnchadh Ó Corráin. *Women in Irish society: the historical dimension*. Westport, CT: Greenwood Press, 1979.

Malcolm, Elizabeth and Greta Jones (eds). *Medicine, disease, and the state in Ireland, 1650–1940*. Cork: Cork University Press, 1999.

Martin, Frank. *The politics of children's rights*. Cork: Cork University Press, 2000.

McCafferty, Nell. *A woman to blame: The Kerry babies case*. Dublin: Attic Press, 1985.

McGee, Hannah. *The SAVI report: Sexual abuse and violence in Ireland*. Dublin: Liffey Press, 2002.

McKay, Susan. *Sophia's story*. Dublin: Gill and Macmillan, 1998.

Milotte, Mike. *Banished babies: The secret history of Ireland's baby export business*. (Dublin: New Island Books, 1997.

Moody, T.W. and F.X. Martin (eds). *The course of Irish history*. Cork: Mercier Press, 1987.

Moore, Chris. *Betrayal of trust: The Father Brendan Smyth affair and the Catholic Church*. Dublin: Marino Books, 1995.

O'Connor, Anne. *Child murderess and dead child traditions: A comparative study*. Helsinki: Suomalainen Tiedeakatemia, 1991.

O'Connor, Anne. *The blessed and the damned: Sinful women and unbaptised children in Irish folklore*. Oxford: Peter Lang, 2005.

O'Doherty, Iseult. *Stolen childhoods: Testimonies of the survivors of child sexual abuse*. Dublin: Poolbeg Press, 1998.

O'Dowd, Mary and Sabine Wichert. *Chattel, servant or citizen: Woman's status in church, state and society*. Belfast: Institute of Irish Studies, 1995.

Ó Drisceoil, Donal. *Censorship in Ireland, 1939–1945: Neutrality, politics and society*. Cork: Cork University Press, 1996.

O'Dwyer, Peter. *Mary: A history of devotion in Ireland*. Dublin: Four Courts Press,

1988.

O'Halloran, Barry. *Lost innocence: The inside story of the Kerry babies mystery*. Dublin: Raytown Press, 1985.

O'Riordan, John. *Irish Catholics: Traditions and transitions*. Dublin: Veritas, 1980.

O'Sullivan, Eoin. "Child welfare in Ireland, 1750–1995: A history of the present." Ph.D. thesis, Trinity College Dublin, 1999.

Owens, Rosemary Cullen. *A social history of women in Ireland 1870–1970*. Dublin: Gill and Macmillan, 2005.

Prunty, Jacinta. *Dublin slums 1800–1925: A study in urban geography*. Dublin: Irish Academic Press, 1998.

Ramblado-Minero, Maria de la Cinta and Auxiliadora Perez-Vides (eds). *Single motherhood in twentieth-century Ireland: Cultural historical, and social essays*. Lewiston, NY: Edwin Mellen Press, 2006.

Ranke-Heinemann, Uta. *Eunuchs for the kingdom of heaven: Women, sexuality, and the Catholic Church*. New York: Doubleday, 1990.

Raftery, Mary and Eoin O'Sullivan, *Suffer the little children: The inside story of Ireland's industrial schools*. Dublin: New Island Books, 1999.

Regan, John. *The Irish counter revolution, 1921–1936*. New York: St Martin's Press, 1999.

Rhodes, Rita. *Women and the family in post-famine Ireland: Status and opportunity in a patriarchal society*. New York: Garland, 1992.

Richard, Maura. *Single issue*. Dublin: Poolbeg Press, 1998.

Robins, Joseph. *The lost children: A study of charity children in Ireland 1700–1900*. Dublin: Institute of Public Administration, 1980.

Robins, Joseph (ed.) *Reflections on health: Commemorating fifty years of the Department of Health 1947–1997*. Dublin: 1997.

Rose, Lionel. *The massacre of the innocents: Infanticide in Britain 1800–1939*. London: Routledge and Kegan Paul, 1986.

Ross, Ellen. *Love and toil: Motherhood in outcast London 1870–1910*. Oxford and New York: Oxford University Press, 1993.

Ryan, Brendan. *Keeping us in the dark: Censorship and freedom of information in Ireland*. Dublin: Gill and Macmillan, 1995.

Ryan, Louise. *Gender, identity, and the Irish press, 1922–1937: Embodying the nation*. Lewiston, NY: E. Mellen Press, 2002.

Sawyer, Roger. *"We are but women": Women in Ireland's history*. London and New York: Routledge, 1993.

Scheper-Hughes, Nancy and Carolyn Sargent (eds). *Small wars: The cultural politics of childhood*. Berkeley, CA: University of California Press, 1998.

Shatter, Alan. *Family law in the Republic of Ireland*. Dublin: Wolfhound Press, 1977.

Skehill, Caroline. *History of the present of child protection and welfare social work in Ireland*. Lewiston, NY: Edwin Mellen Press, 2004.

Smith, James. *Ireland's magdalen laundries and the nation's architecture of containment*. Notre Dame, IN: University of Notre Dame Press, 2007.

Smyth, Ailbhe (ed.) *The abortion papers Ireland*. Dublin: Attic Press, 1992.

Solomons, Michael. *Pro-life? The Irish question*. Dublin: The Lilliput Press, 1992.

Taylor, Lawrence. *Occasions of faith: An anthropology of Irish Catholics*. Philadelphia: University of Pennsylvania Press, 1995.

Tobin, Fergal. *The best of decades: Ireland in the 1960s*. Dublin: Gill and MacMillan, 1996.

Townshend, Charles. *Ireland the twentieth century*. London and New York: Oxford University Press, 1999.

Travers, Olive and Sylvia Thompson. *Behind the silhouettes: Exploring the myths of child sexual abuse*. Belfast: Blackstaff Press, 1999.

Tweedy, Hilda. *A link in the chain: The story of the Irish Housewives Association, 1942–1992*. Dublin: Attic Press, 1992.

Tyrrell, Peter and Diarmuid Whelan. *Founded on fear: Letterfrack industrial school, war and exile*. Dublin and Portland, OR: Irish Academic Press, 2006.

Valiulis, Maryann Gialanella and Mary O'Dowd (eds). *Women and Irish history: Essays in honour of Margaret MacCurtain*. Dublin: Wolfhound Press, 1997.

Viney, Michael. *No birthright: A study of the Irish unmarried mother and her child*. Dublin: Irish Times Press, 1964.

Wagner, Gillian. *Children of the empire*. London: Weidenfeld and Nicolson, 1992.

Walkowitz, Judith. *City of dreadful delight: Narratives of sexual danger in late Victorian London*. Chicago: University of Chicago Press, 1992.

Warner, Marina. *Alone of all her sex: The myth and the cult of the Virgin Mary*. London: Pan Books, 1990.

Whelan, Bernadette. *Women and paid work in Ireland, 1500–1930*. Dublin and Portland, OR: Four Courts Press, 2000.

Whyte, John. *Church and state in modern Ireland: 1923–1979*. Dublin: Gill and Macmillan, 1980

Widdess, J.D.H. *The magdalen asylum, Dublin, 1766–1966*. Dublin, n.p., 1966.

Wood, Kieron. *The Kilkenny incest case*. Dublin: Poolbeg Press, 1993.

Articles/chapters

Beaumont, Caitriona. "Women, citizenship and catholicism in the Irish Free State, 1922–1948," *Women's History Review*, 6:4 (December 1997), pp. 563–85.

Birdwell-Pheasant, Donna. "Irish households in the early twentieth century: Culture, class, and historical contingency," *Journal of Family History*, 18:1 (January 1993), pp. 19–38.

Condren, Mary. "Sacrifice and political legitimation: The production of a gendered social order," *Journal of Women's History*, 6:4 (Winter/Spring 1995), pp. 160–89.

Crowdus, Gary. "The sisters of no mercy: An interview with Peter Mullan," *Cineaste*, 28:4 (Fall 2003), pp. 26–33.

Curtis, B. "Magdalen asylums and moral regulation in Ireland," in *Schools as dangerous places: A historical perspective*, ed. Anthony Potts and T.A. O'Donoghue. Youngstown, NY: Cambria Press, 2007, pp. 119–43.

Daly, Mary E. "Women in the Irish Free State, 1922–1939: The interaction between economics and ideology," *Journal of Women's History*, 4/1:6/7 (Winter/Spring 1995), pp. 99–116.

Daly, Mary. "Marriage, fertility, and women's lives in twentieth-century Ireland (c. 1900–c. 1970)," *Women's History Review*, 15:4 (September 2006), pp. 571–85.

Delay, Cara. "Confidantes or competitors? Women, priests, and conflict in post-famine Ireland," *Éire-Ireland: An Interdisciplinary Journal of Irish Studies*, 40:1/2 (Spring/Summer 2005), pp. 107–25.

Donovan, James. "Infanticide and the juries in France, 1825–1913," *Journal of Family*

History, 16:2 (1991), pp. 157–76.

Earner-Byrne, Lindsey. "The boat to England: An analysis of the official reactions to the emigration of single expectant Irishwomen to Britain, 1922–1972," *Irish Economic and Social History*, 30 (2003), pp. 52–70.

Earner-Byrne, Lindsey. "Managing motherhood: Negotiating a maternity service for Catholic mothers in Dublin, 1930–1954," *Social History of Medicine: The Journal of the Society for the Social History of Medicine*, 19:2 (2006), pp. 261–77.

Ferguson, Harry. "*States of fear*, child abuse, and Irish society," *Doctrine and Life*, 50:1 (2000), pp. 20–31.

Ferguson, Harry. "Abused and looked after children as 'moral dirt': Child abuse and institutional care in historical perspective," *Journal of Social Policy*, 36:1 (January 2007), pp. 123–39.

Finnane, Mark. "The Carrigan committee of 1930–31 and the 'moral condition of the Saorstát'," *Irish Historical Studies*, 32:128 (November 2001), pp. 519–36.

Fletcher, Ruth. "Silences: Irish women and abortion," *Feminist Review*, 50 (Summer 1995), pp. 44–66.

Fuller, Louise. "Religion, politics, and socio-cultural change in twentieth-century Ireland," *European Legacy*, 10:1 (February 2005), pp. 41–54.

Garrett, Paul Michael. "The abnormal flight: The migration and repatriation of Irish unmarried mothers," *Social History*, 25:3 (October 2000), pp. 330–43.

Higginbotham, Ann. "Sin of the age: Infanticide and illegitimacy in Victorian London," in *Victorian scandals: Representations of gender and class*, ed. Kristine Ottesen Garrigan. Athens, OH: Ohio University Press, 1992, pp. 257–88.

Hug, Chrystel. "Moral order and the liberal agenda in the Republic of Ireland," *New Hibernia Review*, 5:4 (Winter 2001), pp. 22–41.

Inglis, Tom. "Origins and legacies of Irish prudery: Sexuality and social control in modern Ireland," *Éire-Ireland: An Interdisciplinary Journal of Irish Studies*, 40:3 (Fall/Winter 2005), pp. 9–37.

Kenneally, James. "Sexism, the church and Irish women," *Eire-Ireland: An Interdisciplinary Journal of Irish Studies*, 21:3 (Fall 1986), pp. 3–16.

Kennedy, Finola. "The suppression of the Carrigan report: A historical perspective on child abuse," *Studies*, 89:356 (Winter 2000), pp. 354–62.

Keogh, Daire. "'There's no such thing as a bad boy': Father Flanagan's visit to Ireland, 1946," *History Ireland*, 12:1 (Spring 2004), pp. 29–32.

Kirke, Deirdre. "Unmarried mothers: A comparative study," *Economic and Social Review*, 10:2 (January 1979), pp. 157–67.

Luddy, Maria. "Moral rescue and unmarried mothers in Ireland in the 1920s," *Women's Studies*, 30 (2001), pp. 797–817.

Luquet, Wade. "The contribution of the Sisters of Mercy to the development of social welfare," *Affilia: Journal of Women and Social Work*, 20:2 (Summer 2005), pp. 153–68.

Maguire, Moira. "The changing face of Catholic Ireland: Conservatism and liberalism in the Kerry babies scandals," *Feminist Studies*, 27:2 (Summer 2001), pp. 335–59.

Maguire, Moira. "Foreign Adoptions and the Evolution of Irish Adoption Policy," *Journal of Social History*, 36:2 (Winter 2002), pp. 387–404.

Maguire, Moira. "The Carrigan committee and child sexual abuse in Ireland," *New Hibernia Review*, 11:2 (Summer 2007), pp. 79–100.

Maguire, Moira and Seamus O'Cinneide. "'A good beating never hurt anyone': The punishment and abuse of children in twentieth-century Ireland," *Journal of Social History*, 38:3 (Spring 2005), pp. 635–52.

McCormick, Leanne. "Sinister sisters? The portrayal of Ireland's magdalen asylums in popular culture," *Cultural and Social History*, 2:3 (September 2005), pp. 373–9.

McKee, Eamonn. "Church–state relations and the development of Irish health policy: the mother-and-child scheme, 1944–53," *Irish Historical Studies*, 25:98 (November 1986), pp. 159–94.

Meehan, Paula. "The statue of the virgin of Granard speaks," in *The man who was marked by winter*. Loughcrew, Oldcastle, Co. Meath: Gallery Press, 1991, pp. 40–42.

Molino, Michael. "The 'house of a hundred windows': Industrial schools in Irish writing," *New Hibernia Review*, 5:1 (Spring 2001), pp. 33–52.

Murphy, Paula. "'A prison of the mind': The magdalen laundries in popular culture," *Doctrine and Life*, 54 (October 2004), pp. 7–15.

O'Brien, George. "The stolen child," *New Hibernia Review*, 9:2 (Summer 2005), pp. 9–24.

O'Donnell, Ian. "Lethal violence in Ireland, 1841–2003: famine, celibacy, and parental pacification," *British Journal of Criminology*, 45:5 (September 2005), pp. 671–95.

Ó hAllmhuráin, Gearóid. "Dancing on the hobs of hell: Rural communities in Clare and the Dance Halls Act of 1935," *New Hibernia Review*, 9:4 (Winter 2005), pp. 9–18.

O'Reilly, James. "Family law in Ireland," *Social Studies*, 2:6 (December 1973), pp. 599–604.

O'Sullivan, Eoin. "'This otherwise delicate subject': Child sexual abuse in early twentieth-century Ireland," in *Criminal justice in Ireland*, ed. Paul O'Mahony. Dublin: Institute of Public Administration, 2002, pp. 176–201.

O'Sullivan, Eoin. "Welfare regimes, housing and homelessness in the Republic of Ireland," *European Journal of Housing Policy*, 4:3 (December 2004), pp. 323–43.

O'Sullivan, Eoin. "Coercive confinement in the Republic of Ireland: The waning of a culture of control," *Punishment and Society*, 9:1 (January 2007), pp. 27–48.

Richter, Jeffrey. "Infanticide, child Abandonment, and abortion in Germany," *Journal of Interdisciplinary History*, 28:4 (Summer 1998), pp. 511–51.

Rowley, Rosmarie. "Women and the constitution," *Administration*, 37:1 (1989), pp. 42–62.

Ryan, Louise. "The massacre of innocence: Infanticide in the Irish Free State," *Irish Studies Review*, 14 (Spring 1996), pp. 17–21.

Ryan, Louise. "Constructing 'Irishwoman': modern girls and comely maidens," *Irish Studies Review*, 6:3 (1998), pp. 263–72.

Ryan, Louise. "Press, police, and prosecution: perspectives on infanticide in the 1920s," in *Irish Women's History*, ed. Alan Hayes and Diane Urquehart (Dublin: Irish Academic Press, 2004), pp. 137–51.

Savage, Robert and James Smith. "Sexual abuse and the Irish church: crisis and response," *The church in the twenty-first century: From crisis to renewal*. Occasional Paper #8.

Shanahan, Suzanne. "The changing meaning of family: Individual rights and Irish adoption policy," *Journal of Family History*, 30:1 (January 2005), pp. 86–108.

Smart, Carol. "Reconsidering the recent history of child sexual abuse," *Journal of Social Policy*, 29:1 (2000), pp. 55–71.

Smyth, Ailbhe. "Paying our respects to the bloody state we're In," *Journal of Women's History*, 6/7:4/1 (Winter/Spring 1995), pp. 190–215.

Smith, James. "The politics of sexual knowledge: The origins of Ireland's containment culture and the Carrigan report (1931)," *Journal of the History of Sexuality*, 13:2 (April 2004), pp. 208–33.

Torode, Ruth and Eoin O'Sullivan. "The impact of *Dear daughter*," *Irish Journal of Feminist Studies*, 3:2 (Autumn 1999), pp. 85–98.

Valiulis, Maryann Gialanella. "Power, gender, and identity in the Irish Free State," *Journal of Women's History*, 6/7:4/1 (Winter/Spring 1995) pp. 117–36.

Wills, Claire. "Women, domesticity, and the family: Recent feminist work in Irish cultural studies," *Cultural Studies*, 15:1 (January 2001), pp. 33–57.

Videos/documentaries

Dear daughter. Crescendo Concepts, producer/director Louis Lentin, 1996.

John Charles McQuaid: What the papers say, presented by John Bowman. Radio Telefis Éireann, RTÉ 1, Dublin, 1998.

Sex in a cold climate, narrated by Dervla Kirwan. Testimony Films, 1998.

States of fear, narrated by Aine Lawlor, written, produced and directed by Mary Raftery, RTÉ, Ireland, 27 April 1999.

20/20: Stolen lives, produced by Louis Lentin. TV3 Ireland, 5 November 2000.

Index